T0345046

Endorsements

This is an excellent book for readers who want to deepen their programming skills. It uses a low-threshold, no-ceiling approach to programming, offering the reader a plethora of practical projects that spark curiosity and demonstrate the versatile contexts of application where refined programming abilities can be applied.

— Calkin Suero Montero, Associate Professor, Uppsala University

This book provides an enjoyable and thought-provoking way to build up your coding skills and explore simple yet fun virtual worlds. Packed with great content, it has something to offer to the reader of any level.

— Iskander Umarov, Game Director, Helium9 Games

Playful Python Projects

This book aims to take beginner and intermediate programming hobbyists to the next level by challenging them with exciting bite-size projects rooted in actual scientific and engineering problems. Each chapter introduces a set of simple techniques and shows a variety of situations where they can be applied.

The main feature of the book is the choice of topics that are designed to be both entertaining and serious. These excursions are a great way to hone coding skills while exploring diverse areas of human knowledge.

The variety of discussed subjects and creative project ideas make the book a perfect choice for aspiring coders thinking where to apply their growing skills.

Maxim Mozgovoy is a senior associate professor at the University of Aizu, Japan. He received his PhD degree in Applied Mathematics from St. Petersburg State University, and his PhD in Computer Science from the University of Joensuu, Finland. His main research interests are focused on educational technologies, natural language processing, and artificial intelligence for games and interactive environments. His current goal is to apply machine learning technologies to the task of creating practical game AI systems. Maxim has industrial-level software development experience and a record of around 100 academic papers. He is a co-founder of Helium9 Games studio, a regular reviewer for IEEE Transactions on Games and Entertainment Computing journals, and a program committee member of IEEE Conference on Games, Foundations of Digital Games, and other international conferences.

Playful Python Projects
Modeling and Animation

Maxim Mozgovoy

CRC Press
Taylor & Francis Group
Boca Raton London New York

CRC Press is an imprint of the
Taylor & Francis Group, an **informa** business

A CHAPMAN & HALL BOOK

Designed cover image: Rabbits. Beauty Art Design of Cute Little Easter Bunny in the Meadow; stock-photo

First edition published 2024
by CRC Press
2385 NW Executive Center Drive, Suite 320, Boca Raton FL 33431

and by CRC Press
4 Park Square, Milton Park, Abingdon, Oxon, OX14 4RN

CRC Press is an imprint of Taylor & Francis Group, LLC

ISBN: 978-1-032-59583-2 (hbk)
ISBN: 978-1-032-59584-9 (pbk)
ISBN: 978-1-003-45529-5 (ebk)

DOI: 10.1201/9781003455295

Typeset in Latin Modent font
by KnowledgeWorks Global Ltd.

Publisher's note: This book has been prepared from camera-ready copy provided by the authors.

Contents

Foreword

The profession of a software developer is becoming more specialized than ever. There are countless technologies to master, and the differences in day-to-day activities of IT professionals of different career paths are incredibly diverse. Over decades, the challenge of making software started to look more and more like a regular *job*, full of inevitable routine tasks, governed by "business processes", "market demands" and other facets of the *real world* many of us are not overly excited about.

This process is natural: our field matures, and maturity comes with certain downsides. However, no manager, employer or market analyst must let us forget that *programming is fun*. It was fun for the hackers who created the world's famous programming languages, games, and operating systems, and it can still be fun today. It probably does not look this way from many current books and blogs that tend to be highly specialized or follow a straightforward "getting things done" approach, but this is just a matter of setting the right goals.

The primary goal of this book is to present a collection of entertaining programming projects aimed at beginner and intermediate coders and hobbyists. In a sense, it fills the gap between introductory programming tutorials and specialized literature. Each project in the book is also supposed to demonstrate a certain interesting practical application of programming skills, to show what can be achieved with simple coding efforts. Most projects aim to simulate or analyze something found in the real world, so we will rarely, if ever, deal with abstract exercises.

Naturally, many of the ideas presented here are hardly new or original. My challenge here is to hand-pick the topics that can bring fun and deliver some useful knowledge: a good hobby project might entertain as well as educate. (As a professional educator, I cannot overlook this aspect!) The primary criterion for including a certain project is my personal taste: what sounds fun to me might not sound fun to someone else. However, my rules of thumb are simple: (1) be fun; (2) provide educational value; (3) be short; (4) do not require pro skills or specialized knowledge; and (5) do not rely on the "magic" functionality of a third-party library.

In practical terms, the last rule means that we are going to rely only on the Python standard library and write the rest ourselves. At the same time, we won't reinvent the wheel: if something is available out of the box, we will use it. This decision sets the scope of the book quite precisely, leaving outside any projects involving larger or smaller building blocks. For example, I like the ideas of making a game with Pygame library or writing my own line-drawing routine, but not for this book.

To wrap up the discussion of objectives, let me add a bit of a personal touch. I have always enjoyed tinkering with things. It could be papercraft, soldering, knitting or stuffed toy-making. Unfortunately, as a kid I grew up in a rather cramped apartment, and my parents had a hard time finding space for my handicrafts. Most of them ended up being thrown away (typically they weren't stellar, I have to concede). Learning a bit of programming gave me a feel for a whole new world of tinkering: I can make stuff that doesn't take space! I can easily make as many copies of a piece as I need! Even after years of professional work, I cherish this attitude to programming—a creative endeavor of making *something* from *nothing*, and I am happy to share it with you, fellow traveler.

Maxim Mozgovoy
The University of Aizu
Japan

Preface

Let me hold your attention for a little longer to discuss our roadmap.

This book is not a textbook on Python, so I expect certain knowledge of programming in general and Python in particular from the readers. Still, we'll start by discussing certain aspects of Python that are central to the content of the subsequent chapters. Even if your Python skills are fine, skim over this chapter to make sure you are familiar with all the concepts mentioned there.

The subsequent six chapters are devoted to actual projects. Chapters are organized by topic, so the material in the last chapters is not necessarily any more difficult than at the beginning of the book. However, new ideas are introduced gradually, so a certain program from a middle chapter might rely on a technique elaborated earlier. Thus, I would advise reading the book in order. On the other hand, there is only a handful of foundational ideas, and their first occurrence is usually mentioned, so jumping between the project randomly is also not impossible.

The discussion of each project in the book ends with its full Python code.[1] This decision did not come easily: if a project is an exercise, its source code is a solution, which is supposed to be at least a few pages away. However, I think there is a major difference between our projects and typical exercises: a project description is an outline of a certain problem to tackle, and the proposed source code is my personal take on the solution. In most cases, its principal feature is brevity: only a couple of listings in the book extend beyond 200 lines of code.

While examining the code, we continue discussing the original problem by considering just one particular way of turning its requirements and constraints into a Python program. You can ignore this part and try implementing the project right away. You can improve and extend my approach. You can take the challenges provided in the "Further Ideas" section at the end of each chapter. In any case, there are ample opportunities for creativity.

Every time an interesting concept or topic is mentioned, I do my best to provide an relevant reference for further reading. Quite often I cite original works or books rather than, say, blog posts. These are not always the easiest texts to read, but they won't disappear suddenly as it unfortunately happens with websites, and their titles might serve as good search queries to retrieve related online material. If you are not interested, just ignore these references. Similarly, feel free to skip any formulas or unclear paragraphs: no part of the book is compulsory for understanding the rest, and no topic is equally enjoyable to everyone. It is perfectly fine to focus on the bits and pieces you personally like.

---

[1] All sources are available at `https://github.com/rg-software/ppp-modeling`

1 A bit of Python

1.1 THE CASE FOR PYTHON

This book is not tied to any particular programming language or coding style. Most projects presented here can be easily reproduced in different programming environments. However, "easy" does not mean "equally easy". Some languages require more *ceremony* than others. A textbook example of *"Hello, world"* program in Java looks like this:

```java
class Hello
{
    public static void main(String[] args)
    {
        System.out.println("Hello, World!");
    }
}
```

This code is not only several lines long, it involves some understanding of what `class` or `public static` mean, and all this for the sake of printing one line of text on your screen. The value of these concepts grows as your project grows, but since we are going to discuss only small and relatively simple programs, their benefit is likely to be minimal.

Python makes an easy choice for our purposes. It is concise, involves little ceremony, and has a reputation of being friendly for beginners, who start their journey with the following piece of code:

```python
print("Hello, world!")
```

I suspect that Python is also the most popular as a first language nowadays, so I expect knowledge of its basics from the reader. Since there is no ironclad list of "Python basics", I will have to propose my own version.

1.2 OUR PYTHON ENVIRONMENT AND TOOLSET

Despite its "beginner-friendliness", Python is not an educational language. It was not designed for beginners, and it hides vast complexities behind a façade of nostalgic BASIC for 1980s 8-bit home computers. A good Python reference manual can easily cross the boundary of 1000 pages.

For this reason, we can probably agree that any beginner should be able to write an `if` statement or a `for` loop, but it is less clear what comes next. Should it be list comprehensions or `match` statements, classes or data structures? It's often hard to decide. Say, a *dictionary* is an essential instrument in Python toolbox, but it is based on a fairly advanced concept. To achieve dictionary-like functionality in a language like C would be quite an advanced exercise.

DOI: 10.1201/9781003455295-1

For the purposes of this book, the following elements are considered "basic":

- Control structures (`if`, `else`, `for`, `break`).
- Common data structures, such lists, sets, tuples, and dictionaries.
- List, dictionary, and set comprehensions.
- Common standard library modules, such as `math` and `random`.
- The idea of an abstract data type (declared using the `class` keyword).

Again, many of them are not simple, but they are part and parcel of Python, and deliberately avoiding them would produce code that feels nothing like Python at all. At least I managed to get around lambda functions without much harm.

Apart from these elements, we will also rely on *data classes* and *turtle graphics*. These concepts are not difficult, but they might be outside of a typical beginner's toolbox. Finally, it should be noted that all the projects are designed and tested in Python 3.9. Python's backward compatibility is far from perfect, but I do not expect any issues with newer versions. As a reminder, no third-party libraries are used.

1.3 DATA CLASSES

A *class* is a basic concept of object-oriented programming, which needs to be understood for creating complex data types having all kinds of interesting properties. A *data class* is a simple type that merely keeps together some pieces of data and possibly provides certain utility functions to handle them. Internally, data classes in Python are built on top of regular classes.

What can be a typical job for a data class? For example, suppose we need to represent N two-dimensional points in our code. One option would be to define two separate arrays for their `x` and `y` components:

```
x = [5, 3, 2] # points (5, 8), (3, 1), and (2, 6)
y = [8, 1, 6]
```

A better option is to keep the components together within the same entity, which can be easily achieved with tuples:

```
points = [(5, 8), (3, 1), (2, 6)]
```

Unfortunately, this method has flaws. In particular, component names (`x` and `y`) are lost now. A data class fixes this issue:

```
from dataclasses import dataclass
```

```
@dataclass
class Point:
    x: float
```

```
    y: float
```

```
points = [Point(5, 8), Point(3, 1), Point(2, 6)]
print(points[1].x) # prints 3
```

This syntax is a bit involved: it relies on relatively advanced concepts of a *decorator* (@dataclass) and *type annotations* (the : float parts). Otherwise, Point is a regular class with a convenient constructor, which converts the input values of x and y into Point objects.

Data classes often benefit from another relatively advanced concept of a *class method*. The objects of type Point can only be constructed from two input numbers (x and y), which is not always convenient. Suppose we often need to create random points with coordinates lying in the given range. The only way to achieve it now is to pass random coordinates to the constructor of Point:

```
from random import uniform

p1 = Point(uniform(0, 10), uniform(0, 10))
p2 = Point(uniform(0, 10), uniform(0, 10))
```

Alternatively, it is possible to implement a method create_random() to simplify this code:

```
from dataclasses import dataclass
from random import uniform


@dataclass
class Point:
    x: float
    y: float

    @classmethod
    def create_random(cls):
        return cls(uniform(0, 10), uniform(0, 10))


p1 = Point.create_random()
p2 = Point.create_random()
```

A class method (declared with a @classmethod decorator) "belongs" to a certain class, so we have to provide a class name to call it. This class is passed as the first argument of the method, so our call to create_random() actually returns Point(uniform(0, 10), uniform(0, 10)).

1.4 TURTLE GRAPHICS AND ANIMATION

In our projects, we will use quite extensively some basic tools for graphics and animation. The only way to achieve what we need in standard Python is to use *turtle graphics*. Making `turtle` module the only option for drawing is a peculiar design decision, but we have what we have.

Turtle graphics was specifically designed as a beginner's gateway to computer graphics, so it is likely that you know about it. However, we'll push turtle a bit farther than required for drawing basic shapes; so let's discuss some relevant aspects of its functionality.

1.4.1 BASIC TOOLS OF TURTLE GRAPHICS

As we all know, a Python program by default operates in text mode: if you run a .py file with a Python interpreter, you will see an empty text console, where all the output is going to appear. To start drawing, we will need to create a *drawing canvas* first:

```
import turtle


turtle.setup(800, 600) # make a 800 x 600 canvas
```

Next, suppose we need to draw a line between two given points (20, 0) and (300, 200). Just issuing a single-line command to do it would have been too simple. Instead, we have to create a "robotic turtle" and give it some instructions:

```
m = turtle.Turtle()
m.color("blue")    # choose a drawing color
m.penup()          # no drawing mode
m.goto(20, 0)      # source point
m.pendown()        # drawing mode
m.goto(300, 200)   # destination point
```

If you run this code, you will first see a drawing canvas appear, then a quick stroke over the canvas, performed by a visible arrow-like "robot", and then everything will be closed.

To keep the drawn picture on the screen, you can add a pause using `sleep()` function of the `time` module:

```
import time
...

time.sleep(5) # a 5-second pause
```

This solution would, however, *freeze* the canvas for 5 seconds: you will not be able to move it around the screen or close it. A better option is to end your code with a `turtle.done()` call. In a nutshell, it turns the drawing canvas into a regular window, which can be moved, resized, and closed.

Note that the turtle in the example above moves away from the screen center toward its top-right corner. The default turtle coordinate system presumes that the screen center is $(0, 0)$, the x-axis points right, and the y-axis points up.

Each `Turtle` object keeps track of its movements, which makes it possible, for example, to undo some actions or even completely remove the drawn shape from the screen:

```python
m = turtle.Turtle()
... # draw something with m
m.clear() # remove everything drawn with m
```

We will not use this capability much, but it comes in handy in one specific case. Suppose we need an updatable text label on the screen. A turtle can be used to output text as follows:

```python
writer = turtle.Turtle()
writer.hideturtle()
writer.penup()
writer.goto(100, 100)
writer.write("Hello")
```

If we try updating the label by printing Good-bye at the same position, we'll simply get a mess of both labels printed one on top of another. A call to `m.clear()` before updating the label fixes this issue.

Line-drawing animation is helpful to understand what is going on, but it also obviously slows down the program. There are ways to make animation faster, but we can also shut it down completely:

```python
turtle.tracer(0, 0) # call before drawing
...
turtle.update()      # call to perform a screen update
```

Turning off animation also turns off screen updates, meaning that we will not see any graphics at all. Calling `turtle.update()` forces a screen update to make the changes visible.

1.4.2 TURTLE ROBOT COMMANDS

The role of the turtle in this book is to be a mere device of animation and graphic output. However, turtle graphics, first introduced in Logo programming language in the late 1960s, is an interesting concept on its own.

Unlike Python, Logo was specifically designed as an educational language, targeted at children. Turtle graphics was conceived as a simple and appealing method to learn both geometry and computer programming. In many experiments, an actual physical turtle-like robot was used, so the kids could type commands and see it moving and drawing with an attached pen.

The original set of turtle commands provided no options for moving and drawing in absolute coordinates: a simple robot had no way to reach a location

(x, y) from its current place. What it could do is turn around and move forward. Seymour Papert, one of the original creators of Logo, thought that the ability to "*identify* with the Turtle" was very important [39]. The point is that we can easily imagine being a robot that executes commands like "turn 90 degrees to the right, then go 10 steps forward", and it helps to internalize what programming is all about.

Naturally, Python turtles also support such "native" commands, and we will use them occasionally:

```
# draw an L-shaped figure
m = turtle.Turtle()
m.forward(30)
m.left(90)
m.forward(15)
```

Turtle graphics is also a great example of how the right *mental model* of a certain process can sometimes simplify our tasks. Imagine we need to draw a simple 100×100 square (see Figure 1.1, left). It is equally easy to do with conventional drawing functions and with turtle robot commands:

```
# option 1: conventional drawing functions
m = turtle.Turtle()
m.goto(100, 0)
m.goto(100, 100)
m.goto(0, 100)
m.goto(0, 0)

# option 2: "the real" turtle graphics
# when created, a turtle stands at (0, 0)
# and looks to the right
m = turtle.Turtle()
for _ in range(4):
    m.forward(100)
    m.left(90)
```

Now, how difficult it is to draw a slightly rotated square (Figure 1.1, right)?

The first option looks much more complicated now, because the coordinates of vertices of the square are not obvious anymore, while the turtle graphics version is still a piece of cake:

```
m = turtle.Turtle()
m.left(20)
for _ in range(4):
    m.forward(100)
    m.left(90)
```

1.4.3 MOVING OBJECTS

Most of our projects will include some kind of animation. In general, animation is achieved by drawing successive frames at regular intervals. Fortunately, in

FIGURE 1.1: Two equal squares drawn at different rotation angles.

our case we will only need simple moving objects, which can be achieved by leveraging the existing functionality of the `turtle` module.

The trick is to use robotic turtles of different shapes and sizes. By default, the turtle looks like a little arrowhead, but this shape can be changed or made invisible:

```
...
m = turtle.Turtle()
m.shape("circle")
...
m.hideturtle()
```

Python turtle library comes with six shapes ("classic", "arrow", "turtle", "triangle", "circle", and "square"), but this list can be extended with custom user-created shapes.

Likewise, it is possible to adjust turtle size. This functionality is slightly less straightforward to use, however. All built-in turtle shapes fit into a 20×20-pixel square. This fact can be checked from a Python shell:

```
>>> import turtle
>>> turtle.Screen()._shapes['square']._data
((10, -10), (10, 10), (-10, 10), (-10, -10))
```

The square shape is defined as a list of connected vertices. As it can be seen, each vertex coordinate in the list lies within the range [-10, 10]. To make a turtle larger or smaller, we have to specify "stretch factors" for its shape:

```
m = turtle.Turtle()
m.shapesize(2)          # make the turtle twice larger
```

Thus, if we pass `size` to `shapesize()`, the actual shape would fit into a 20×`size` pixel-wide square. If a certain robotic turtle is visible, we can simply change its color and appearance as needed, and move it around to obtain the effect of a motion.

1.4.4   KEYBOARD AND TIMER EVENTS

Event handling is going to be a minor yet vital part of our projects. Suppose we want to move a turtle around using the keyboard. How can it be done? The turtle module lets us register *handlers* for various kinds of *events*. A handler is just a function that is going to be called when a certain event occurs. An event is, well, "something that happens", but this "something" must belong to a list of supported events. Python's turtle module supports only five event types: a key is pressed, a key is released, the drawing canvas is clicked, the mouse is dragged, and a timer alarm goes off. To detect a certain event, we need to register an event handler and to turn on the listening mode:

```
# every time the user presses the space key,
# the turtle makes 10 steps forward

m = turtle.Turtle()

def move_forward():
    global m
    m.forward(10)

turtle.onkeypress(move_forward, "space")
turtle.listen()
turtle.done()
```

We will use keyboard event handlers to monitor specific keys, such as "space" in the code above.

Timer alarm is an interesting type of event, because it has to be generated inside our program rather than occur as a result of user input. The ontimer() function sets up a timer alarm and specifies its handler:

```
m = turtle.Turtle()

def move_forward():
    global m
    m.forward(10)

turtle.ontimer(move_forward, 1000) # move forward after 1000 milliseconds
turtle.listen()
turtle.done()
```

1.4.5 TURTLE TOOLSET: A WRAP-UP

The turtle library of Python is quite large, and we are going to use only a fraction of its instruments. Table 1.1 and Table 1.2 provide a quick summary of the functions we'll need in the subsequent projects.[1]

TABLE 1.1: Selected methods of `Turtle` objects.

Method	Description
forward(d)	Moves the turtle by the distance `d` in the current direction.
right(a)	Turns the turtle right by `a` degrees.
left()	Turns the turtle left by `a` degrees.
goto(x, y)	Moves the turtle into the location (x, y).
setx(x)	Sets the turtle's x-coordinate to `x`.
sety(y)	Sets the turtle's y-coordinate to `y`.
setheading(a)	Sets turtle's orientation to the angle `a`.
towards(x, y)	Returns the orientation angle toward the point (x, y).
xcor()	Returns the turtle's x-coordinate.
ycor()	Returns the turtle's y-coordinate.
distance(p)	Returns the distance from the turtle to the coordinate pair or turtle object `p`.
pendown()	Enables drawing mode.
penup()	Disables drawing mode.
color(c)	Sets the turtle's pen color and fill color to `c`. Color is specified with a color string[2] or a triple of (R, G, B) components.
fillcolor(c)	Sets the turtle's fill color (specified as a color string or a triple) to `c`.
reset()	Deletes the turtle's drawings made so far and moves the turtle to its initial position.
clear()	Deletes the turtle's drawings made so far.
write(str)	Writes the string `str` at the current turtle position.
showturtle()	Makes the turtle visible.
hideturtle()	Makes the turtle invisible.
isvisible()	Returns `True` if the turtle is visible, `False` otherwise.
shape(name)	Sets turtle shape to `name`. Built-in shapes include "classic", "arrow", "turtle", "triangle", "circle", and "square".
shapesize(n)	Resizes turtle shape according to the stretch factor `n`.
clone()	Returns a clone of the current turtle, having the same position and orientation.

---

[1] From Python documentation: https://docs.python.org/3.9/library/turtle.html

[2] Supported color strings are listed in Tcl/Tk documentation: https://www.tcl.tk/man/tcl8.4/TkCmd/colors.html

TABLE 1.2: Selected functions of `turtle` module.

Method	Description
`clearscreen()`	Deletes the drawings of all the turtles.
`setworldcoordinates` `(x1, y1, x2, y2)`	Sets up user coordinate system. Four passed values become new coordinates of screen corners.
`tracer(n, delay)`	Sets up turtle update mode. Only each n-th screen update will be performed, and the delay between the updates will be set to `delay` milliseconds.
`update()`	Forces screen update.
`listen()`	Sets the currently active turtle screen as the receiver of keyboard events.
`onkeypress(fun, key)`	Sets `fun()` as the handler of a key press event for the given `key`[3].
`ontimer(fun, t)`	Sets a timer event to call `fun()` after t milliseconds.
`done()`	Starts the main event loop, responsible for the proper event handling.
`colormode(cmode)`	Sets the range of (R, G, B) values for `color()` to [0, 1.0] or [0, 255]. The value of `cmode` must be either 1.0 or 255.
`setup(width, height)`	Sets the size of the main window to `width` × `height`.
`title(titlestr)`	Sets the title of the main window to `titlestr`.

---

[3]Supported key names include "Tk keysyms", listed in Tcl/Tk documentation: `https://www.tcl.tk/man/tcl8.4/TkCmd/keysyms.html`

2 Motion and reflections

Computational modeling of real-life phenomena is one of the earliest and most important application of computer technologies. Scientific theories can be viewed as *models* of reality, as more or less accurate descriptions or the processes we see around us. The significance of these descriptions lie in their predictive power: if we understand what is going on, we can predict the outcomes.

The best predictions can be made when the underlying process is relatively simple, and its accurate mathematical description is available. For example, if I want to know how much time it would take to fill a bathtub with tap water, I can simply measure the time needed to fill a one-liter bottle and multiply it by the bathtub volume. The alternative approach would be to perform an actual *experiment* by timing the whole process.

The bathtub example relies on a simple theory: it takes N times longer to fill a vessel of an N-times larger volume. The theory will be much more complex if the task is to drain a bathtub instead, since the rate of outflow is going to decrease over time. In any case, mathematicians over centuries have developed a vast collection of methods for solving many intricate problems when they can be described in mathematical terms.

Sometimes, a process we are interested in happens to be too complex for a straightforward mathematical solution, and experimental data is difficult to obtain. For example, experimenting with rocket engines is dangerous and expensive, and experiments with social policies might take decades to complete.

Computers give us a third option: *virtual experiments.* If we understand something enough to build its computer model, we can perform a *simulation* to obtain experimental data. Computer model can be simpler than a mathematical description, and if it is sufficiently accurate, the results will also be accurate. Computational modeling is used literally everywhere, and computer simulations became an integral part of today's science and technology.

Obviously, a model has to be accurate enough to produce reliable results, and the primary point of a simulation is usually to provide numerical data. In contrast, our models are going to be simple and "visual". After all, our primary purpose is to have fun. Still, you will see that even simple models and simulations are able to produce some interesting results.

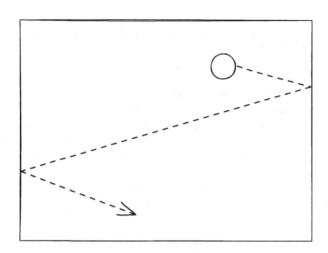

FIGURE 2.1: Trajectory of a molecule of gas in a closed vessel.

2.1   A MOLECULE OF GAS

Let's begin our journey with several simple models, inspired by the *kinetic theory of gases*.[1] Imagine a glass vessel that contains nothing but a single molecule of gas, such as oxygen or hydrogen. To make this picture even less realistic, let's presume that the molecule behaves similar to a solid, elastic ball on a billiard table without pockets and other balls (see Figure 2.1). In other words, it will move straight with a constant speed until it collides with a vessel wall and continues moving toward the opposite wall.

In addition, let's presume there is no friction, so the molecule would never stop moving, since its initial kinetic energy is never lost. Finally, for the sake of simplicity we will operate in a 2D space, which makes our vessel even more similar to a billiard table.

This little model is a good starting point for our subsequent experiments, so I suggest implementing it right away.

2.1.1   IMPLEMENTATION

Fortunately, Python syntax is close enough to pseudocode, so usually we can proceed straight to the real program. However, in this case let's look at the general picture first, and then sort out the missing details:[2]

---

[1] A great beginner-friendly resource to explore the kinetic theory is HyperPhysics, available at `http://hyperphysics.phy-astr.gsu.edu/`. Its design is certainly outdated, but the topics are presented in easily explorable bite-size chunks of pure knowledge. Click on "Heat and Thermodynamics", then open "Kinetic Theory".

[2] As a quick reminder: *speed* is a scalar (directionless) value, denoting the distance covered by a moving object in one time unit. *Velocity* is a vector, referring to the distance covered in one time unit in a certain direction. Our molecule is moving with a constant speed, but its vertical and horizontal velocities may change.

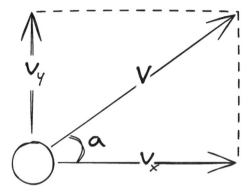

FIGURE 2.2: Calculating vertical and horizontal velocity constituents of a molecule.

```
create a molecule in a random point (x, y)
assign it a random direction
calculate vertical (vy) and horizontal (vx) velocity constituents
LOOP
    move the molecule to the point (x + vx, y + vy)
    IF the molecule is outside the vertical vessel bounds
        invert vx
    IF the molecule is outside the horizontal vessel bounds
        invert vy
END LOOP
```

Let's first note that our simulation is *discrete*: we cannot obtain the position of the molecule in any arbitrary moment of time. Instead, time is treated as a series of steps, and our molecule "jumps" from (x, y) to $(x + v_x, y + v_y)$ on every step. Consequently, its speed will be expressed in "pixels per step".

Our first task would be to obtain the values of v_x and v_y if we know the molecule's speed v and initial direction a (see Figure 2.2). This can be done with the formulas

$$v_x = v \cdot cos(a)$$

$$v_y = v \cdot sin(a)$$

Since the model is discrete, it is easy to understand how our molecule might end up being outside the vessel borders: if, for example, $v_x = 15$, the molecule makes a 15-pixel jump on each step of our simulation. If it is already close to the wall, it might very well cross it.

We will push the molecule back to the vessel on the next step of simulation, but such "jumps outside" do not look nice and make the simulation less accurate, because some points of molecule-wall collision will not be determined correctly. While there are ways to fix this issue, in practice it can usually be ignored. We can always opt for smaller speed values to minimize inevitable inaccuracies.

Now we can consider the complete program (see Listing 2.1).

Listing 2.1: A molecule of gas in a closed vessel (preliminary version).

```python
import turtle
import time
import math
from random import uniform


WIDTH = 600       # drawing canvas dimensions
HEIGHT = 400
V = 10            # molecule speed
R = 10            # molecule radius

# vessel borders (molecule's "fly zone")
left_wall, right_wall = -WIDTH / 2 + R, WIDTH / 2 - R
top_wall, bottom_wall = HEIGHT / 2 - R, -HEIGHT / 2 + R

# set up the molecule
turtle.setup(WIDTH, HEIGHT)
turtle.tracer(0, 0) # turn off turtle animation
turtle.title("A molecule of gas") # set the main window title
m = turtle.Turtle()
m.shape("circle")
m.penup()

# place it in a random screen point
m.goto(uniform(left_wall, right_wall), uniform(bottom_wall, top_wall))

angle = uniform(0, 2 * math.pi) # assign it a random direction
vx = V * math.cos(angle)        # and find velocity constituents
vy = V * math.sin(angle)

while True:
    m.goto(m.xcor() + vx, m.ycor() + vy)        # move the molecule

    # reflect if necessary
    if m.xcor() < left_wall or m.xcor() > right_wall:
        vx *= -1

    if m.ycor() < bottom_wall or m.ycor() > top_wall:
        vy *= -1

    turtle.update()    # update drawing canvas
    time.sleep(0.02)   # small pause between frames
```

As you can see, the actual simulation code takes less than one third of the complete program, and most space is devoted to setup and preparation. Let's make sure this fragment has no unclear parts.

We start by setting up vessel borders. The center of our molecule should never come closer than R pixels to any border, so we have to make the molecule's fly zone a bit smaller than the actual drawing canvas. The molecule itself is represented with a circular-shaped turtle of a default size, so its radius is going to be 10 pixels.

As explained previously, we do not need built-in turtle animation, so we have to turn it off. This also means that we need to call `turtle.update()` explicitly every time we want to display any changes made on the drawing canvas. We can make animation faster or slower without changing any model parameters by adjusting a delay between two subsequent frames.

Now you can run the code and enjoy the view of a ball bouncing around the screen. However, before proceeding to the next simulation, I suggest making some improvements.

Note that the only way to stop the simulation now is to interrupt program execution by pressing Ctrl+C / Cmd+C or closing the turtle window. It would be good to give the user a better option, such as pressing the space key. In principle, this capability can be easily incorporated into our current code:

```
. . .
done = False       # a global "simulation is done" flag

def set_done():    # will be called when the user presses space
    global done
    done = True

. . .
turtle.listen()
turtle.onkeypress(set_done, "space")

while not done:
    # move the molecule here
    . . .
```

Unfortunately, while this method seems to work fine in our case, it mixes together two poorly compatible approaches to control flow organization. Our current program is based on a traditional "active" control flow: instructions immediately follow one another, and the application shuts down after executing the last statement. In contrast, Python's turtle is based on a different, *event-driven* architecture, which treats a program mainly as a collection of functions, being called in response to certain events. A typical event-driven program is not doing anything most of the time, and its functionality is only triggered by external signals, such as user input or timer alarms (think how an application like a calculator or a text editor works).

The turtle is designed to operate in an event-driven environment. The call to `turtle.done()` (missing in our current code) actually starts a so-called *event loop*, which enables proper event handling. For this reason, a well-designed turtle-based application should quickly start an event loop, and only react to incoming events. This type of program structure requires quite a different thinking style. Our code is still simple, so the changes are going to be minimal: all we need to do is to transfer the main molecule-moving functionality inside a timer event handler.

In this new version of the code, the `while` loop will be replaced with the following fragment:

```
def tick():
    if not done:
        ... # move the molecule here
        turtle.ontimer(tick, 20) # call tick() after 20 milliseconds

tick()
turtle.done()
```

Instead of starting the main `while` loop, we are going to call `tick()`, which performs only one step of simulation. At the end, however, it sets up a timer alarm: we generate an artificial event, which will occur after 20 milliseconds and is going to be handled by `tick()`.

Other improvements are going to be less substantial. First, I think it would be good to vessel borders to make it visible (the drawing canvas has to be made a bit larger to accommodate a vessel with its borders). Second, since our vessel is symmetrical, we can simplify the condition for a bounce.

These additions turn our program into its final form (see Listing 2.2). A screenshot of the working program is shown in Figure 2.3.

Listing 2.2: A molecule of gas in a closed vessel (final version).

```
import turtle
import math
from random import uniform

WIDTH = 600
HEIGHT = 400
V = 10
R = 10
MARGIN = 50 # additional space for the drawing canvas

done = False # a global "simulation is done" flag
right_wall = WIDTH / 2 - R
top_wall = HEIGHT / 2 - R


def set_done(): # will be called when the user presses space
    global done
    done = True


turtle.setup(WIDTH + MARGIN, HEIGHT + MARGIN)
turtle.tracer(0, 0)
turtle.title("A molecule of gas")

turtle.listen()
turtle.onkeypress(set_done, "space")

m = turtle.Turtle()
m.shape("circle")
```

```
m.penup()

# let's draw a vessel (four lines)
m.goto(-WIDTH / 2, -HEIGHT / 2)
m.pendown()
m.sety(HEIGHT / 2)
m.setx(WIDTH / 2)
m.sety(-HEIGHT / 2)
m.setx(-WIDTH / 2)
m.penup()

m.goto(uniform(-right_wall, right_wall), uniform(-top_wall, top_wall))

angle = uniform(0, 2 * math.pi)
vx = V * math.cos(angle)
vy = V * math.sin(angle)


def tick():
    if not done:
        global vx, vy
        m.goto(m.xcor() + vx, m.ycor() + vy)

        if abs(m.xcor()) > right_wall:
            vx *= -1

        if abs(m.ycor()) > top_wall:
            vy *= -1

        turtle.update()
        turtle.ontimer(tick, 20)


tick()
turtle.done()
```

2.1.2 AFTERTHOUGHTS

Let me pause for a moment to appreciate how much the turtle helps us to implement moving onscreen objects.

Suppose our task is to move a black circle over a white background. Each step of this process breaks down into three actions: delete the circle by turning each of its pixels white, update its coordinates, and draw the circle at its new position.

An obvious flaw of this simple method is an inevitable *flickering* effect it produces. By deleting the circle before drawing it elsewhere, we create situations when nothing is drawn on the screen at all. As short as these periods may be, they still make the circle visibly flicker when moving. In addition, simple removal of onscreen objects might work only if the background is empty; if the circle is moving over a graphical pattern, it has to be preserved somehow.

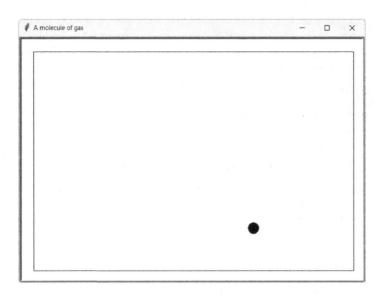

FIGURE 2.3: Molecule of gas in a closed vessel (screenshot).

This difficulty can be resolved with a popular technique of *double buffering*. An invisible virtual screen (buffer) is used to draw the whole onscreen scene from scratch on each animation frame. When the scene is ready, it is transferred to the main screen at once. Thus, there is no need to save and restore the screen areas hidden behind the moving objects, since they are redrawn on every frame. This method also removes flickering but is still prone to *tearing*.

Computer monitor updates screen content at a certain fixed rate (60 times per second is typical for conventional non-gaming monitors; gaming devices have refresh rate of 100 times per second or higher). While the virtual screen is transferred "at once", this process still takes time, and if screen refresh happens when half of virtual screen content is already on the main screen, you'll see a picture made of this new half and the previously drawn frame. This issue is resolved by synchronizing frame drawing with screen refresh rate (a technique known as *VSync*).

The turtle at least implements proper double buffering, so we will never have to deal with tearing or think what happens when a turtle crosses a patterned background or other moving objects. In addition, we don't have to do anything to restore screen content when the main application window is minimized and restored or temporarily covered by another window.

2.2 IDEAL GAS

Our starting point—the kinetic theory of gases—dates back to 18th and 19th centuries, when the modern view of microscopic particles did not yet emerge [10]. What was available is Newtonian mechanics, which could explain how

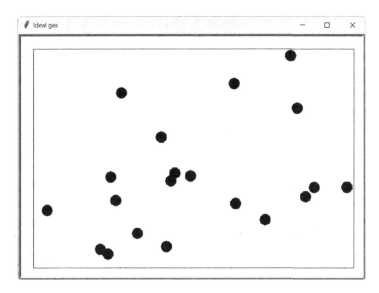

FIGURE 2.4: Ideal gas (screenshot).

macroscopic objects behave when they move and collide. The kinetic theory developed a notion of *ideal gas*, based on the following assumptions:

1. A gas consists of a large number of randomly moving molecules.
2. The molecules obey Newtonian laws of motion, and collide elastically with each other and with vessel walls.
3. The space occupied by the molecules is small compared to the total gas volume, so that possible intermolecular forces can be ignored.

The idea that molecules behave like rubber balls is obviously inaccurate, and no real gas is "ideal". Yet, the kinetic theory produced numerous important results, and still can be used under certain conditions. Our "molecule" model is actually a molecule of an ideal gas.

Let's introduce additional molecules to our code to obtain an ideal gas simulation. For now, we will presume that all the molecules have the same speed, and will ignore possible collisions between the molecules: this task is harder to accomplish, so it deserves a separate project.

2.2.1 IMPLEMENTATION

I think in this case we can proceed directly to Python code. Generalization from one molecule to a list of N molecules is quite straightforward. However, as our program grows, it makes sense to improve its organization by creating a dedicated Molecule data class, a keypress handler class SimState, and separate functions for preparing the screen and drawing a vessel (see Listing 2.3 and Figure 2.4).

Listing 2.3: Ideal gas.

```python
import turtle
import math
from random import uniform
from dataclasses import dataclass

WIDTH = 600
HEIGHT = 400
V = 10
R = 10
MARGIN = 50
SLEEP_MS = 20
N = 20          # number of molecules in our vessel

right_wall = WIDTH / 2 - R
top_wall = HEIGHT / 2 - R


@dataclass
class SimState:
    done: bool

    def set_done(self):
        self.done = True

    @classmethod
    def setup(cls):
        r = cls(False)
        turtle.listen()
        turtle.onkeypress(r.set_done, "space")
        return r


@dataclass
class Molecule:
    m: turtle.Turtle
    vx: float
    vy: float

    def move(self):
        self.m.goto(self.m.xcor() + self.vx, self.m.ycor() + self.vy)

        if abs(self.m.xcor()) > right_wall:
            self.vx *= -1

        if abs(self.m.ycor()) > top_wall:
            self.vy *= -1

    @classmethod
    def create(cls):
        m = turtle.Turtle()
        m.shape("circle")
        m.penup()
        m.goto(uniform(-right_wall, right_wall), uniform(-top_wall, top_wall))
```

```
        angle = uniform(0, 2 * math.pi)
        return cls(m, V * math.cos(angle), V * math.sin(angle))


def setup_screen(title):
    turtle.setup(WIDTH + MARGIN, HEIGHT + MARGIN)
    turtle.tracer(0, 0)
    turtle.title(title)


def draw_vessel():
    m = turtle.Turtle()
    m.hideturtle()
    m.penup()
    m.goto(-WIDTH / 2, -HEIGHT / 2)
    m.pendown()
    m.sety(HEIGHT / 2)
    m.setx(WIDTH / 2)
    m.sety(-HEIGHT / 2)
    m.setx(-WIDTH / 2)


sim_state = SimState.setup()
setup_screen("Ideal gas")
draw_vessel()
molecules = [Molecule.create() for _ in range(N)]


def tick():
    if not sim_state.done:
        for m in molecules:
            m.move()

        turtle.update()
        turtle.ontimer(tick, SLEEP_MS)


tick()
turtle.done()
```

2.2.2 AFTERTHOUGHTS

Turtle graphics capabilities definitely help us with visualization. Turtle's event-driven architecture might look like a less clear-cut bargain.

Nothing beats the simplicity of a command-line utility. Read input data from a file or a console, do something, write output data. It is tempting to preserve this simplicity in an interactive animation-heavy application. It is easy to do on a game console, where all your users share the same hardware, and your application can use computational resources exclusively. Things get more difficult if available resources vary from device to device, and your software has to play well with other processes in the memory.

Event-driven architecture not only helps to solve these issues, but also provides a way to deal with them separately. We will rarely have to think about performance or responsiveness of user interface, but our programs also benefit from this approach.

First of all, note that our simulations do not consume processor power between timer events. They won't cause your operating system to freeze. Next, consider a subtle difference between *physics* and *animation*. Our ideal gas simulation works fine for a small number of molecules. On my machine, when N is set to 5, and SLEEP_MS is zero, the program is able to produce 500-600 frames per second. If N is increased to 500, the framerate drops to 10, and the movements look slow. Computational resources are spent on two separate activities: moving molecules and drawing them. Which one is more expensive? It is easy to test: if I remove the call to turtle.update(), the framerate rises to 150 frames per second. Removing move() while keeping turtle.update() intact barely makes any difference.

Thus, in this particular case the expensive part is animation, while the actual simulation costs next to nothing. Now, suppose we need to keep 500 molecules in the vessel, but make them move faster. The easy way would be to increase their speed, but it is bad for accuracy. Even now the molecules might get outside vessel borders, and higher speeds will make this effect even more pronounced. Such "jumps" are also very bad for any kinds of interaction between moving objects. A smarter approach would be to keep the physics accurate and sacrifice only the smoothness of animation. For example, we can still update molecule coordinates at a fast rate, increasing the time between screen updates only. This is easy to achieve with two independent timers:

```
SLEEP_MS = 10
VIS_SLEEP_MS = 40
...

def tick_draw():
    if not sim_state.done:
        turtle.update()
        turtle.ontimer(tick_draw, VIS_SLEEP_MS)


def tick():
    if not sim_state.done:
        for m in molecules:
            m.move()
        turtle.ontimer(tick, SLEEP_MS)


tick()
tick_draw()
turtle.done()
```

Here animation smoothness is controlled by the VIS_SLEEP_MS delay, while physics works with the same rate. To achieve clockwork accuracy, you can also adjust frame delays to take into account that some frames take longer to process than others:

```python
import time

SLEEP = 50


def tick():
    start = time.perf_counter()  # hi-resolution timer (in seconds)
    # do something
    ...
    elapsed = int(1000 * (time.perf_counter() - start))  # milliseconds
    turtle.ontimer(tick, max(0, SLEEP - elapsed))
```

A similar approach is often used in game development. For example, games created with a popular engine Unity rely on two independent kinds of timer events. The "fixed time step system" operates at a constant rate and is typically used for physics. The "variable time step system" generates timer events as often as possible on the given hardware and it is typically used for user input handling and animation.[3]

In games, animation often works faster than physics. In Unity, physics by default operates at the rate of 50 frames per second, while an animation subsystem may produce much higher values. This is good, in particular, for camera controls: a little mouse nudge changes the camera angle instantly. This functionality does not modify the game world, and can be implemented entirely within the variable time step system.

2.3 BOYLE-MARIOTTE'S LAW

As noted by George Box, *"All models are wrong, but some are useful"* [5]. It is easy to criticize the kinetic theory as naïve, and yet it managed to connect certain macroscopic properties of gases with behavior of molecules, and establish a few laws with reasonable accuracy. For example, gas in a vessel has a certain temperature, which can be checked with a thermometer, while an individual molecule cannot be hot or cold. How can it be? Similarly, by pumping air into a rubber tire, we increase pressure, but what does it mean for a molecule to "push stronger"?

Within the kinetic theory, it is presumed that a temperature of gas grows proportionally with the average kinetic energy of molecules. Thus, a thermometer actually detects how fast gas molecules are moving. Likewise, pressure is considered to be the observable result of force exerted by molecules colliding with vessel walls. By employing Newtonian mechanics, it is possible to calculate some specific numbers, which makes the whole theory useful.

---

[3] According to Unity documentation:
https://docs.unity3d.com/2023.3/Documentation/Manual/TimeFrameManagement.html

Our ideal gas simulation also can demonstrate certain properties of gasses. Perhaps, the easiest one to test is *Boyle-Mariotte's law*:

The pressure of a given quantity of gas varies inversely with its volume at constant temperature.[4]

In other words, the product of pressure and volume is constant: $P \cdot V = const$.

The quantity of gas is the number of molecules in the vessel, and its temperature depends on the average speed of molecules. These values remain the same in our simulations, so it is enough to try vessels of different sizes and see how these changes affect the resulting gas pressure.

Now only one missing piece of the puzzle prevents us from testing Boyle-Mariotte's law experimentally: how to calculate the pressure. In the kinetic theory, it is presumed to be equal to the average force exerted by the molecules on vessel walls *per unit area* (a single collision exerts more pressure on a small wall than on a large wall) [32]. Now, suppose a molecule with horizontal velocity v_x hits a side wall. Its change in momentum would be

$$\Delta p = 2mv_x$$

According to Newton's second law of motion, the force is the rate of change of momentum:

$$F = \frac{\Delta p}{\Delta t}$$

In our case, Δt is the time between two subsequent collisions of a molecule with a wall, so in a large vessel the pressure is lower, because it takes more time for a molecule to travel from one side to another and hit a wall again.

Naturally, we are not really interested in the contribution of every single molecule: it is enough to calculate the average force, which in practice means adding up all the calculated Δp values and dividing the result by the total running time. As a further simplification, we can presume that the mass of each molecule is 0.5, so the formula for Δp becomes simply

$$\Delta p = |v_x|$$

Let's also remember that every collision adds up to the pressure, so we don't need to take into account velocity signs: all contributions are positive. Since we know the force, it is finally possible to calculate the pressure:

$$P = \frac{F}{(wall\ area)}$$

---

[4]From *Encyclopaedia Britannica*: https://www.britannica.com/science/Boyles-law

In our two-dimensional simulations, a vessel volume is simply the bounding box area:

$$V = (vessel\_height) \times (vessel\_width)$$

Similarly, the total wall area is the box perimeter:

$$wall\ area = 2(vessel\_height + vessel\_width)$$

If you are not convinced, think about our vessel as having a depth of 1, and no molecules (by luck!) collide with its front and back walls.

2.3.1   IMPLEMENTATION

This simulation can be easily obtained from Listing 2.3 ("Ideal gas"). The changes are going to be very straightforward:

1. Modify the SimState class to incorporate Δp and Δt as follows:

```
@dataclass
class SimState:
    done: bool
    delta_p: float
    delta_t: int

    def set_done(self):
        self.done = True

    def pressure(self):
        area = 2 * (2 * top_wall + 2 * right_wall)
        force = self.delta_p / self.delta_t
        return force / area

    @classmethod
    def setup(cls):
        r = cls(False, 0, 0)
        turtle.listen()
        turtle.onkeypress(r.set_done, "space")
        return r
```

2. Modify the value of delta_p every time a molecule collides with a wall:

```
@dataclass
class Molecule:
    ...
    def move(self):
        ...
        if abs(self.m.xcor()) > right_wall:
            self.vx *= -1
            sim_state.delta_p += abs(self.vx)

        if abs(self.m.ycor()) > top_wall:
            self.vy *= -1
            sim_state.delta_p += abs(self.vy)
```

3. Increase `delta_t` before calling `turtle.update()` and print the value of $P \cdot V$:

```
def tick():
    ...
    sim_state.delta_t += 1

    # do it on every 100th iteration
    if sim_state.delta_t % 100 == 0:
        vol = (2 * top_wall) * (2 * right_wall)
        print(round(sim_state.pressure() * vol, 2))

    turtle.update()
    turtle.ontimer(tick, SLEEP_MS)
```

Finally, run the program with different values of HEIGHT and WIDTH to see whether the value of $P \cdot V$ remains the same. In my test runs, I consistently get something within a range of 460-500 for two vessels, one four times larger than the other one in terms of volume.

2.4   THERMODYNAMICS

Thermodynamics is a branch of physics that *"deals with the transfer of energy from one place to another and from one form to another"*.[5] As one might expect, it is an established and well-developed discipline with all kinds of theories and laws, so it might seem strange to name any single simulation simply "Thermodynamics". I owe this name to Vaillencourt's book [55] thanks to the following statement:

*"As far as using energy is concerned, thermodynamics can be boiled down to one simple rule. <...> **ENERGY ALWAYS MOVES FROM HOT TO COLD"**.*

This rule (with all the necessary refinements) is also known as *the second law of thermodynamics*. Despite its simplicity, this law possibly means grave consequences for our beloved universe: according to the "heat death" hypothesis, if the energy always moves to the colder objects, eventually all the objects will reach the same temperature, and no further processes, essential to our being, are going to be possible. However, there are other views on this subject, and in any case humankind has more pressing issues than "heath death" at the moment.

What we really can do now is to show that the second law indeed works. As previously noted, according to the kinetic theory of gases, a temperature is presumed to be proportional to the average kinetic energy of molecules. Thus, we can create two communicating vessels—one with cold gas, another one with hot gas—and see what happens (Figure 2.5).

---

[5] From *Encyclopaedia Britannica*:
https://www.britannica.com/science/thermodynamics

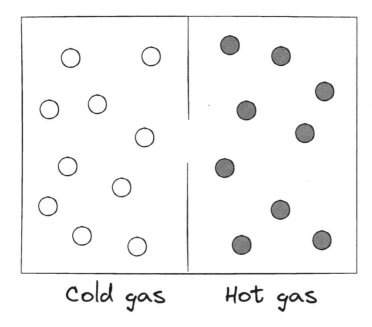

Cold gas   Hot gas

FIGURE 2.5: Communicating vessels with gases of different temperatures.

I believe at this point it should be crystal-clear how the kinetic theory explains the second law of thermodynamics: fast and slow molecules mix together until the average speed in both vessels is the same. At a macroscopic level, it means that the right vessel cools down while the left vessel heats up. Let's demonstrate this effect with a simulation.

2.4.1 IMPLEMENTATION

Let's again rely on our trusty "Ideal gas" model (Listing 2.3) and review the necessary modifications. Instead of the same speed value for all the molecules, we'll need "cold" slow molecules and "hot" fast molecules now:

```
V_COLD = 5
V_HOT = 15
```

We will also need to separate our vessel into two compartments, leaving a hole in the separating wall. The radius of this hole affects the ability of gases to mix together, so it's better to make it a dedicated constant:

```
R_HOLE = 30
```

Next, let's modify the `draw_vessel()` function to draw an additional wall:

```
def draw_vessel():
    ...
    m.penup()
    m.goto(0, -HEIGHT / 2)  # draw a straight vertical line
    m.pendown()             # from the screen top toward the center
    m.sety(-R_HOLE)
    m.penup()
    m.sety(R_HOLE)          # draw a similar line from the screen bottom
    m.pendown()             # toward the center, leaving a gap in the middle
    m.sety(HEIGHT / 2)
```

The changes in `Molecule` class are going to be more complicated. Most importantly, its `move()` method will have to reflect a molecule from a new vertical wall in the middle of the vessel:

```
@dataclass
class Molecule:
    m: turtle.Turtle
    v: float          # let's store the original speed value
    vx: float
    vy: float

    def move(self):
        # same as before
        self.m.goto(self.m.xcor() + self.vx, self.m.ycor() + self.vy)

        if abs(self.m.xcor()) > right_wall:
            self.vx *= -1

        if abs(self.m.ycor()) > top_wall:
            self.vy *= -1

        # new functionality: reflecting from the central wall
        near_hole = abs(self.m.ycor()) <= R_HOLE - R
        moves_right = -R < self.m.xcor() < 0 and self.vx > 0
        moves_left = 0 < self.m.xcor() < R and self.vx < 0

        if not near_hole and (moves_left or moves_right):
            self.vx *= -1

    # a molecule will be created in the specified vessel part
    # and will have a custom color
    @classmethod
    def create(cls, v, left, right, color):
        m = turtle.Turtle()
        m.shape("circle")
        m.color(color)
        m.penup()
        m.goto(uniform(left, right), uniform(-top_wall, top_wall))

        angle = uniform(0, 2 * math.pi)
        return cls(m, v, v * math.cos(angle), v * math.sin(angle))
```

The logic is simple: if a molecule is approaching the wall from either side and its vertical coordinate does not match the hole, we have to reflect it back.

The molecules have to be created in two steps now:

```
# create cold gas, then hot gas
mcold = [Molecule.create(V_COLD, -right_wall, -R, "blue") for _ in range(N)]
mhot = [Molecule.create(V_HOT, R, right_wall, "red") for _ in range(N)]
molecules = mcold + mhot
```

At this point, it is possible to run the program and see blue and red balls flying around the screen just as expected. However, there is no way to check the real-time temperature in either vessel, so we can only guess which side is hotter. As mentioned above, the temperature of gas is presumed to be proportional to the average kinetic energy of its molecules. The kinetic energy of an individual molecule is $\frac{mv^2}{2}$, but since in our case all masses are equal, we can simply use v^2 and calculate the temperature of the list of molecules as follows:

```
def temperature(gas):
    return sum(mol.v**2 for mol in gas) / len(gas)
```

Finally, we'll have to call `temperature()` for both vessels in our `tick()` function and show both values on the screen:

```
writer = turtle.Turtle()
writer.hideturtle()
writer.penup()


def tick():
    if not sim_state.done:
        for m in molecules:
            m.move()

        m_left = [mol for mol in molecules if mol.m.xcor() < 0]
        m_right = [mol for mol in molecules if mol.m.xcor() > 0]

        writer.clear()
        writer.goto(-100, HEIGHT / 2)              # left vessel's temperature
        writer.write(round(temperature(m_left)))
        writer.goto(100, HEIGHT / 2)               # right vessel's temperature
        writer.write(round(temperature(m_right)))

        turtle.update()
        turtle.ontimer(tick, SLEEP_MS)


tick()
turtle.done()
```

Finally, we can run the program and wait for some time to let the gases mix together (see Figure 2.6). You can adjust the size of the hole to speed up or slow down this process.

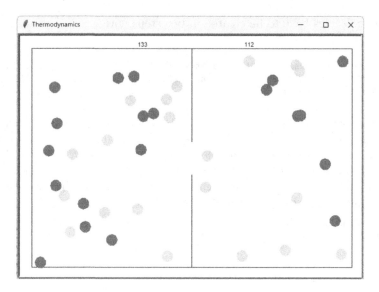

FIGURE 2.6: "Thermodynamics" (screenshot).

2.5 CENTRAL COLLISION

Our model of an ideal gas has an obvious flaw: it does not handle collisions between the molecules. One might ask whether modeling collisions is worth the effort: after all, molecules are not balls, and making them collide would not bring much benefit in terms of model accuracy. However, collisions are interesting in case of macroscopic objects, so I will use our model of an ideal gas simply as a good excuse to bring them up.

In the subsequent simulations, we will consider three different cases of a collision:

1. Central collision of two balls.
2. Collision of two balls moving in arbitrary directions.
3. Collision of a ball with an arbitrarily placed wall.

We will start with the simplest case of a *central collision*. Imagine two balls of different masses and velocities approaching each other. Eventually they collide *elastically* (meaning there is no loss of energy due to a collision) and continue their motion. Let's presume that the collision is *central*, meaning that the original ball trajectories lie on the same line (see Figure 2.7).

The primary challenge of modeling this situation lies in calculating ball velocities after the collision. Their values can be obtained from the laws of conservation of energy and momentum.

Suppose the masses of the balls are m_1 and m_2, and their initial velocities are v_1 and v_2. If the balls move in the same direction, both velocities would have the same sign. Let's denote ball velocities after the collision as v_1' and

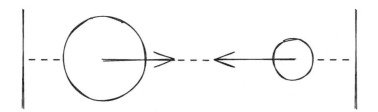

FIGURE 2.7: Central collision of two balls.

v_2'. According to the laws of conservation:

$$m_1 v_1 + m_2 v_2 = m_1 v_1' + m_2 v_2' \qquad \text{(conservation of momentum)}$$

$$\frac{m_1 v_1^2}{2} + \frac{m_2 v_2^2}{2} = \frac{m_1 v_1'^2}{2} + \frac{m_2 v_2'^2}{2} \qquad \text{(conservation of energy)}$$

These equations can be regrouped as follows:

$$m_1(v_1 - v_1') = m_2(v_2' - v_2) \qquad (1)$$

$$m_1(v_1^2 - v_1'^2) = m_2(v_2'^2 - v_2^2) \qquad (2)$$

Since $a^2 - b^2 = (a - b)(a + b)$, we can rewrite (2) as

$$m_1(v_1 - v_1')(v_1 + v_1') = m_2(v_2' - v_2)(v_2' + v_2) \qquad (3)$$

Now let's divide (3) by (1):

$$\frac{m_1(v_1 - v_1')(v_1 + v_1')}{m_1(v_1 - v_1')} = \frac{m_2(v_2' - v_2)(v_2' + v_2)}{m_2(v_2' - v_2)}$$

After simplification, this equation becomes

$$v_1 + v_1' = v_2' + v_2$$

Therefore,

$$v_2' = v_1 + v_1' - v_2 \qquad (4)$$

By substituting v_2' in (1) with the right-hand side of (4), we obtain

$$m_1(v_1 - v_1') = m_2(v_1 + v_1' - v_2 - v_2)$$

From this equation, we can derive v_1':

$$v_1' = \frac{v_1(m_1 - m_2) + 2m_2 v_2}{m_2 + m_1} \qquad (5)$$

That's all. By calculating (5), we can obtain the resulting velocity of the first ball. The obtained value can then be used in (4) to calculate the velocity of the second ball.

2.5.1 IMPLEMENTATION

This model can be implemented by modifying one of our previous programs ("Ideal gas" seems to be an easy choice in most cases). This time we will have to deal with the balls of different masses and velocities. The tricky part is mass, as it would be good to adjust ball sizes to show the differences in their masses. In the real world, a mass of a ball is proportional to its volume, meaning that it grows as a cube of radius. Since we are operating in a two-dimensional world, I suggest to presume that the mass is proportional to the ball's area, i.e., to the square of its radius. Let's recall that the size of the robotic turtle is specified via "stretch factors", so if we pass a value of size to the shapesize() function, the actual values for the ball radius and ball mass will be

```
r = size * R              # R = 10
mass = math.pi * (r ** 2)   # ball area
```

Note that the code for wall collision detection also has to take into account different ball sizes. Apart from this change, the new program relies on roughly the same Molecule class (renamed as Ball), with now-unnecessary vy velocity component removed (see Listing 2.4). A screenshot of the working program is shown in Figure 2.8.

Listing 2.4: Central collision of two balls.

```
# central_collision.py
import turtle
import math
from random import uniform
from dataclasses import dataclass

WIDTH = 600
HEIGHT = 400
MIN_V = 5
MAX_V = 15
MIN_SIZE_FACTOR = 0.7
MAX_SIZE_FACTOR = 4
START_DISTANCE = 400
R = 10
MARGIN = 50
SLEEP_MS = 20


@dataclass
class SimState:
    ... # same as in "Ideal gas"


@dataclass
class Ball:
    m: turtle.Turtle
    vx: float
```

```
    r: float

    def move(self):
        self.m.setx(self.m.xcor() + self.vx)

        if abs(self.m.xcor()) >= WIDTH / 2 - self.r:
            self.vx *= -1

    def mass(self):
        return math.pi * (self.r ** 2)

    @classmethod
    def create(cls, x, v_factor):
        size = uniform(MIN_SIZE_FACTOR, MAX_SIZE_FACTOR)
        r = size * R
        m = turtle.Turtle()
        m.shape("circle")
        m.shapesize(size)
        m.penup()
        m.goto(x, 0)

        return Ball(m, v_factor * uniform(MIN_V, MAX_V), r)


def setup_screen(title):
    ... # same as in "Ideal gas"

def draw_vessel():
    ... # same as in "Ideal gas"

# balls b1 and b2 collide if their centers are closer than b1.r + b2.r
def balls_collide(b1, b2):
    return abs(b1.m.xcor() - b2.m.xcor()) <= b1.r + b2.r


# obtain new ball velocities after the collision
# according to the formulas (4) and (5)
def process_collision(b1, b2):
    m1, m2 = b1.mass(), b2.mass()
    v1n = (b1.vx * (m1 - m2) + 2 * m2 * b2.vx) / (m1 + m2)
    v2n = b1.vx + v1n - b2.vx

    b1.vx = v1n
    b2.vx = v2n


sim_state = SimState.setup()
setup_screen("Central collision")
draw_vessel()

ball1 = Ball.create(-START_DISTANCE / 2, 1)
ball2 = Ball.create(START_DISTANCE / 2, -1)


def tick():
    if not sim_state.done:
```

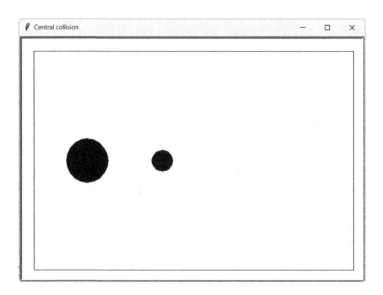

FIGURE 2.8: Central collision of two balls (screenshot).

```
ball1.move()
ball2.move()

if balls_collide(ball1, ball2):
    process_collision(ball1, ball2)

turtle.update()
turtle.ontimer(tick, SLEEP_MS)


tick()
turtle.done()
```

Before moving on to the next project, let's test our formulas in two interesting edge cases:

1. Suppose that both balls have the same mass $(m_1 = m_2 = M)$. Then

$$v_1' = \frac{v_1(M - M) + 2Mv_2}{M + M} = \frac{2Mv_2}{2M} = v_2$$

$$v_2' = v_1 + v_1' - v_2 = v_1 + v_2 - v_2 = v_1$$

Therefore, when the balls of equal masses collide, they exchange velocities. In particular, when a moving ball hits a still ball, it stops,
and the previously still ball starts moving with the same velocity as
the ball that hit it.

2. Suppose that the mass of the first ball is very large $(m_1 = M)$, and
its speed is zero. This case is equivalent to hitting a wall, and our

formula works perfectly fine:

$$v_1' = \frac{0(M - m_2) + 2m_2v_2}{M + m_2} = \frac{2m_2v_2}{M + m_2} \approx 0$$

$$v_2' = v_1 + v_1' - v_2 = 0 + 0 - v_2 = -v_2$$

This means the first ball stands still, while the second ball's velocity value changes its sign.

2.6   FREE KICK

A natural way to extend the previous project would be to support collision of two balls moving in arbitrary directions. Obviously, math becomes more complicated here, so the most difficult part of this challenge is to figure out how ball velocities change as a result of collision.[6]

Suppose two balls have collided. The first ball is located in the point (x_1, y_1) and the angle between its trajectory and the x-axis is A_1. Likewise, the second ball is currently at (x_2, y_2), and its trajectory is defined with the angle A_2 (see Figure 2.9). Horizontal and vertical ball velocities $(v_{x1}, v_{y1}, v_{x2},$ and $v_{y2})$ are also known.

Let's first find the angle a between the x-axis and the line connecting the centers of both balls (let's denote this line as m):[7]

$$a = atan2(y_2 - y_1, x_2 - x_1)$$

Now let's rotate the coordinate system to make the x-axis parallel to m, and the y-axis parallel to its normal n. To do it, we simply need to subtract a from A_1 and A_2:

$$A_1' = atan2(v_{y1}, v_{x1}) - a$$

$$A_2' = atan2(v_{y2}, v_{x2}) - a$$

Each ball's movement consists of radial (along m) and tangential (along n) velocity constituents. As a result of collision, no tangential constituent is affected, while radial constituents have to be modified according to the laws of conservation, just like in the previous model.

At this point we need to know ball speeds. They can be calculated from velocity constituents using the Euclidian distance formula:

---

[6]A simpler algorithm can be obtained with vector operations. However, it relies on slightly more advanced math [29].

[7]A math textbook would say that the angle between the x-axis and a line connecting (0, 0) with (x, y) is equal to $arctan(y/x)$. However, $arctan$ produces results between -90° and 90°, and it won't work if $x = 0$, so various corrections are necessary to convert it to the value in the range from -180° to 180° we are looking for. Python's $atan2()$ is able to make these corrections and produce the result in the target range because it knows the signs of both input values.

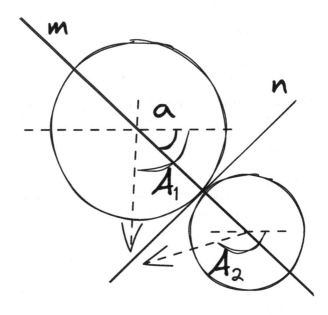

FIGURE 2.9: Sketch of two colliding balls.

$$v_1 = \sqrt{v_{x1}^2 + v_{y1}^2} \qquad \text{(velocity of the first ball)}$$

$$v_2 = \sqrt{v_{x2}^2 + v_{y2}^2} \qquad \text{(velocity of the second ball)}$$

Since coordinate axes are parallel to m and n, radial and tangential velocity constituents are simply projections onto axes:

$$v_{r1} = v_1 \cdot cos(A_1') \qquad \text{(radial velocity of the first ball)}$$

$$v_{t1} = v_1 \cdot sin(A_1') \qquad \text{(tangential velocity of the first ball)}$$

$$v_{r2} = v_2 \cdot cos(A_2') \qquad \text{(radial velocity of the second ball)}$$

$$v_{t2} = v_2 \cdot sin(A_2') \qquad \text{(tangential velocity of the second ball)}$$

Now we can obtain radial velocity constituents after the collision (presuming that ball masses are m_1 and m_2) using the formulas from the previous project:

$$v_{r1}' = \frac{v_{r1}(m_1 - m_2) + 2m_2 * v_{r2}}{m_1 + m_2}$$

$$v_{r2}' = v_{r1} + v_{r1}' - v_{r2}$$

Since one of the velocity constituents of each ball has changed, we have to recalculate v_1 and v_2:

$$v_1' = \sqrt{v_{r1}'^2 + v_{t1}^2}$$

$$v_2' = \sqrt{v_{r2}'^2 + v_{t2}^2}$$

New values for the trajectory angles can be obtained using arctangents, just like before. We also have to turn back the coordinate axes by adding a:

$$A_1'' = atan2(v_{t1}, v_{r1}') + a$$

$$A_2'' = atan2(v_{t2}, v_{r2}') + a$$

Finally, we have to calculate new velocity constituents of both balls:

$$v_{x1}' = v_1' \cdot cos(A_1'')$$

$$v_{y1}' = v_1' \cdot sin(A_1'')$$

$$v_{x2}' = v_2' \cdot cos(A_2'')$$

$$v_{y2}' = v_2' \cdot sin(A_2'')$$

2.6.1 IMPLEMENTATION

The easiest way to create "Free kick" is to modify our previous program, "Central collision" (Listing 2.4). Let me save some space and only show the changes (see Listing 2.5). In a nutshell, we have to:

1. Add the second velocity component to the `Ball` class, so it can move in the vertical direction.
2. Handle both velocity components in `move()`.
3. Modify `balls_collide()` so it takes into account both x and y ball coordinates.
4. Introduce our formulas into `process_collision()`.
5. Create both balls in random vessel locations.

Listing 2.5: A collision of two balls moving in arbitrary directions (fragments).

```
... # same as before

@dataclass
class Ball:
    m: turtle.Turtle
    vx: float
    vy: float
    r: float

    def move(self):
        self.m.goto(self.m.xcor() + self.vx, self.m.ycor() + self.vy)
```

```python
        if abs(self.m.xcor()) > WIDTH / 2 - self.r:
            self.vx *= -1

        if abs(self.m.ycor()) > HEIGHT / 2 - self.r:
            self.vy *= -1

    def mass(self):
        return math.pi * (self.r ** 2)

    @classmethod
    def create(cls):
        size = uniform(MIN_SIZE_FACTOR, MAX_SIZE_FACTOR)
        r = size * R
        x = uniform(-WIDTH / 2 + r, WIDTH / 2 - r)      # create in a
        y = uniform(-HEIGHT / 2 + r, HEIGHT / 2 - r)  # random location
        m = turtle.Turtle()
        m.shape("circle")
        m.shapesize(size)
        m.penup()
        m.goto(x, y)
        v = uniform(MIN_V, MAX_V)
        angle = uniform(0, 2 * math.pi) # set a random direction
        return Ball(m, v * math.cos(angle), v * math.sin(angle), r)


def setup_screen(title):
    ... # same as before


def draw_vessel():
    ... # same as before


def balls_collide(b1, b2):
    return b1.m.distance(b2.m) <= b1.r + b2.r


def process_collision(b1, b2): # use our new formulas
    a = math.atan2(b2.m.ycor() - b1.m.ycor(), b2.m.xcor() - b1.m.xcor())
    A1n = math.atan2(b1.vy, b1.vx) - a
    A2n = math.atan2(b2.vy, b2.vx) - a

    v1 = math.sqrt(b1.vx ** 2 + b1.vy ** 2)
    v2 = math.sqrt(b2.vx ** 2 + b2.vy ** 2)

    vr1 = v1 * math.cos(A1n)
    vt1 = v1 * math.sin(A1n)

    vr2 = v2 * math.cos(A2n)
    vt2 = v2 * math.sin(A2n)

    m1, m2 = b1.mass(), b2.mass()
    vr1n = (vr1 * (m1 - m2) + 2 * m2 * vr2) / (m1 + m2)
    vr2n = vr1 + vr1n - vr2
```

```
    v1n = math.sqrt(vr1n ** 2 + vt1 ** 2)
    v2n = math.sqrt(vr2n ** 2 + vt2 ** 2)

    A1nn = math.atan2(vt1, vr1n) + a
    A2nn = math.atan2(vt2, vr2n) + a

    b1.vx = v1n * math.cos(A1nn)
    b1.vy = v1n * math.sin(A1nn)

    b2.vx = v2n * math.cos(A2nn)
    b2.vy = v2n * math.sin(A2nn)


sim_state = SimState.setup()
setup_screen("Free kick")
draw_vessel()

ball1 = Ball.create()
ball2 = Ball.create()


def tick():
    ... # same as before
```

A screenshot of the running program is virtually indistinguishable from "Central collision", so it is hardly worth showing. However, I really recommend running it! In this age, we are used to the most fascinating visual effects, and yet there is still something captivating about watching moving and colliding balls. It isn't on the same level as watching burning fire or falling water, but definitely feels like a step in the right direction.

2.7   VERY IDEAL GAS

There is no such concept called "very ideal gas" in physics, of course, but we have already created the model called "Ideal gas", and the goal of our next project is to improve it.

Let's recall that the theoretical concept of "ideal gas" presumes the molecules behave like rubber balls, and, in particular, they collide with each other. Since we already know how to handle collisions, we can increase the count of moving particles in "Free kick" and obtain a better model.

2.7.1   IMPLEMENTATION

The required modifications are going to be very minor.[8] First, we'll need to declare the number of molecules in the vessel, rename the `Ball` class back to `Molecule`, and let the user supply a custom molecule size:

---

[8]The code can be simplified by removing the support of arbitrary molecule sizes, but I wanted to keep the changes minimal.

```
N = 10
...

@dataclass
class Molecule:
    ...

    def create(cls, size):
        # remove the line
        # size = uniform(MIN_SIZE_FACTOR, MAX_SIZE_FACTOR)
        ...
```

Next, we'll have to place all our molecules into a list (just like in "Ideal gas"), and modify the tick() function to handle their collisions:

```
...
molecules = [Molecule.create(1) for _ in range(N)]


def tick():
    if not sim_state.done:
        for m in molecules:
            m.move()

        for i in range(len(molecules)): # process collision once
            for j in range(0, i):        # for each pair of molecules
                if balls_collide(molecules[i], molecules[j]):
                    process_collision(molecules[i], molecules[j])

        turtle.update()
        turtle.ontimer(tick, SLEEP_MS)
```

Theoretically, it should be the end of the story. However, if you run the modified program, eventually you will notice its flaws: sometimes a stray molecule gets stuck somewhere outside the edge of the vessel, and sometimes a pair of molecules gets "glued" together and continues moving as a single blob.

This is how our discrete model meets the continuous reality. Consider, for example, a molecule approaching the right vessel wall with v_x of 5 pixels per step. Suppose that its current x-coordinate is WIDTH / 2 - 11, so it is very close to the wall. This molecule is being chased by another molecule with v_x of 10 pixels per step, and its x-coordinate is WIDTH / 2 - 32. Since R is 10, the molecules do not collide with each other yet. Now let's see what happens next:

- The first molecule's coordinates get updated:

```
self.m.goto(self.m.xcor() + self.vx, self.m.ycor() + self.vy)
# x becomes WIDTH / 2 - 11 + 5 = WIDTH / 2 - 6

if abs(self.m.xcor()) > WIDTH / 2 - self.r:
    self.vx *= -1
# vx becomes -5
```

- The second molecule's coordinates similarly get updated. Its x becomes WIDTH / 2 - 22.
- Since the molecules collide now (the distance between them is 16 pixels), we have to update their velocities. By calling process_collision(), we obtain $v_x = 10$ for the first molecule, and $v_x = -5$ for the second molecule.
- Note that the first molecule's v_x is positive again, so on the next simulation step it will fly away *further* to the right! Even worse, it will be too far away from the wall to get back into the vessel. The fragment

```
if abs(self.m.xcor()) > WIDTH / 2 - self.r:
    self.vx *= -1
```

will keep changing the sign of v_x on every step, so the molecule will keep oscillating outside the wall until some other molecule helps it get unstuck.

The trouble with moving blobs of molecules has a somewhat similar nature: it is possible that two molecules end up in a collision resolved in such a way that they still collide on the next step of simulation. These multiple collisions may lead to all kinds of strange behavior.

Moving blobs, however, rarely happen in "Very ideal gas", so for now let's just add a small fix for the molecules stuck outside the vessel. The easiest way to do it is to make sure that all the coordinates in our program are inside the vessel:

```
# make sure -max_v <= v <= max_v
def clamp(v, max_v):
    return math.copysign(min(abs(v), max_v), v)


@dataclass
class Molecule:
    ...

    def move(self):
        ...
        self.m.setx(clamp(self.m.xcor(), WIDTH / 2 - self.r))
        self.m.sety(clamp(self.m.ycor(), HEIGHT / 2 - self.r))
```

The final lines of move() force the molecule back into the vessel by "clamping" the molecule's coordinates. Python's function copysign(x, y) applies the sign of y to abs(x) and returns the obtained value, so our clamp() first takes the smaller of values abs(v) and max_v, and then uses copysign() to preserve the original sign of v.

2.8 BROWNIAN MOTION

In 1827, a botanist Robert Brown was examining pollen of the recently discovered plant *Clarkia pulchella*. Being suspended in water, the grains of pollen released certain particles that could be seen under a microscope. Brown noticed and reported the irregular, jittery motion of these particles but could not provide a good explanation for what he had seen.[9]

Much later it was discovered that the jittery motion of particles, now known as *Brownian motion*, is the result of their collisions with the molecules of water. A particle behaves somewhat like a large inflated ball in the middle of a crowd of people moving in random directions.

Believe it or not, my proposal would be to simulate Brownian motion on a computer.

2.8.1   IMPLEMENTATION

Essentially, "Brownian motion" is "Very ideal gas" with one large particle surrounded by much smaller molecules. Its initial speed is equal to zero, and all the collisions are handled according to the rules of "Free kick".

The only important modification I am about to introduce deals with the "moving blobs" problem that we encountered in "Very ideal gas". The particle is going to be large and is likely to form blobs with surrounding molecules. Furthermore, some molecules will inevitably appear *inside* the particle if we scatter them randomly within the vessel bounds. For these reasons we should finally get rid of "moving blobs".

Fortunately, there is an easy solution. Since blobs form when we handle a collision between the same pair of objects on two successive iterations, we can simply stop doing it. It is enough to form the list of colliding pairs while working on collision resolution and ignore any collisions from this list on the next step of simulation. This way, only the pairs that collide now but did not collide at the previous step are going to be processed.

Let's review the changes to be made in "Very ideal gas". Since our particle is much larger than a molecule, we'll need to increase its size while reducing the size of regular molecules. It also makes sense to increase the overall molecule count:

```
PARTICLE_SIZE_FACTOR = 7
MOLECULE_SIZE_FACTOR = 0.5
N = 50
```

The `SimState` class will now have to store the pairs of particles colliding at the previous simulation step:

```
@dataclass
class SimState:
    done: bool
```

---

[9] As further reading, I wholeheartedly recommend the site "What Brown Saw and You Can Too", available at https://physerver.hamilton.edu/Research/Brownian/. The particles he saw were starch organelles *amyloplasts* and lipid organelles *spherosomes*.

```
prev_collisions: set
    ...

def setup(cls):
    r = cls(False, set())
        ...
```

Our Brownian particle behaves just like an ordinary molecule; the only difference is its larger size. Thus, the easiest way to incorporate it into the simulation is to keep it in the same list with other molecules and handle it with the same code:

```
molecules = [Molecule.create(MOLECULE_SIZE_FACTOR) for _ in range(N)]

particle = Molecule.create(PARTICLE_SIZE_FACTOR)
particle.vx = particle.vy = 0
particle.m.goto(0, 0)
particle.m.color("blue")
molecules.append(particle)
```

Here we make the molecules smaller (in reality, they are *much* smaller than a Brownian particle) and place the still particle into the screen center. Finally, the tick() function will have to prevent repeated collisions of the same pairs of objects:

```
def tick():
    if not sim_state.done:
        for m in molecules:
            m.move()

        collisions = set()
        for i in range(len(molecules)):
            for j in range(0, i):
                if balls_collide(molecules[i], molecules[j]):
                    collisions.add((i, j))
                    if not (i, j) in sim_state.prev_collisions:
                        process_collision(molecules[i], molecules[j])

        sim_state.prev_collisions = collisions

        turtle.update()
        turtle.ontimer(tick, SLEEP_MS)
```

That's all. Now we can run the program and enjoy the result (see Figure 2.10).

2.9   FURTHER IDEAS

1. All our current simulations stop when the space key is pressed. Modify the basic code template to support three keyboard commands: pause, resume, and exit.

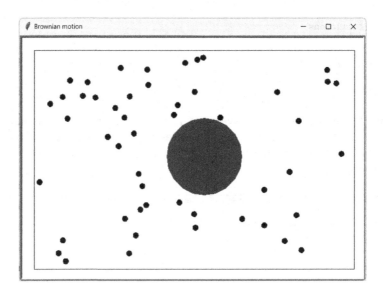

FIGURE 2.10: Brownian motion (screenshot).

2. Modify the "Boyle-Mariotte's law" simulation to see in real time how the size of the vessel affects gas pressure. You can start with a large vessel and calculate the pressure over 100 iterations of the model, then reduce the vessel slightly and repeat the process until the vessel is only one-quarter of its original size. Plot the obtained values on a two-dimensional chart with axes representing pressure and volume.

3. Boyle-Mariotte's law examines the relationship between the pressure and volume under a constant temperature. It is possible to lock another value instead: for example, if the pressure is constant, heating causes expansion of the volume occupied by gas (Charles's law[10]). Develop a program demonstrating this phenomenon.

4. *Maxwell's demon* is a hypothetical scenario where the second law of thermodynamics is violated. James Maxwell thought that it is possible to reverse the process demonstrated in our "Thermodynamics" simulation if a tiny creature ("the demon") opens the path between the communicating vessels only when a fast molecule moves to the right or a slow molecule moves to the left. In the beginning, both vessels are filled with the same mixture of fast and slow molecules, but gradually the temperature difference between the vessels increases. Maxwell's demon has been and remains the subject of debate for over a century [27]. My proposal is to modify "Thermodynamics" to demonstrate the demon's work instead.

---

[10]From *Encyclopaedia Britannica*:
https://www.britannica.com/science/Charless-law

5. Modify the "Brownian motion" model to show the trajectory of the Brownian particle.
6. Use the "Free kick" model to trace the path of a laser beam reflecting from mirrors. Arrange a certain number of lines that would serve as mirrors and a beam source. A turtle representing the tip of the beam should continue moving until it leaves the screen.

3 Gravity and rotation

All projects from the previous chapter featured entities moving with constant speed and direction. Collisions with walls and other moving objects could change them, but only to set a new route, straight and steady as before.

In this chapter we will extend our arsenal with *acceleration*. Conceptually, velocity is the rate of change of an entity's distance from the starting point. Acceleration is simply the rate of change of velocity. Introducing acceleration is technically easy, but it opens a door to the world of more interesting kinds of motion, which will especially shine in the projects of Chapter 5, devoted to behavior of living things.

In the current chapter we will keep dealing with inanimate objects, but their choice is going to be wide: from balls to planets, and from pendulums to toothed wheels.

3.1 JUMPING BALL

Let's again start with something very simple. Imagine a ball resting on a pedestal. How would it move if we apply a horizontal force to it (in other words, give it a kick)? Under the influence of Earth's gravity, it would reach the surface, lose some fraction of its energy, and bounce back. Then it would reach a slightly lower height and continue in this manner until stopping in its final resting place on the ground.

Unlike molecules of ideal gas, the ball moves with *uniform acceleration:* approaching the surface, it moves faster and faster, and after bouncing back it gradually slows down until its vertical velocity reaches zero, and it starts falling again. In the absence of loss of energy at the moment of collision and resistance of the atmosphere, the ball would continue moving forever.

3.1.1 IMPLEMENTATION

Taking into account acceleration is not hard. In the "Ideal gas" and related models we had to change the coordinates of the moving entity on each step of the simulation. Here we will also have to change its vertical velocity:

```
vy += ACCELERATION
```

Bouncing works exactly like in the case of a molecule reflecting from a vessel wall: we simply inverse the sign of the ball's velocity. Before moving on to the actual code, let's review other presumptions and simplifications:

1. We will presume that the horizontal ball velocity is constant.

DOI: 10.1201/9781003455295-3

2. Loss of energy upon collision with the surface is simulated by multi-plying velocity value by a certain "coefficient of loss". The horizontal velocity is not going to be affected, which is somewhat believable: recall that the real ball still rolls for quite a while after it stopped jumping.

3. We will ignore the loss of energy due to atmospheric resistance.

Full implementation of this simulation is shown in Listing 3.1. Just for fun, I decided to keep ball trajectory visible (see Figure 3.1).

Listing 3.1: Jumping ball.

```python
import turtle

WIDTH = 600
HEIGHT = 400
V = 3
MINV = 0.01
LOSS_COEFF = 0.7
ACCELERATION = -0.5   # negative is downward
R = 10
MARGIN = 50
SLEEP_MS = 20

done = False
right_wall = WIDTH / 2 - R
bottom_wall = -HEIGHT / 2 + R


def set_done():
    global done
    done = True


turtle.setup(WIDTH + MARGIN, HEIGHT + MARGIN)
turtle.tracer(0, 0)
turtle.title("Jumping ball")

turtle.listen()
turtle.onkeypress(set_done, "space")

m = turtle.Turtle()
m.shape("circle")
m.penup()
m.goto(WIDTH / 2, -HEIGHT / 2)
m.pendown()
m.setx(-WIDTH / 2)

vx = V
vy = 0
m.sety(HEIGHT / 3)


def tick():
    if not done:
```

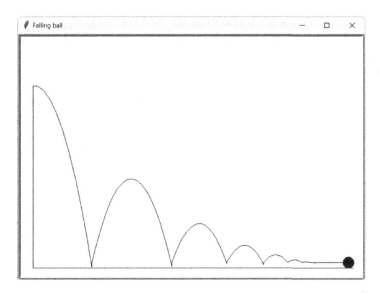

FIGURE 3.1: Trajectory of a jumping ball.

```
global vx, vy

m.goto(m.xcor() + vx, m.ycor() + vy)

# stop if the ball is about to leave the screen
if m.xcor() > right_wall:
    set_done()

if m.ycor() < bottom_wall:
    m.goto(m.xcor(), bottom_wall)
    vy *= -LOSS_COEFF

vy += ACCELERATION

turtle.update()
turtle.ontimer(tick, SLEEP_MS)


tick()
turtle.done()
```

3.2 NEWTON'S CANNONBALL

The "Jumping ball" simulation presumes that the ground surface is flat, which is perfectly fine for any realistic ball speed and pedestal height. What would happen, however, if we consider *really* high pedestals and *really* fast balls? In this case the curvature of Earth cannot be ignored anymore.

This scenario, first discussed by Newton, is often referred to as "Newton's cannonball". Instead of a ball on a pedestal, Newton imagined a cannon firing from the summit of a very tall mountain, and there is no jumping after the cannonball hits the surface, but otherwise it is exactly the same situation. It is also presumed that Earth is a sphere, and there is no air resistance.

Taking into account the round shape of Earth is easier than it might seem. Just like before, gravity merely accelerates the ball, and the only difference from the previous simulation is the direction and the magnitude of this acceleration. In "Jumping ball", acceleration always points down, toward the flat surface. In our new simulation, this is still the case, but "toward the surface" should mean "toward the center of the planet". As the ball moves, the direction of the acceleration vector changes. In addition, according to Newton's *law of universal gravitation*, the force of gravity (and, therefore, acceleration) is inversely proportional to the square of the distance between the centers of Earth and the cannonball, so the effect of gravity diminishes as the cannonball moves away from the planet's surface.

3.2.1 IMPLEMENTATION

Generally speaking, we had to update our "Jumping ball" on every simulation step as follows:

```
x += vx
y += vy
vy += acceleration
```

Our new project will use a modified scheme with variable acceleration:

```
x += vx
y += vy
vx += ax
vy += ay
ax, ay = calc_acceleration()
```

Acceleration is a vector that should point to the center of Earth. If it is located in (E_x, E_y), and the cannonball is currently at (x, y), acceleration has the same direction as the vector $dir = (x - E_x, y - E_y)$ (see Figure 3.2).

In our case Earth can be drawn in the center of the screen $(0, 0)$, so the direction becomes simply (x, y). Now we know the direction of acceleration, but not yet its length. In the previous project acceleration was set to a constant value ACCELERATION. Now it has to be inversely proportional to the distance between the cannonball and Earth's center. If this distance is r, we should aim for the value of $\frac{ACCELERATION}{r^2}$.

Thus, we can take the vector dir, rescale it to the desired length, and then use its horizontal and vertical constituents as acceleration values ax and ay.

In general, if the task is to rescale the given vector v to a new desired length L, both constituents of v must be multiplied by $\frac{L}{length(v)}$. In our case, the multiplier of dir is

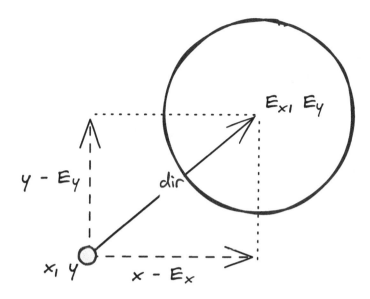

FIGURE 3.2: Calculating acceleration direction.

$$\frac{\text{ACCELERATION}}{r^2} \cdot \frac{1}{r} = \frac{\text{ACCELERATION}}{r^3}$$

Now we can proceed to the code (Listing 3.2).

Listing 3.2: Newton's cannonball.

```
import turtle

WIDTH = 600
HEIGHT = 400

V = 2.7
R = 5
R_EARTH = 100
PEDESTAL_H = 14
ACCELERATION = -1000
MARGIN = 50
TURTLE_SIZE = 20
SLEEP_MS = 20

done = False
right_wall = WIDTH / 2 - R
bottom_wall = -HEIGHT / 2 + R


def set_done():
    global done
```

```
    done = True


turtle.setup(WIDTH + MARGIN, HEIGHT + MARGIN)
turtle.tracer(0, 0)
turtle.title("Newton's cannonball")

turtle.listen()
turtle.onkeypress(set_done, "space")

# draw the planet
earth = turtle.Turtle()
earth.shape("circle")
earth.color("blue")
earth.shapesize(2 * R_EARTH / TURTLE_SIZE)

m = turtle.Turtle()
m.shape("circle")
m.shapesize(2 * R / TURTLE_SIZE)
m.goto(0, R + R_EARTH + PEDESTAL_H)

vx = V
vy = 0


def tick():
    if not done:
        global vx, vy
        m.goto(m.xcor() + vx, m.ycor() + vy)

        r = m.distance((0, 0))

        if r < R_EARTH + R:
            set_done()

        ax = m.xcor() * ACCELERATION / (r**3)
        ay = m.ycor() * ACCELERATION / (r**3)

        vx += ax
        vy += ay

        turtle.update()
        turtle.ontimer(tick, SLEEP_MS)


tick()
turtle.done()
```

The default parameters of the simulation show a "low-speed case", where the cannonball falls to the planet surface (see Figure 3.3), and the program is stopped.

Faster cannonballs can leave Earth forever. The lowest *orbital speed* in our simulation is approximately 2.9. A cannonball shot with this speed follows a nearly circular trajectory and comes back to the cannon's location to continue

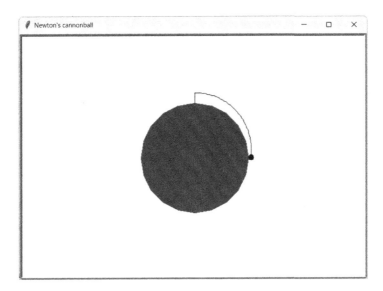

FIGURE 3.3: Newton's cannonball falling to the surface (screenshot).

revolving around Earth. Higher orbital speeds produce various elliptic orbits (see Figure 3.4).

An even faster cannonball fired with an *escape velocity* will leave the planet without ever returning to its original location. For the real planet Earth escape velocity is around 11.2 km/s.[1]

3.3 LISSAJOUS FIGURES

Let me approach the next simulation in a somewhat roundabout way. Imagine running our "Jumping ball" program with a horizontal velocity of zero and no energy loss. The ball would simply jump forever on the same spot. Its speed would gradually decrease as it flies higher and then increase as it approaches the surface. The point of collision with the ground is the only moment where the ball experiences a sudden change in velocity. Let's modify our setup to remove this collision point.

Now imagine there is no ground: instead of hitting the surface, the ball falls into a tunnel dug through the center of Earth (see Figure 3.5). In this case, the ball would approach the center with a maximal speed but zero acceleration, and start decelerating, reaching the other side of the planet with zero

---

[1] From *Encyclopaedia Britannica*:
https://www.britannica.com/science/escape-velocity

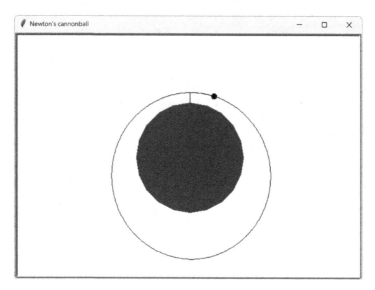

FIGURE 3.4: Elliptic orbit of Newton's cannonball ($v = 3.2$).

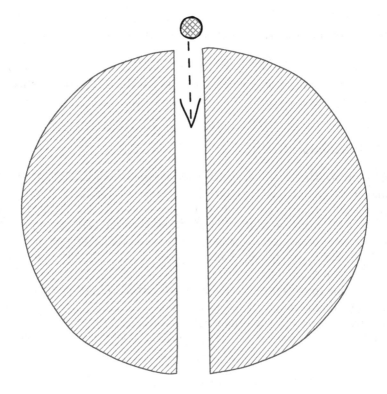

FIGURE 3.5: Ball falling into a tunnel through the center of Earth.

speed. Then the ball would fall again into the tunnel to continue its endless oscillation.[2]

This kind of movement is know as *simple harmonic motion*: the ball moves back and forth under the influence of force directed toward the center of Earth and proportional to the distance from it.[3]

The same pattern can be seen in a movement of a simple pendulum: tie a string to the ceiling and attach a weight to its loose end, pull the weight (now known as a *bob*) closer to yourself and release. The pendulum would swing approaching both ends of its trajectory with zero speed and accelerating when moving back to the center.[4]

The movement of a pendulum is interesting in terms of speed and acceleration, but its trajectory is a simple straight line, when looked at from above. A more complex pattern of motion can be obtained by combining movements in two perpendicular directions.

This is not a trivial task in the real world. If you pull the pendulum bob toward yourself, it will move back and forth. If you pull the bob to the left, it will move sideways. However, pulling the bob toward yourself and to the left will simply make it swing diagonally rather than in both directions.

The easiest way to make the bob move back-and-forth *and* left-and-right is to employ a Y-shaped device known as the *Blackburn pendulum* [59]. It consists of two secured threads tied with their loose ends, and a third thread connected to the resulting knot. The bob is attached to the loose end of the third thread (see Figure 3.6).

Obviously, the V-shaped part of this device can only move back and forth, so if you pull the bob toward yourself and to the left, the resulting motion would be the combination of movements in both directions. By plotting possible trajectories of the bob, we obtain *Lissajous figures*, named after Jules Antoine Lissajous, who produced them by attaching a leaky funnel with sand to the bob [16].

Fortunately, our previous projects provide a solid foundation for drawing Lissajous figures without any need to mess with strings and sand. Let's see how it can be done with our trusty turtles.

3.3.1 IMPLEMENTATION

Before proceeding to implementation, let's sort out the differences between these recently considered cases of accelerated motion:

---

[2]If you are interested in details of this process, check out the "Journey through the center of the Earth" section on HyperPhysics:
http://hyperphysics.phy-astr.gsu.edu/hbase/Mechanics/earthole.html

[3]From *Encyclopaedia Britannica*:
https://www.britannica.com/science/simple-harmonic-motion

[4]Strictly speaking, a pendulum does not exhibit simple harmonic motion, but it works as a reasonably accurate approximation for small-amplitude pendulums.

FIGURE 3.6: Y-shaped Blackburn pendulum.

- "Jumping ball". For a ball moving near the surface of Earth, the acceleration is constant.
- "Newton's cannonball". For large distances (comparable to planet radius), the acceleration is inversely proportional to the square of the distance between the ball and the planet center.
- "Lissajous figures" (and a fall-through-tunnel scenario). For simple harmonic motions, the acceleration is proportional to the distance between the moving object and the central point (*equilibrium*), according to *Hooke's law*.

The HyperPhysics article explains why the tunnel case can serve as an example of simple harmonic motion. In brief, the so-called "shell theorem" states that: (1) the ball inside the planet can be treated as tucked between a smaller planet and an "outer shell"; (2) the gravity of the shell can be ignored; (3) the gravity of a planet depends on its radius, so the gravitational force applied to the ball is actually the force exerted by the smaller planet, which gradually diminishes as the ball approaches the center of Earth.

Now we can finally look at the implementation shown in Listing 3.3.

Listing 3.3: Lissajous figures.

```python
import turtle

WIDTH = 600
HEIGHT = 400
MARGIN = 50
SLEEP_MS = 20

AX_COEFF = -0.003
AY_COEFF = -0.001
START_COORDS = (200, 200)

done = False


def set_done():
    global done
    done = True


turtle.setup(WIDTH + MARGIN, HEIGHT + MARGIN)
turtle.tracer(0, 0)
turtle.title("Lissajous figures")

turtle.listen()
turtle.onkeypress(set_done, "space")

m = turtle.Turtle()
m.shape("circle")
m.penup()
m.goto(START_COORDS[0], START_COORDS[1])
m.pendown()

vx, vy = 0, 0


def tick():
    if not done:
        global vx, vy

        m.goto(m.xcor() + vx, m.ycor() + vy)

        vx += m.xcor() * AX_COEFF
        vy += m.ycor() * AY_COEFF

        turtle.update()
        turtle.ontimer(tick, SLEEP_MS)


tick()
turtle.done()
```

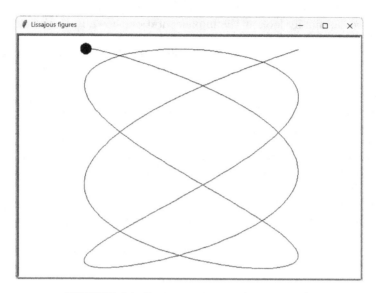

FIGURE 3.7: Lissajous figures (screenshot).

This time, the program is surprisingly short. All we have to do on each step of the simulation is update the turtle position according to its velocity constituents and then recalculate these constituents:

```
vx += m.xcor() * AX_COEFF
vy += m.ycor() * AY_COEFF
```

Vertical and horizontal acceleration values are calculated independently. According to Hooke's law, acceleration increases as the ball moves away from its point of equilibrium:

$$a = k(x - e_x)$$

In our program, $e_x = e_y = 0$. The value of k is characteristic of a particular oscillating device. In case of a pendulum it depends on string length. Thus, different pictures can be obtained by varying vertical and horizontal acceleration values, and the initial location of the ball (see Figure 3.7).

3.4 DIGITAL ORRERY

So far, our simulations of non-straight motion involved the application of force to moving objects, resulting in Lissajous figures or cannonball trajectories. However, there are common cases of movement along curves, which can be implemented with simpler methods.

Consider, for example, any app that displays time via traditional analog clock face with hands. The ends of clock hands move in circles, and the underlying code draws them most likely without any resorts to velocity, acceleration or other concepts of physics.

FIGURE 3.8: Simple orrery.

To explore circular motion, I propose implementing a project that is a bit more advanced than an imitation analog clock: an imitation analog *orrery*.

An orrery is a mechanical device that demonstrates the motions of planets of the Solar system.[5] Actual orreries greatly vary in terms of their sophistication and accuracy. Simple devices are sometimes used just to illustrate the general idea of planetary motion, and they may include just a handful of celestial objects, such as the Sun, Mercury, Venus, Earth, and the Moon (see Figure 3.8).

Advanced orreries may show all the planets of the solar system with (some) of their moons, and represent the relations between orbital periods of planets and moons quite accurately [23]. For example, Venus takes a full circle approximately 1.6 times faster than Earth. On the other hand, no attempt is usually made to preserve realistic proportions between the distances and planet sizes, and orbits are circular rather than elliptic.

For our purposes, it would be sufficient to implement an even simpler model, consisting of the Sun, Earth, and the Moon.

3.4.1 IMPLEMENTATION

We already know how to implement motion along a straight line. Let's think how to obtain a circular trajectory. Suppose our moving object revolves around a central point (x_0, y_0), just like Earth revolves around the Sun, and the distance from the object to the central point is constant and equal to L. Then the current position (x, y) of the object can be described by the angle a between the line connecting (x_0, y_0) and (x, y), and the line that goes parallel to the x-axis through the point (x_0, y_0) (see Figure 3.9).

Such *polar coordinates* (L, a) are just as good as Cartesian (x, y), and are especially handy for our purposes: to make the object move around a central

---

[5]From *Encyclopedia Britannica*:
https://www.britannica.com/science/orrery-astronomical-model

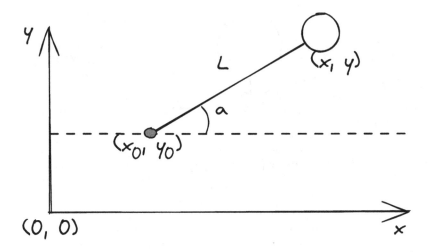

FIGURE 3.9: Using polar coordinates (L, a) to define the position of an object.

point, we simply have to gradually increase the value of a on each simulation step:

```
a += AV
```

The value of AV here is *angular velocity*, defined in radians per simulation step.

Since the (x, y) coordinates are still necessary to draw the object on the screen, we'll need the following conversion formulas:

$$x = x_0 + L \cdot cos(a)$$

$$y = y_0 + L \cdot sin(a)$$

Now we have everything to show how Earth orbits the Sun. The Moon might seem a bit more tricky because it orbits around Earth, which orbits around the Sun. However, the central point (x_0, y_0) is not required to remain constant: it can be set to the center of Earth, and the conversion formulas will do the rest. The complete program is shown in Listing 3.4, and the screenshot of the working application in Figure 3.10.

Listing 3.4: Digital orrery.

```
import turtle
import math

WIDTH = 600
HEIGHT = 400
```

```
MARGIN = 50
SLEEP_MS = 20
TURTLE_SIZE = 20

R_SUN = 60
R_EARTH = 20
L_EARTH = 130
AV_EARTH = 0.02
R_MOON = 3
L_MOON = 30
AV_MOON = AV_EARTH * 13 # the real Moon makes approx 13 turns per year

done = False


def set_done():
    global done
    done = True


def init_object(color, r, distance):
    m = turtle.Turtle()
    m.shape("circle")
    m.color(color)
    m.shapesize(2 * r / TURTLE_SIZE)
    m.penup()
    m.goto(distance, 0)
    return m


turtle.setup(WIDTH + MARGIN, HEIGHT + MARGIN)
turtle.tracer(0, 0)
turtle.title("Digital orrery")

turtle.listen()
turtle.onkeypress(set_done, "space")

sun = init_object("yellow", R_SUN, 0)
earth = init_object("blue", R_EARTH, L_EARTH)
moon = init_object("black", R_MOON, L_EARTH + L_MOON)
a_earth = a_moon = 0


def tick():
    if not done:
        global a_earth, a_moon

        earth.goto(L_EARTH * math.cos(a_earth), L_EARTH * math.sin(a_earth))
        moon.goto(
            earth.xcor() + L_MOON * math.cos(a_moon),
            earth.ycor() + L_MOON * math.sin(a_moon),
        )

        a_earth += AV_EARTH
        a_moon += AV_MOON
```

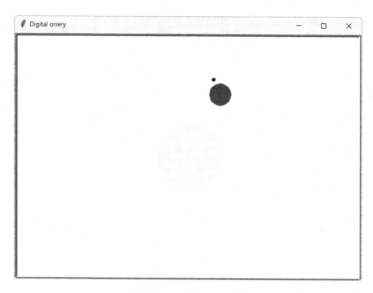

FIGURE 3.10: Digital orrery (screenshot).

```
        turtle.update()
        turtle.ontimer(tick, SLEEP_MS)

tick()
turtle.done()
```

3.5 SPIROGRAPH CURVES

Spirograph is a toy drawing device capable of producing intricate curvy patterns. In its basic form, it includes a frame with a large cog-shaped opening and a number of holed cogs of various sizes (see Figure 3.11).

In preparation for drawing, the frame is mounted on a piece of paper, a cog is pushed against the opening, and a colored pen is inserted into one of the cog holes. The cog is rolled around the opening several times to produce a curve. The teeth are only needed for better friction: the same picture can be obtained by carefully rolling a wheel inside a circular hole. Different curves can be obtained with different cogs and holes.

Spirograph produces curves technically known as *hypotrochoids*.[6] Our next task will be to figure out how to draw them on a computer.

---

[6]From *Wolfram MathWorld*: https://mathworld.wolfram.com/Hypotrochoid.html

FIGURE 3.11: Sketch of a Spirograph.

3.5.1 IMPLEMENTATION

The previous project, "Digital orrery", includes all the necessary pieces to simulate a Spirograph. Earth revolving around a fixed center works like a Spirograph cog, and the trajectory of the Moon is similar to the curve made by a pen inserted into a cog hole.

What sets these two simulations apart is their treatment of relationships between moving objects. In "Digital orrery", each angular velocity can be set independently: the Moon can spin around Earth faster or slower. In contrast, a cog traveling around the circular opening always makes the same number of revolutions on its path. Furthermore, if the cog travels clockwise, it revolves anticlockwise.

To determine the angular velocity of a moving cog, we need a formula for the distance covered by an object moving along the arc of the radius R and the central angle a:

$$D = R \cdot a$$

Suppose the radius of the frame opening is R_f, and the radius of the cog is R_c., so the cog is moving along the arc of radius $L = R_f - R_c$. When a freshly painted cog moves by the angle A along the arc, it stains the strip of length $L \cdot A$ on the frame (see Figure 3.12).

It also means that the outer side of the cog has to cover the same distance and turn by the angle $-a$ ("minus" because the cog rotates in the opposite direction):

$$L \cdot A = -R_c \cdot a$$

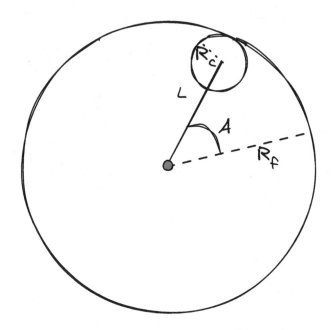

FIGURE 3.12: Moving a cog along the frame opening.

Therefore, if we know A, we can calculate a and vice versa:

$$a = -\frac{L \cdot A}{R_c}$$

$$A = -\frac{R_c \cdot a}{L}$$

To draw our cog on the screen, we'll need its Cartesian coordinates, calculated just like in the previous project:

$$x = L \cdot cos(A)$$

$$y = L \cdot sin(A)$$

If the drawing pen is located on the edge of the cog, its coordinates are

$$x_{pen} = x + R_c \cdot cos(a)$$

$$y_{pen} = y + R_c \cdot sin(a)$$

However, since Spirograph cogs have multiple holes, a pen may be located at a different distance R_p from the cog center, so these formulas become

$$x_{pen} = x + R_p \cdot cos(a)$$

$$y_{pen} = y + R_p \cdot sin(a)$$

The complete listing of the project is shown in Listing 3.5. I decided to modify the value of a inside the main loop and to calculate A, but it could have been done in the opposite way. An example curve is shown on the screenshot (Figure 3.13).

Listing 3.5: Spirograph curves.

```python
import turtle
import math

WIDTH = 600
HEIGHT = 400
MARGIN = 50
SLEEP_MS = 20

# astroid
# R_FRAME = 25 * 4
# R_COG = 25
# R_PEN = 25

R_FRAME = 154
R_COG = 55
R_PEN = 30

L = R_FRAME - R_COG
AV = 0.1 # angular velocity

done = False


def set_done():
    global done
    done = True


turtle.setup(WIDTH + MARGIN, HEIGHT + MARGIN)
turtle.tracer(0, 0)
turtle.title("Spirograph curves")

turtle.listen()
turtle.onkeypress(set_done, "space")

pen = turtle.Turtle()
pen.shape("circle")
pen.penup()
pen.goto(L + R_PEN, 0)
pen.pendown()

a = 0


def tick():
    if not done:
```

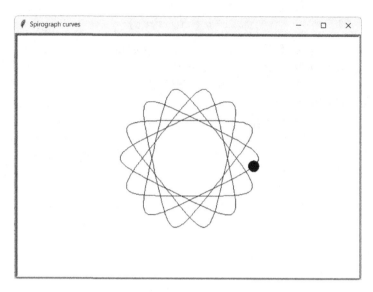

FIGURE 3.13: Screenshot of working program (Rf=154, Rc=55, Rp=30).

```
        global a

        A = -a * R_COG / L
        x = L * math.cos(A)
        y = L * math.sin(A)
        pen.goto(x + R_PEN * math.cos(a), y + R_PEN * math.sin(a))

        a += AV

        turtle.update()
        turtle.ontimer(tick, SLEEP_MS)


tick()
turtle.done()
```

3.6 FURTHER IDEAS

1. Introduce friction into "Free kick" project. Friction is a constant force affecting a moving object, so it translates into a constant negative acceleration. The resulting program can be turned into a variation of a billiards game.
2. By combining "Free kick", friction, and the laser beam tracer, you can get a minigolf-like game. The player has to guide a ball through a complex-shaped, wall-surrounded course and reach the goal point.
3. Create a customizable orrery simulator, reading planet configuration from an input file. Each item in the file should specify the size of a

certain body, its distance from its "parent" planet, and its angular velocity. Planets with no parent should orbit around the screen center.

4. Introduce the idea of the tilt angle into "Jumping ball". The ball in our model starts moving in horizontal direction, but you can imagine it being fired from a cannon pointing in an arbitrary direction.

5. The code of "Lissajous figures" can actually produce only figures with zero *phase difference*. Both pendulums are started in their farthest positions from the central point with their velocities set to zero. However, it does not have to be so: one of the pendulums can be started when another one is already in motion. Extend our program with a capability to simulate this scenario.

6. The Spirograph can be also used to draw *epitrochoids*—the curves obtained by rolling one toothed wheel around another toothed wheel instead of a frame. Implement this capability.

4 Stochastic processes

In the next projects we will discuss simple experiments where results are obtained via numerous repetitions of a certain *stochastic* (randomized) process.

It might sound counterintuitive to rely on something random to obtain something more or less precise, but this idea lies behind a family of *Monte Carlo methods*, widely used in science and engineering. While the idea of analyzing randomized processes is centuries old, Monte Carlo methods in the present form appeared in the 1940s, and they are directly associated both with nuclear physics, where it was applied at the time, and the rise of computing machinery, which is great at doing repetitive work fast.

The advantage of randomized repetitions is its simplicity. Large systems are complex and hard to simulate. However, large systems often consist of simple small parts, moving and interacting with each other. By simulating these microscopic interactions, Monte Carlo methods manage to grasp the complexity of the whole [3]. Some processes, such as dice games, are stochastic by their nature, so throwing "electronic dice" is the only right way to simulate them accurately.

Now let's see how order and chaos play together, reflecting our complex reality. We'll start with simple artificial examples and consider some real-world scenarios closer to the end of the chapter.

4.1 CALCULATING PI

Imagine a mug with one black and three white tokens. Let's take out a random token without looking into the mug. Is the token more likely to be white? It is intuitively clear that it is indeed so, and the chance to fish out the black token is just one out of four. However, how to *prove* it? A straightforward experimental proof can be performed by actually repeating this draft-a-token process a number of times and to examine the outcomes.

While the experimentally obtained answer is going to be approximate, the *law of large numbers* states that by increasing the number of trials it is possible to produce more and more accurate results.[1] Thus, despite inevitable hiccups on the way, hundreds or thousands of token drafts should yield a proportion of black tokens close to $\frac{1}{4}$.

For our next task, we will consider a more interesting example: experimental derivation of the value of π. This can be done in a variety of ways, so let's choose the simplest one.

---

[1] From *Wolfram MathWorld*:
https://mathworld.wolfram.com/LawofLargeNumbers.html

DOI: 10.1201/9781003455295-4

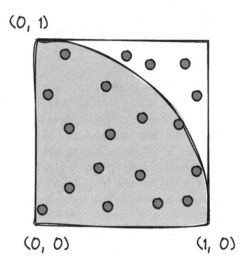

(0, 1)

(0, 0)   (1, 0)

FIGURE 4.1: Square poster of a quarter-circle.

Take a 1m×1m square piece of paper and draw a quarter-of-a-circle, as shown in Figure 4.1. Hang this poster on the wall and throw some darts into its random areas. The chance to hit any point on the poster should be the same, so in the real world it might be a tricky task (which is fortunately not in our agenda). Next, count the number of darts that happened to land inside the quarter-circle.

It can be proved that the ratio between the darts inside the quarter-circle (N_c) and the total number of darts (N) is proportional to the areas of the quarter-circle and the bounding square:

$$\frac{N_c}{N} \approx \frac{area\ of\ quarter\text{-}circle}{area\ of\ square}$$

This observation lies behind the method of complex shape area calculation, known as *Monte Carlo integration*.[2] Naturally, it works best when the number of thrown darts is large.

The area of a quarter-circle of radius r is $\frac{\pi r^2}{4}$, so for our case it is simply $\frac{\pi}{4}$, and the area of the bounding square is simply 1. Thus,

$$\frac{N_c}{N} \approx \frac{\pi}{4}$$

---

[2]From *Wolfram MathWorld*:
https://mathworld.wolfram.com/MonteCarloIntegration.html

This formula gives us the final estimation for π:

$$\pi \approx 4\frac{N_c}{N}$$

4.1.1 IMPLEMENTATION

The implementation of this project will follow a simple "text in—text out" approach without any turtle-based visualizations. Graphics would certainly look nice here, but it would take a disproportionately large piece of the code without adding much value.

The only missing bit in the formulas above is the method for checking whether a certain point lies within a quarter-circle. An obvious way to do it is to employ Euclidian distance. It should be smaller than one for the inside points:

$$\sqrt{x^2 + y^2} < 1$$

By squaring both sides of this inequality, we can also get rid of the square root:

$$x^2 + y^2 < 1$$

The compete listing of this project gets the prize for the shortest program in the book (see Listing 4.1). Still, it illustrates an interesting concept and is well worth our attention.

Listing 4.1: Calculating Pi.

```python
from random import uniform

N = 100000
Nc = 0

for _ in range(N):
    x = uniform(0, 1.0)
    y = uniform(0, 1.0)
    if x * x + y * y < 1:
        Nc += 1

print(f"Pi is {4*Nc/N}")
```

Subsequent runs of this code provide relatively accurate estimations of π:

```
Pi is 3.14124
Pi is 3.14312
Pi is 3.13384
...
```

4.2   MONTY HALL PROBLEM

The previous program demonstrated the "experimental" approach to the calculation of π. While a random number generator can certainly be used to simulate dart throwing, it feels like quite a roundabout way to find the desired value by means of a rather exotic setup. Far more often, Monte Carlo methods are used to directly simulate a certain process and find out its outcome.

In our next project we will perform such a simulation of a fictional, but widely discussed scenario, known as *Monty Hall problem*. This "problem", which should actually be called a mathematical puzzle, seems to experience regular surges of attention since its first publication in 1959 as the "Three prisoners problem" [13]. The original plot involved a grim prison setting, while its later revision is much more upbeat, featuring a fictional game show, and named after the real-life TV show host Monty Hall.

The problem can be formulated as follows. As a participant of a game show, you have to choose one of three doors. Behind one of the doors is a prize, behind two other doors is nothing. After you pick a door, the game host, who knows where the prize is, selects a door with no prize from the two remaining doors, and opens it. Then the host tells you that you may stick to your original choice or switch to another closed door. Should you do it?

This question was answered affirmatively by *Parade* magazine columnist Marilyn vos Savant in her Q/A column appeared in 1990, which caused a torrent of letters claiming she got it wrong [54]. While some readers seemed to rely on convoluted interpretations of the original problem definition, the bulk of them, including professional mathematicians, apparently trusted their intuition. My personal intuition isn't any better: what difference could the host have made, really?

Gardner's piece starts with a note on false beliefs of famous mathematicians regarding probabilistic processes, where intuition is indeed a poor advisor. Fortunately, we can very quickly run thousands of experiments and see for ourselves whether vos Savant was right or not.

4.2.1   IMPLEMENTATION

The simulation will repeatedly play out the following scenario. A prize is randomly placed behind one of the three doors. The player chooses a random door, then the host opens another door without a prize. Then we'll compare how two distinct strategies perform. Player A would always stick to the original choice, while Player B would always switch the door. Full implementation is shown in Listing 4.2.

Listing 4.2: Monty Hall problem.

```
from random import choice

N = 100000
```

```
player_a = 0
player_b = 0


def choose_empty(prize, options):
    if options == [False, False]:
        return choice(options)
    return options[1] if prize[options[0]] else options[0]


for _ in range(N):
    prize = [False, False, False]
    prize[choice([0, 1, 2])] = True

    options = [0, 1, 2]
    player_choice = choice(options)
    options.remove(player_choice)
    monty_choice = choose_empty(prize, options)
    options.remove(monty_choice)

    if prize[player_choice]:
        player_a += 1
    if prize[options[0]]:
        player_b += 1

print(f"Player A: {player_a/N}")
print(f"Player B: {player_b/N}")
```

The code is straightforward: every time a choice is made, it is removed from the list of choices. If the host has two empty doors to choose from, a random door is taken. My test run provides the following results:

```
Player A: 0.33511
Player B: 0.66489
```

Player B, who always switches doors, wins twice more often! Thus, the experiment shows vos Savant was right.

If your intuition still rebels, here is an easy way to think about this game. Suppose you have initially chosen a door with the prize. The chances of this lucky event are 1 out of 3. In this case, switching doors means failure: you move away from your prize. However, in any other case (2 out of 3) you choose between your empty door and another closed door with the prize behind. Therefore, "always switch" strategy wins in $\frac{2}{3}$ of all the games.

4.3 THE BUS STOP

The next project is another good test for your intuition.[3] Imagine a bus line between two points A and B. There is only one bus on the line: it starts

---

[3]Unfortunately, I don't know the original source of this problem. It was discussed at one now-defunct online forum around 2005.

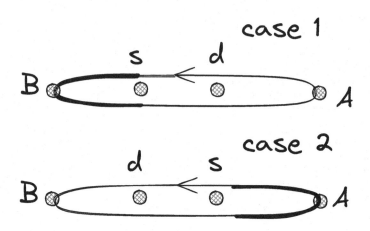

FIGURE 4.2: Two scenarios favorable for the passenger.

moving from A to B, then makes a U-turn and proceeds back to A, cruising in this manner till the end of the day. A bus would stop at any point to pick up or drop off a passenger. Now suppose a passenger who needs to ride to a random location on the line, shows up at some other random location at a random moment of time. When the bus reaches the passenger, is it more likely that the bus drives toward the passenger's goal or in the opposite direction?

My personal intuition is that the chances are equal. Yes, it often seems that the buses are against us, but isn't it yet another variation of the buttered toast phenomenon? Let's find out.

4.3.1 IMPLEMENTATION

Let's formalize our experimental setup. A bus makes a full circle by driving from A to B and back. If the distance between these points is D, the length of the loop is $2D$. If the time since bus departure is t, and the bus is moving with unit speed (one unit of distance per unit of time), its location on the route is

$$busloc = t \bmod 2D$$

The bus makes a full loop in $2D$ time units. If $busloc$ is smaller than D, the bus moves in the forward direction, and backward otherwise. From a passenger's point of view, there are two randomly chosen points, source s and destination d, on the road, and either of these points can be closer to B. In a scenario favorable for the passenger, the bus is either to the left side of s if s is closer to B, or to the right side of s if s is closer to A (see Figure 4.2).

The complete text of the program is shown in Listing 4.3.

Listing 4.3: The bus stop.

```
from random import uniform

N = 100000
DIST = 10
DAYLEN = 5 * 2 * DIST   # 5 loops

wins = 0
for _ in range(N):
    t = uniform(0, DAYLEN)
    src = uniform(0, DIST)
    dst = uniform(0, DIST)
    busloc = t % (2 * DIST)

    bus_sbs = src <= busloc <= 2 * DIST - src
    bus_sas = busloc <= src or busloc >= 2 * DIST - src

    if src >= dst and bus_sbs or src < dst and bus_sas:
        wins += 1

print(wins / N)
```

Five full loops are simulated here. We choose random source and destination points, and random time, and check favorable scenario conditions. My test run yields the following output:

```
0.33357
```

In other words, there is only a 33% chance of being lucky; so, as passengers we should keep our expectations low.

4.4 PLAYING PIG

The combination of luck and well-calculated strategy is a foundation of many popular games. The player of the "Monty Hall" game can be advised to switch the doors, but this still does not guarantee victory. The optimal strategy at best can maximize a player's chances.

Seeking the winning strategy in a stochastic environment is not an easy task. Even very simplistic worlds often turn out to be more complex than they might seem at a glance. A good example of such an environment is a little dice game known as *Pig*.

In its most basic variation, Pig is a game for two players, who take turns until either of them scores 100 points and wins. The first player starts the turn by rolling a regular six-sided die. If "one" is rolled, the turn ends: the player scores nothing in this turn and passes the die to the second player. If any other number is rolled, the player adds it to the current turn score and decides whether to continue rolling the die or to hold. If the player decides to hold, the total turn score is added to the player's final score, the turn ends, and the die is passed to another player.

This type of game mechanics is called "push your luck". By rolling the die, the player continues to score (while the opponent doesn't), but the stakes are rising: one unlucky roll, and all the earnings evaporate. Anyway, what is the optimal strategy in Pig? Discovering it will be our next challenge.

Let's base our efforts on two quite strong presumptions. First, since the player's objective is to earn 100 points as quickly as possible, it makes sense to strive to maximize the score of each turn. Second, the player chooses between rolling and holding after each roll on the basis of the current round score. The player should hold when the score is too high to justify the risk of rolling "one" and losing everything.

These presumptions make finding the optimal strategy a very straightforward task. We will try out different values of "holding scores" and run experiments to understand how they influence the average per-round earnings.

4.4.1 IMPLEMENTATION

The complete program is shown in Listing 4.4. For each possible holding score from 2 to 100, we play 10,000 games and report the holding score yielding the best overall performance.

Listing 4.4: Playing Pig.

```python
from random import randint

N = 10000


def turn_score(target):
    r = 0
    while r < target:
        die = randint(1, 6)
        if die == 1:
            return 0
        r += die
    return r


best_target = 0
best_total = 0

for target in range(2, 101):
    total = 0
    for _ in range(N):
        total += turn_score(target)

    if total > best_total:
        best_total, best_target = total, target
```

```
print(f"best target: {best_target}, best total (avg): {best_total/N}")
```

It seems that 10,000 games are not enough to obtain a reliable definitive answer. Consequent runs of the program may produce different answers:

```
best target: 19, best total (avg): 8.1802
...
best target: 23, best total (avg): 8.3056
```

Playing more games takes more time, but at this point we can safely presume that the answer lies somewhere between 18 and 24, and play 100,000 games for each value in this range, which yields 20 in most cases:

```
best target: 20, best total (avg): 8.17995
best target: 21, best total (avg): 8.16088
best target: 20, best total (avg): 8.15719
best target: 20, best total (avg): 8.15575
```

4.4.2 AFTERTHOUGHTS

Our experiments show that the optimal strategy in Pig is "hold at 20". While this is indeed a good rule of thumb, the real optimal strategy is not that simple, because our initial presumptions about it are not entirely correct. For starters, the game is more favorable for the first player, because if both players score equally per turn, the first player has one extra turn available to win before the second player has a chance to catch up. For this reason, being the second player you might decide to accept higher risk. There is a variation of Pig with the "leveling" rule: if the first player holds with a score of 100+, the second player has a chance to play one more turn to score higher.

Another important factor affecting the optimal strategy is the current opponent score. Suppose it's your turn. You have 75 points, while the opponent has 95. Clearly, you should strive for victory rather than hold at 20, because the opponent is likely to win on the next turn. In general, the optimal strategy depends on the current scores of both opponents, and it significantly deviates from "hold at 20" closer to the end of the game [33], [34].

4.5 GALTON BOARD

Random numbers generated by Python's functions uniform() and randint() are *uniformly distributed*, meaning that any number in the target range is equally likely to be produced. This situation is similar to a coin flip or a roll of a standard six-sided die. However, take a pair of dice instead of a single die and consider the sum of dots obtained in a throw. Some numbers are going to be less likely to appear. For example, only one dice combination $(1 + 1)$ yields the sum of two; in contrast, there are six possible ways to obtain the sum of seven: $1 + 6, 2 + 5, 3 + 4, 4 + 3, 5 + 2, 6 + 1$.

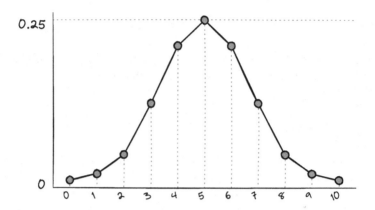

FIGURE 4.3: The likelihood of obtaining 0 to 10 heads in 10 coin tosses.

It is easy to propose a similar setup for a coin. Let's toss a coin N times and count the number of obtained heads. The least likely outcomes would be 0 and N, while the most likely sums huddle around $\frac{N}{2}$. The sums of heads are *binomially distributed*: their probabilities[4] form a nice-looking "bell curve" when plotted (see Figure 4.3)[5].

This result is just an example of a more fundamental law called *central limit theorem*[6], which, in particular, states that the bell curve appears when independent and identically distributed random variables are summed up.

Our coin tosses are independent in a sense that one toss "knows" nothing about other tosses, and their outcomes are not connected. (A popular erroneous belief that five heads in a row means growing chances for a tail is known as "gambler's fallacy" [53].) The requirement of mere "identical distribution" means that the law works even for non-uniformly distributed variables. If we replace a coin with a six-sided die with faces marked 1, 2, 2, 3, 3, 3 and start counting sums of points obtained over N throws instead of coin heads, we'll get the same bell curve picture.

A great way to visualize this process was proposed by Sir Francis Galton in 1873 [51]. He designed a device consisting of a board with a mounted funnel and several rows of pegs, arranged in a chessboard-like pattern. The bottom of the board hosted isolated compartments. The idea is to fill the funnel with beads and let them fall through the board, bouncing off the pegs and finally resting in the bottom compartments (see Figure 4.4).

---

[4]For our purposes, the *probability* of an event can be defined as the number of times this event occurred in trials (its *frequency*), divided by the total number of trials made.

[5]Note that the sum of two dice is *not* binomially distributed, see
https://math.stackexchange.com/questions/1204396

[6]From *Wolfram MathWorld*:
https://mathworld.wolfram.com/CentralLimitTheorem.html

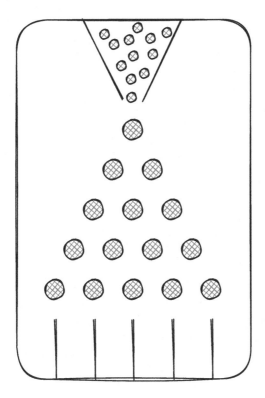

FIGURE 4.4: Galton board.

As a rough approximation, such Galton board (or "quincunx", as he called it), can be seen as a simulation of successive coin tosses: upon reaching the next peg, a bead bounces to the left (heads) or to the right (tails). The leftmost compartment corresponds to the all-heads outcome, which is as unlikely as the rightmost all-tails, so the bead will probably end up in one of the central compartments.

Simulating the operation of this device is going to be our next challenge.

4.5.1   IMPLEMENTATION

The proposed implementation will merely provide a textual output of the resulting placement of beads. While visualization of a probabilistic process *is* the point of the real Galton board, let's concentrate on its inner workings for now. Fortunately, the underlying mechanics can be implemented just in a few lines of code (see Listing 4.5).

Listing 4.5: Galton board.

```
from random import randint

N = 100000
PEGS = 7

bins = [0 for _ in range(PEGS + 1)]

for _ in range(N):
    bin_idx = 0
    for _ in range(PEGS):
        if randint(0, 1) == 1:
            bin_idx += 1
    bins[bin_idx] += 1

print(f"bins: {bins}")
print(f"prob: {[b / N for b in bins]}")
```

Intuitively it feels natural to assign the central peg to the next incoming bead, and shift the bead to the left or to the right on each subsequent step. However, thinking in terms of the target compartments leads to simpler code. A generated random value of 1 corresponds to coin tails, or shifting the bead to the right. Initially, a bead is projected to fall into the leftmost compartment, and each toss of tails promotes the bead to the next compartment. As expected, the final list generated by our code is quite close to binomial distribution:

```
bins: [773, 5426, 16474, 27272, 27493, 16339, 5457, 766]
prob: [0.00773, 0.05426, 0.16474, 0.27272, 0.27493, 0.16339, 0.05457, 0.00766]
```

4.5.2 AFTERTHOUGHTS

I have to note that this code is not a very accurate representation of the real Galton board. Imagine the process simulated here. A bead falls into the funnel, meets the first peg and bounces off to land precisely onto the next peg. These bounces continue with clockwork accuracy until the bead reaches its compartment, and the next bead starts its journey.

The physical board works quite differently. The funnel is usually wide enough to pour a small stream of beads, and both the pegs and the distances between them are quite large to allow a great deal of random jumping and bumping into walls, pegs, and other beads.[7] Still, all the beads live in the same environment, and their jumps are *identically distributed*, so thanks to the central limit theorem the bottom of the board still forms a perfect bell curve. This mechanism of transforming the chaos of beads into a neat

---

[7]Watch how it works, for example, at https://galtonboard.com

binomial distribution is a little wonder, and a chance to see it working is a major attraction of the Galton board.

4.6 ZIPF'S LAW

The effect of the central limit theorem, visualized by the Galton board, can be often observed in nature. Say, measure the height of each person in a city. Distribute people into several groups according to their height, from shortest to tallest, count the members of each group, and plot these numbers. You'll get the same "bell curve": the number of people of average height is going to be the largest, while both "tails" will have few very tall and very short individuals.

The idea that the average values are the most common feels quite natural, but it is easy to find examples where it does not hold up. Imagine we use the Galton board to simulate how people choose their favorite YouTube channels. Incoming beads will represent people, and the bottom compartments will correspond to individual channels. As a result, we'll see every channel accumulating a certain number of viewers (to simplify, let's presume each person watches just one channel).

It turns out this simulation method is going to be very inaccurate. In reality, there is a short list of very popular channels, taking the lion's share of viewers, and a long "tail" of countless YouTubers watched only by their friends and family. Scenarios like this one follow the "80/20 rule" (also known as the *Pareto principle*): 80% of something comes from 20% of something. In particular, 80% of all YouTube visitors come to watch just 20% of channels. We can't say that a typical (randomly chosen) channel probably has an average number of watchers. It is more likely that a typical channel has very, very few visitors, while the top YouTubers attract an immense audience.

Another variation of the same pattern can be observed in natural language. The most common English word is "the", followed by "of" and "and". However, their frequencies decline sharply: "the" accounts for 7% of *all* the words in a typical text, "of" takes around 3.3%, and the share of "and" is 2.9% [2].

In general, the frequency of the k-th most frequent word is approximately proportional to $\frac{1}{k}$. It is far from obvious why this rule (*Zipf's law*) holds true [61], but at least we can confirm its validity ourselves, and this will be the goal of our next exercise.

4.6.1 IMPLEMENTATION

There are two points to clarify in this task before we can proceed to the code. First: what texts to analyze? Second: how to show that the formula of Zipf's law is approximately correct?

While any reasonably large text would work fine, we can stay strictly within the Python environment by utilizing a built-in help system. Just type, for example,

```
help('LISTS')
```

in the interactive Python shell to read the section on *lists*. The complete
list of topics is available by typing:

```
help('topics')
```

Some parts of the documentation can be accessed from code. The above-
mentioned section on lists, for instance, can be retrieved from the dictionary
topics, located in the module pydoc_data.topics:

```
from pydoc_data.topics import topics
```

```
print(topics['typesseq-mutable'])
```

By concatenating all the elements of this dictionary, we can obtain a relatively lengthy document:

```
input_text = " ".join(topics.values())
```

Now let's decide how to evaluate the correctness of the formula for the
given list of words and their frequencies. Fortunately, there is a very easy way
to do it: if Zipf's law is correct, word ranks and frequencies should form a
nearly straight line on a *log-log plot*, which is a two-dimensional graph with
logarithmic scales on both axes. If the frequency of the k-th frequent word is
F_k, we draw a dot at the screen location $(\log k, \log F_k)$, and the resulting line
would be expected to connect the top-left and the bottom-right corners of the
chart.

The complete text of the program is shown in Listing 4.6. A turtle is used
to create a log-log plot, shown in Figure 4.5.

Listing 4.6: Zipf's law.

```
import math
import turtle
from collections import defaultdict
from pydoc_data.topics import topics

WIDTH = 600
HEIGHT = 400


def setup_screen(title, width, height):
    turtle.setup(WIDTH, HEIGHT)
    turtle.tracer(0, 0)
    turtle.title(title)
    turtle.setworldcoordinates(0, 0, math.ceil(width), math.ceil(height))
```

```
input_text = " ".join(topics.values())
words = input_text.split()
freq = defaultdict(int)

for word in [w.lower() for w in words if w.isalpha()]:
    freq[word] += 1

values = sorted(freq.values(), reverse=True)

setup_screen("Zipf's law", math.log(len(values)), math.log(values[0]))
drawer = turtle.Turtle()
drawer.hideturtle()
drawer.penup()

for x, y in enumerate(values):
    drawer.goto(math.log(x + 1), math.log(y))
    drawer.pendown()

turtle.update()
turtle.done()
```

The input text is transformed into the list of words using `split()`. Words are converted to a lowercase to make sure we don't process entries like "List" and "list" separately, and all non-alphabetic entries are removed. The frequencies are stored in the dictionary `freq`, which has to be initialized with zeroes. The easiest way to do it is to use the type `defaultdict(int)`, which returns zero as a value for any key not found in the dictionary. When `freq` is ready, we simply retrieve all the frequency values it stores (we don't need the words anymore) and sort them in the descending order. The first element of the resulting list

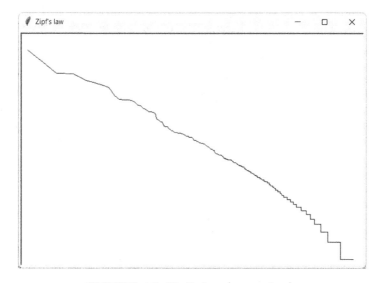

FIGURE 4.5: Zipf's law (screenshot).

is the 1st frequent word, so the x-coordinate of its dot on the graph should be $\log 1$.

While not a perfectly straight line, our chart is quite close to it. The right end of the picture shows a very typical step-like pattern, which usually appears at low frequencies. A frequency is a whole number: there is no way for a word to occur 1.5 or 2.7 times in the text. Thus, the differences between the adjacent low frequencies can be large in relation to their values, and these "jumps" are quite noticeable.

In our case, there are 2355 distinct words in the dictionary, and the most frequent of them appears 4269 times (yes, it is "the"). Thus, the values on the vertical axis range from zero to $\log 4269 \approx 8.36$. Two least frequent elements that occur once and twice, respectively, occupy, vertical positions $\log 1 = 0$ and $\log 2 \approx 0.69$. This means the vertical "jump" between these elements takes around $\frac{1}{12}$ of the total chart height.

4.7 RISE OF CITIES

As already mentioned, Zipf's law is empirical: it is easy to check whether it works in a particular situation, but harder to propose a simulation that would demonstrate its emergence. However, it is still possible, and even not very difficult to do.

One commonly employed case for illustrating Zipf's law is the population of cities. It is proposed that the list of cities, ranked by their population, would follow the same pattern as words in text: the population of the k-th most populous city is going to be approximately proportional to $1/k$. (For other interesting examples, see [36].)

The validity of Zipf's law for cities is often disputed [1], but it is hard to agree on a definitive answer, because there is no single "right" way to create a list of cities. Should we consider only cities within a certain country? How to deal with international borders? Should separate cities belonging to the same metropolitan area be treated as a single entity? Should certain cities be excluded from consideration because their role is somehow special and unique?

In any case, it turns out that a simple model of city attractiveness and intercity migration produces a list of cities, well conforming to Zipf's law [26]. It is based on the principles, which we will simplify even further:

1. We start with a rectangular board having a "proto-city" in each cell.
2. A certain number of people is randomly distributed among the cities.
3. Each person is characterized with a randomly chosen maximum distance they are willing to move away from the current location if a better living option is available.
4. Each city's attractiveness score is determined by its population according to the formula

$$score\ (points) = population - C \cdot population^2,$$

where C is a very small constant. A growing population makes a city more attractive by creating more opportunities for work and leisure. On the other hand, overcrowded regions are often associated with higher crime, pollution, and prices, so after a certain size these "disagglomerating forces" start to dominate. Since x^2 grows faster than x, at some point the increase of population will make a city less attractive.

5. On each simulation step we move every person to the most attractive city within the allowed travel distance, if its score at least MS points higher than of the current city. The process is repeated until nobody is willing to move anymore.

4.7.1 IMPLEMENTATION

This simulation will work in two steps. First, we will simulate the growth of cities until their population stabilizes. Next, we'll draw a log-log plot to check how the cities agree with Zipf's law.

Let's start with the initial quick sketch of the program shown in Listing 4.7.

Listing 4.7: The rise of cities (a sketch).

```python
import math
import turtle
from random import randint
from dataclasses import dataclass

H = 25
W = 25
SLEEP_MS = 50
CELLSIZE = 20   # pixels


@dataclass
class SimState:
    done: bool

    def set_done(self):
        self.done = True

    @classmethod
    def setup(cls):
        r = cls(False)
        turtle.listen()
        turtle.onkeypress(r.set_done, "space")
        return r


@dataclass
class WorldState:
    ...
    is_stable: bool = False
```

```
    @classmethod
    def setup(cls):
        ...

    def update(self):
        ...

    def rankings(self): # return a sorted list of city populations
        ...


def setup_screen(title):
    turtle.setup(W * CELLSIZE, H * CELLSIZE)
    turtle.tracer(0, 0)
    turtle.title(title)
    turtle.setworldcoordinates(0, 0, W, H)


def draw_chart(rankings):
    ...


setup_screen("The rise of cities")
sim_state = SimState.setup()
world_state = WorldState.setup()


def tick():
    if not sim_state.done:
        if not world_state.is_stable:
            world_state.update()
            turtle.update()
        turtle.ontimer(tick, SLEEP_MS)
    else:
        draw_chart(world_state.rankings())


tick()
turtle.done()
```

As you can see, this is our usual template for an interactive simulation. The internal state of the model is updated on each step, and the user can stop it at any time by pressing the space key. In this case, however, there is an extra stage where the resulting chart is drawn.

Now let's make one step forward by implementing the initial distribution of people among the cities (Listing 4.8).

Listing 4.8: The rise of cities: `City` and `Person` classes.

```
...
SHAPE_SIZE_FACTOR = 0.01
SHAPE_SIZE = SHAPE_SIZE_FACTOR * CELLSIZE / 20   # turtle size
POPULATION = 25000
SHAPE_SIZE_FACTOR = 5000
```

```
DAC = 0.0005
MS = 3


@dataclass
class City:
    shape: turtle.Turtle
    population: int = 0

    def increase(self):
        self.update(self.population + 1)

    def decrease(self):
        self.update(self.population - 1)

    def update(self, p):
        self.population = p

        if self.population == 0:
            self.shape.hideturtle()
        else:
            self.shape.shapesize(SHAPE_SIZE * math.sqrt(self.population))

    def score(self):
        return self.population - DAC * self.population**2

    @classmethod
    def create(cls, x, y):
        p = turtle.Turtle()
        p.penup()
        p.shape("circle")
        p.goto(x, y)
        return cls(p)


@dataclass
class Person:
    city: object
    max_distance: int

    def move_to(self, new_city):
        self.city.decrease()
        self.city = new_city
        new_city.increase()

    @classmethod
    def create(cls, cities):
        c = cities[randint(0, W - 1)][randint(0, H - 1)]
        c.increase()
        return cls(c, randint(1, max(H, W) // 2))


@dataclass
class WorldState:
    cities: list
    population: list
```

```
@classmethod
def setup(cls):
    cells = [[City.create(x, y) for y in range(H)] for x in range(W)]
    population = [Person.create(cells) for _ in range(POPULATION)]
    return cls(cells, population)
```

The WorldState object keeps a list of cities and a list of people. Each cell of the W × H board contains a city, and there are POPULATION people in total. Each city "knows" how many people live there by keeping a counter of its current population. City objects can be updated by calling increase() and decrease() methods, and each update triggers redrawing. A city is drawn as a circle of a radius, proportional to the square root of its population (because by linearly increasing a city radius, we quadratically increase its livable area). Empty cities are hidden. The most important attribute of a city is its attractiveness score, calculated in score() method:

```
def score(self):
    return self.population - DAC * self.population**2
```

Here DAC stands for "disagglomeration coefficient", which can be fine-tuned.

The Person class is even simpler. Every person is initially placed into a random city on the board and gets a random maximal distance to move. Some will only move as far as the adjacent cell, while others are going to be ready to cross up to one-half of the board. When a person moves from one city to another, we update the current population counters of both cities and the mover's current city of residence.

Finally, let's fill the missing functionality of WorldState and draw_chart(), as shown in Listing 4.9.

Listing 4.9: The rise of cities: final touches.

```
@dataclass
class WorldState:
    ...
    prev_ranks: list = None

    def better_neighbor(self, city, dist):
        best_city = city
        xc, yc = int(city.shape.xcor()), int(city.shape.ycor())
        for x in range(max(0, xc - dist), min(W - 1, xc + dist) + 1):
            for y in range(max(0, yc - dist), min(H - 1, yc + dist) + 1):
                dst = self.cities[x][y]
                if dst.score() > best_city.score():
                    best_city = dst
        will_move = best_city.score() - city.score() >= MS
        return best_city if will_move else city

    def rankings(self):
        p = [self.cities[x][y].population for x in range(W) for y in range(H)]
        return sorted([v for v in p if v > 0], reverse=True)
```

```
def update(self):
    for p in self.population:
        dest = self.better_neighbor(p.city, p.max_distance)
        p.move_to(dest)

    if self.rankings() == self.prev_ranks:
        self.is_stable = True
        print(f"The cities ({len(self.prev_ranks)}) have stabilized")
    self.prev_ranks = self.rankings()


def draw_chart(rankings):
    turtle.clearscreen()
    drawer = turtle.Turtle()
    drawer.hideturtle()
    drawer.penup()

    width = math.log(len(rankings))
    height = math.log(rankings[0])
    turtle.setworldcoordinates(0, 0, math.ceil(width), math.ceil(height))

    print(rankings)
    for x, y in enumerate(rankings):
        drawer.goto(math.log(x + 1), math.log(y))
        drawer.pendown()
```

The core loop of the simulation (`world_state.update()`) is straightforward: for each person in the list, find the best city within `max_distance` form their current residence, and move there. Once the population of cities stabilizes (no more changes in rankings), let the user know.

Cities of higher score are searched within the `max_distance` × `max_distance` square with the current city residence at the center. This decision makes code simpler, but lets the people move a bit further that `max_distance` in the diagonal direction.

Final stats are visualized in the same way as in our previous simulation: the resulting ranked list is displayed on a log-log chart using a dedicated turtle-based drawer object.

The typical map of cities obtained by a test run of this program is shown in Figure 4.6. As a result, 105 cities with the following populations are produced:

```
[12302, 2667, 1719, 1510, 1243, 680, 511, 333, 243, 240, 203, 183, 178, 159,
 155, 143, 140, 139, 126, 112, 110, 109, 108, 103, 99, 87, 66, 65, 58, 53, 51,
 50, 49, 48, 47, 44, 43, 39, 37, 36, 36, 35, 34, 33, 33, 25, 25, 24, 23, 23,
 22, 21, 17, 17, 17, 17, 17, 16, 16, 16, 14, 14, 12, 12, 11, 11, 11, 11, 11,
 11, 10, 8, 8, 7, 7, 7, 6, 6, 5, 5, 5, 5, 4, 4, 4, 4, 3, 3, 3, 3, 2, 2, 2, 2,
 2, 1, 1, 1, 1, 1, 1, 1, 1, 1, 1]
```

The corresponding log-log plot (see Figure 4.7) shows a certain lack of small-sized cities in our simulation: the graph falls down somewhat abruptly at its right end. However, considering the simplicity of the underlying model, its ability to produce mostly realistic distribution of cities is impressive.

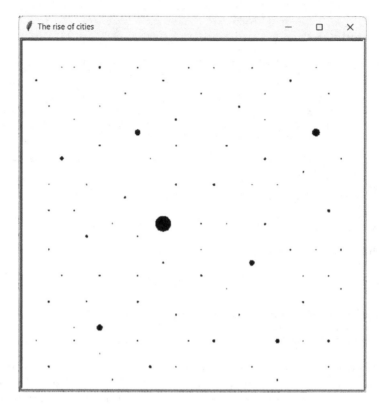

FIGURE 4.6: The rise of cities (screenshot).

4.8 TRAFFIC SHOCKWAVES

The next project brings together circular motion, stochastic (randomized) processes, and system-wide effects resulting from interaction between independent moving entities.

Traffic jams are not among the most pleasant experiences in life. Large city dwellers know it very well: central streets are quite congested all the time, and minor roadworks or a traffic accident may cause noticeable inconveniences. However, complex networks of city streets are not the only places where jams occur: a high-speed intercity road isn't immune either. However, these are different kinds of disruptions requiring different kinds of measures. City jams can be made tolerable with careful management of traffic streams, while highways are sensitive to speed and distance control.

Let's consider a simplified model of a narrow one-lane road. If it is moderately congested, cars proceed at steady rate, observing speed limits and keeping safe distance.[8] Now imagine that one of the drivers has to quickly

---

[8]Yes, it is a *very* simplified model.

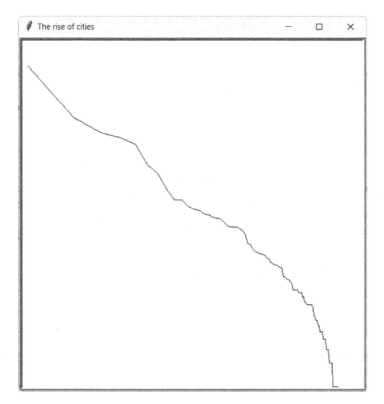

FIGURE 4.7: The rise of cities (city populations on a log-log plot).

slow down for a few seconds due to a certain distraction, obstacle, or technical trouble.

If cars are moving not too fast, and the distance between the cars is reasonable, nothing noteworthy would happen: after a while, the "rhythm" of the road would go back to normal. In contrast, if the cars approach airplane speeds, every random delay might trigger a major obstruction, known as a *traffic shockwave*.

The slowed-down car creates a "tail" of cars behind it. Over time, the density of this "tail" (cars per unit of distance) decreases, while its length grows. Eventually the "tail" density approaches the usual density for the road, and the jam dissolves.

This effect can be observed even in very basic computer models of traffic flow, which will be demonstrated in our next project (adopted with simplifications from Wetherell [58]). Interestingly, similar experiments with real cars were performed only recently, showing how shockwaves actually happen in the physical world [52].

Our task would be to simulate a simple case of a circular road, uniformly populated with N cars. Each car moves with its preferred speed (randomly chosen within predefined limits) and tries to respect certain distance rules. A car coming uncomfortably close to its front neighbor starts to decelerate at a steady rate. A car moving slower than it prefers and keeping a safe distance may accelerate. Safe distance is bound to car speed: it is safer to come closer to a slowly moving car, so it makes sense to formulate the distance rule in terms of "simulation steps before the collision" if both cars continue moving with their current speeds.

The main capability of our program would be to let the user simulate a disruption. A random car will slow down to a full stop, stay for a certain time, then resume its normal operation. If a car ever comes to a full stop, it won't be able to resume immediately as the driver needs some time to notice that the car in the front is now moving, and press the acceleration pedal. Acceleration rate is typically lower than the deceleration rate: it is easier to lose speed when braking than to gain speed when accelerating. It is of course possible to choose unfortunate parameter values leading to car crashes. In case of a crash, the program is stopped.

4.8.1 IMPLEMENTATION

The description above may look a bit overwhelming, but the required functionality is not very hard to separate into small independent functions. Let's start with the general structure of our program, shown in Listing 4.10.

Listing 4.10: Traffic shockwaves (incomplete).

```python
import turtle
import math
from random import uniform, randint
from dataclasses import dataclass

WIDTH = 600
HEIGHT = 400
MARGIN = 50
SLEEP_MS = 20

N = 25


@dataclass
class SimState:
    done: bool
    cars: list

    def set_done(self):
        self.done = True

    def gen_disruption(self):
        self.cars[randint(0, N - 1)].disrupt()
```

```
    @classmethod
    def setup(cls, cars):
        r = cls(False, cars)
        turtle.listen()
        turtle.onkeypress(r.set_done, "space")
        turtle.onkeypress(r.gen_disruption, "Return")
        return r


@dataclass
class Car:
    ...
    def disrupt(self):
        ...

    def move(self):
        ...


def setup_screen(title):
    turtle.setup(WIDTH + MARGIN, HEIGHT + MARGIN)
    turtle.tracer(0, 0)
    turtle.title(title)


def setup_cars():
    ...


setup_screen("Traffic shockwaves")
cars = setup_cars()
sim_state = SimState.setup(cars)


def tick():
    if not sim_state.done:
        for c in cars:
            c.move()

        turtle.update()
        turtle.ontimer(tick, SLEEP_MS)


tick()
turtle.done()
```

This code is based on our usual template, which served as a base for "Ideal gas" and related simulations. We'll make a list of N cars, which will be moved inside tick(). The sim_state object stops program execution when the user presses space, as usual. It can also generate a disruption for a random car when the enter key is pressed ("Return" keysym).

Now let's fill some gaps in Car class (see Listing 4.11).

Listing 4.11: Car class (incomplete).

```
MIN_SPEED = 4
MAX_SPEED = 7
R = 200
...


@dataclass
class Car:
    m: turtle.Turtle
    angle: float
    pref_speed: float
    speed: float
    front_car: object = None
    in_disrupt: bool = False
    ...

    def disrupt(self):
        self.in_disrupt = True

    def adjust_speed(self):
        ...

    def move(self):
        self.adjust_speed()
        self.angle += self.speed / R
        self.m.goto(R * math.cos(self.angle), R * math.sin(self.angle))

    @classmethod
    def create(cls, angle):
        m = turtle.Turtle()
        m.shape("circle")
        m.shapesize(0.2)
        m.penup()
        speed = uniform(MIN_SPEED, MAX_SPEED)
        return cls(m, angle, speed, speed)


def setup_cars():
    cars = [Car.create(i * 2 * math.pi / N) for i in range(N)]
    for i in range(N):
        cars[i].front_car = cars[(i + 1) % N]
    return cars
...
```

Initially, each car is moving with its preferred speed, randomly chosen between MIN_SPEED and MAX_SPEED. To distribute cars uniformly along the circular road, we assign each car its unique angle, calculated as

$$i \cdot \frac{2\pi}{N}$$

Since a car watches its front neighbor, it needs a reference to the next car in the list. The last car gets a reference to the first car.

Conceptually, cars move along a straight road. Circular onscreen motion is merely a way to visualize their movement: we could have easily opted for two straight lanes with U-turns at both ends instead. Therefore, distance, speed, and acceleration are regular units, while "car angle" appears only when we draw the car on the screen. A car moving with the speed *speed* along the circle with radius R has the angular velocity $\frac{speed}{R}$. Thus, to update the onscreen car location, we adjust its current angle and use polar to Cartesian conversion formulas to obtain new car coordinates:

$$x = R \cdot cos(angle)$$
$$y = R \cdot sin(angle)$$

The main logic of the program is hidden in `adjust_speed()`. It is a bit involved, so let's proceed carefully (see Listing 4.12).

Listing 4.12: `Car` class with speed adjustment functionality.

```
EPSILON = 0.0001

SAFE_DIST_STEPS = 15
CRASH_DISTANCE = 2
...

@dataclass
class Car:
    ...

    def accelerate(self):
        ...

    def decelerate(self):
        ...

    def front_distanace(self):
        angle = self.front_car.angle - self.angle
        return R * (angle if angle >= 0 else angle + 2 * math.pi)

    def front_distance_steps(self):
        return self.front_distanace() / (self.speed + EPSILON)

    def adjust_speed(self):
        if self.front_distanace() < CRASH_DISTANCE:
            print("Crash!")
            sim_state.set_done()
        elif self.front_distance_steps() < SAFE_DIST_STEPS or self.in_disrupt:
            self.decelerate()
        elif self.speed < self.pref_speed:
            self.accelerate()
```

We need to make a distinction between the absolute distance between the cars and the distance in simulation steps. The absolute distance matters when detecting crashes: if cars are too close, we have to report a crash and stop the program. Steps are necessary to determine safe following distance, as already discussed.

To calculate the distance between two cars, we use the arc length formula, just like in "Spirograph curves". For the last car in the list, the value

```
angle = self.front_car.angle - self.angle
```

is going to be negative and needs to be adjusted.

The distance in steps can be obtained by simply dividing the absolute distance by the current car speed. For a fully stopped car, this formula produces a divide by zero error, and the easiest way to fix it is to make sure the speed is never zero (hence, we divide by `self.speed + EPSILON`).

Now we have a car that decelerates when it comes too close to the front car or is disrupted, and accelerates if its speed is lower than the driver prefers, and the distance is safe. Only the final piece of the puzzle remains at this point: when a car comes to a full stop, it has to stay still for some time before resuming its motion. This time depends on the reason of a stop. If it is due to disruption, we'll keep it still for `DISRUPT_TIME` steps. If it merely came close to another non-moving car, the pause will be shorter (`REACT_TIME`). Consequently, a car may accelerate only when its waiting time expires (see Listing 4.13).

Listing 4.13: `Car` class with acceleration and deceleration functionality.

```
DECEL = 0.4
ACCEL = 0.1
REACT_TIME = 15
DISRUPT_TIME = 70
...


@dataclass
class Car:
    ...
    pause_steps: int = 0

    def accelerate(self):
        if self.pause_steps > 0:
            self.pause_steps -= 1
        else:
            self.speed = min(self.pref_speed, self.speed + ACCEL)

    def decelerate(self):
        self.speed = max(0, self.speed - DECEL)
        if self.speed == 0:
            self.pause_steps = DISRUPT_TIME if self.in_disrupt else REACT_TIME
            self.in_disrupt = False
    ...
```

A screenshot of the working program is shown in Figure 4.8. With the current parameter values, shockwaves can be clearly observed. They take time

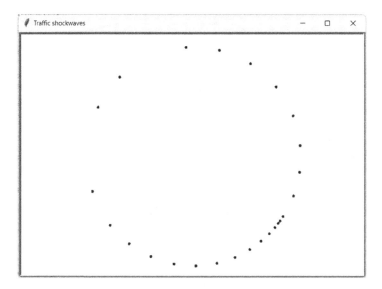

FIGURE 4.8: Traffic shockwaves (screenshot).

to dissipate, but they are not fatal. By playing with the values, it is easy to simulate both ends of the spectrum: low speeds and high safe distances make shockwaves barely noticeable, while high speeds and low distances cause immediate crashes.

4.9 FURTHER IDEAS

1. Use "Free kick" as a starting point to create a more realistic version of the Galton board simulation, where ball-shaped beads can bounce off pegs, walls, and other beads.
2. Use Monte Carlo integration to find out the area of a complex shape. You can use the shape shown in Figure 4.9 or any similar combination of circles and polygons.
3. Find the optimal "hold at N" strategy for the following variation of Pig. Instead of one die, a player throws two dice and adds their sum to the turn score. Doubles multiply the score by two (so, for example, $3 + 3$ scores 12). The combination of two "ones" scores 25. Any other combination having "one" on either die ends the turn with zero score for the player. Draw a chart showing the average per-turn player score for different values of N.
4. Check the validity of Zipf's law for the frequency of individual letters rather than words in English-language documents.

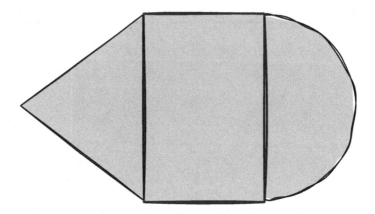

FIGURE 4.9: Example of a complex shape.

5 Living things

The world of living organisms has always been a great source of interest for scientists and engineers. It is commonly mentioned that gliders are inspired by birds, flippers are designed after duck feet, and velcro works like thistle burrs. Such *biomimicry* is not foreign to computer science, either. There are concepts like "ant colony optimization", "genetic algorithms", and "artificial neural networks". Being inspired by nature is not the same as striving for an exact copy of nature's solution. Just as gliders don't flap wings, artificial ant colonies don't reflect every aspect of real ant behavior.

On the other hand, modeling the behavior of real living nature is an important research task on its own. Besides helping in numerous practical problems like simulating fish population dynamics or paths of birds migration, computers are indispensable in testing out theories. The idea of already mentioned "virtual experiments" applies well to biological systems. Having a theory, say, of plant development, we can grow "virtual plants" and see how similar they are to the real ones. Even a rough theory can be good enough for certain purposes, and computational modeling is often a vital part of its evaluation and refinement.

The present chapter offers a quick excursion to the world of living things by approaching it with the tools developed in our previous projects. We will see how the techniques used to simulate the motion of molecules or celestial bodies work for birds and insects. Closer to the end of the chapter, we will finally depart from motion physics and concentrate on other interesting aspects of our virtual worlds and their inhabitants.

5.1 A MOTH AND A LIGHTBULB

As most of us can attest, moths are attracted to light. Curiously, there is no definitive explanation why exactly it happens. Existing theories seem to have shortcomings, which is good news for the ambitious researchers who still have a chance to unravel this mystery.

The dance of a moth around a lightbulb looks quite complicated, so it might be surprising how easily this kind of movement can be simulated on a computer. This simulation will be inaccurate, but still reasonably believable from the perspective of a non-expert observer. It might also be surprising that such a simulation will be a close relative of our recent ball motion models.

Let's start with a very simple scenario, which can be described as follows. A moth starts its journey in a random screen location. Its initial direction is random, and its movement speed is constant. Next, a lightbulb, located in a certain point, is turned on. The moth, attracted by the light, changes its direction and starts moving toward the lightbulb.

DOI: 10.1201/9781003455295-5

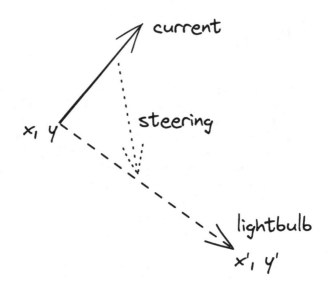

FIGURE 5.1: Scheme of moth steering toward the lightbulb.

So far, this sounds very much like the motion of a molecule of gas. The key difference between these models is made by *inertia*. We will presume that the moth cannot turn instantaneously, so any change of movement direction takes time. Naturally, this presumption creates much more life-like models of real macroscopic objects, such as cars, animals, or spaceships. The resulting *steering behavior*, thoroughly discussed in the influential Reynolds paper [45] is indeed often employed in animation, virtual simulations, and computer games.

With or without inertia, our simulation will end when the hapless moth smacks into the lightbulb. To make things more interesting, let's also presume that the lightbulb is really tiny, and the moth can't hit it. Instead, it will fly through it, turn around and resume its endless chase.

In general, this simulation works very much like "A molecule of gas": on every step, we simply update the moth's coordinates according to velocity constituents v_x and v_y. The trick here is to modify these constituents on every step as well. This procedure is also familiar to us from "Newton's cannonball", where Earth served as a really large and attractive lightbulb.

Suppose our moth wants to reach the lightbulb at (x', y') but is currently moving somewhere else (see Figure 5.1).

In terms of velocity constituents, the moth is moving with (v_x, v_y), but its desired constituents are (v'_x, v'_y) that go along the vector pointing toward the lightbulb.

It is not hard to calculate their values. If we had no speed limit, these constituents would have been as follows:

$$v_x^* = x' - x$$

$$v_y^* = y' - y$$

However, we need to scale them to make up the original moth speed (let's denote it as V). The length of the vector (v_x^*, v_y^*) is

$$|(v_x^*, v_y^*)| = \sqrt{v_x^{*2} + v_y^{*2}},$$

so we can divide each constituent by $|(v_x^*, v_y^*)|$ and then multiply by V to obtain the desired values:

$$v_x' = V \frac{v_x^*}{|(v_x^*, v_y^*)|}$$

$$v_y' = V \frac{v_y^*}{|(v_x^*, v_y^*)|}$$

If we set v_x' and v_y' as moth's velocity constituents, the moth will instantly turn in the direction of the lightbulb. What we want, however, is to *gradually* transform v_x into v_x', and v_y into v_y'. To do it, we need to introduce another constant: a *force F* that is applied to the moth on each step to alter its direction (larger force increases moth's maneuverability).

A force modifies velocity via *acceleration*, calculated as $a = \frac{F}{m}$ according to Newton's second law. Here m is the mass of a body, which can be set to 1 in this case, so for us $a = F$.

To apply the force, we'll need a *steering* vector (s_x, s_y), calculated as

$$s_x = v_x' - v_x$$

$$s_y = v_y' - v_y$$

Now we'll simply scale the steering vector to the length of F to obtain the force (and, hence, the acceleration) to be applied to each velocity constituent:

$$a_x = F \frac{s_x}{|(s_x, s_y)|}$$

$$a_y = F \frac{s_y}{|(s_x, s_y)|}$$

Finally, let's calculate moth's new velocity constituents (v_x^{**}, v_y^{**}), making sure the resulting speed is V:

$$v_x'' = v_x + a_x$$

$$v_y'' = v_y + a_y$$

$$v_x^{**} = V \frac{v_x''}{|(v_x'', v_y'')|}$$

$$v_y^{**} = V \frac{v_y''}{|(v_x'', v_y'')|}$$

5.1.1 IMPLEMENTATION

It might take some time to fully comprehend the formulas used to implement
steering behavior, but the actual code is straightforward and follows the same
approach as in our previous simulations. The only notable difference is the use
of vector arithmetic. The explanations above look quite repetitive, because
most formulas appear twice (once per constituent). However, we can clean up
the code a bit by using variables that represent two-dimensional vectors, and
implementing some basic arithmetical functions for them.

Since we are about to draw a moth rather than a molecule, I also suggest
keeping the original arrow-like shape of the turtle. The complete code is shown
in Listing 5.1, and the screenshot of the working program in Figure 5.2.

Listing 5.1: A moth and a lightbulb.

```python
import turtle
import math
from random import uniform
from dataclasses import dataclass

WIDTH = 600
HEIGHT = 400
MARGIN = 50
R = 10
SLEEP_MS = 20
V = 15
FORCE = 9
BULB = (0, 0)


@dataclass
class SimState:
    done: bool

    def set_done(self):
        self.done = True

    @classmethod
    def setup(cls):
        r = cls(False)
        turtle.listen()
        turtle.onkeypress(r.set_done, "space")
        return r


def setup_screen(title):
```

```
        turtle.setup(WIDTH + MARGIN, HEIGHT + MARGIN)
        turtle.tracer(0, 0)
        turtle.title(title)


sim_state = SimState.setup()
setup_screen("A moth and a lightbulb")

bulb = turtle.Turtle()
bulb.shape("circle")

moth = turtle.Turtle()
moth.penup()
moth.setx(uniform(-WIDTH / 2 + R, WIDTH / 2 - R))
moth.sety(uniform(-HEIGHT / 2 + R, HEIGHT / 2 - R))

angle = uniform(0, 2 * math.pi)
v = (V * math.cos(angle), V * math.sin(angle))


def mult(vec, factor):
    return (vec[0] * factor, vec[1] * factor)


def length(vec):
    return math.sqrt(vec[0] ** 2 + vec[1] ** 2)


def scale(vec, new_len):
    return mult(vec, new_len / length(vec))


def vecsum(v1, v2):
    return (v1[0] + v2[0], v1[1] + v2[1])


def vecdiff(v1, v2):
    return (v1[0] - v2[0], v1[1] - v2[1])


def tick():
    if not sim_state.done:
        global v

        bulb_direction = vecdiff(BULB, (moth.xcor(), moth.ycor()))
        v_desired = scale(bulb_direction, V)
        steering = vecdiff(v_desired, v)
        acceleration = scale(steering, FORCE)
        v = scale(vecsum(v, acceleration), V)

        x_new, y_new = moth.xcor() + v[0], moth.ycor() + v[1]
        moth.setheading(moth.towards(x_new, y_new))
        moth.goto(x_new, y_new)

        turtle.update()
        turtle.ontimer(tick, SLEEP_MS)
```

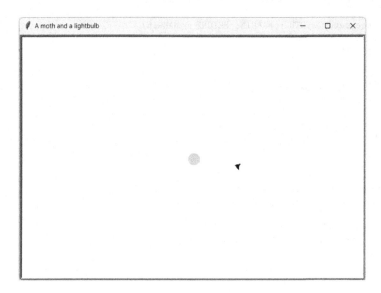

FIGURE 5.2: A moth and a lightbulb (screenshot).

```
tick()
turtle.done()
```

5.2 DANCING MOTH

I think the largest downside of the previous simulation is the "fly-through" behavior. Yes, the lightbulb can be tiny, and our moth can indeed buzz next to it, but in real life lamps are usually much larger than a moth, and insects manage to steer away from them.

Implementing this lamp-avoidance effect is surprisingly easy, because all we have to do is reverse the desired direction as soon as the moth comes too close to the lamp (Reynolds calls these types of behavior "seek" and "flee").

5.2.1 IMPLEMENTATION

This change is really a matter of three new lines of code:

```
BULB_RANGE = 70
...

def tick():
    if not sim_state.done:
        global v
```

```
bulb_direction = vecdiff(BULB, (moth.xcor(), moth.ycor()))

if length(bulb_direction) < BULB_RANGE:
    bulb_direction = (-bulb_direction[0], -bulb_direction[1])
...
```

Please try out this program, if you haven't done it yet. It's hard to believe that just a few lines of Python can create such a fascinating effect.

5.3   HOMING PIGEON

In both projects considered so far, we had to update moth's velocity components on each simulation step, while the overall speed remained constant. It is also easy to imagine a case when the speed needs to be adjusted on the go.

For example, the current "seeking" behavior can be reprogrammed into "arrival", such as exhibited by a bird coming back to its nest. When the bird (let it be a bird rather than a moth now) comes closer than the predefined "nest range" to the target, its speed starts decreasing.

If deceleration is constant (which is a realistic presumption), the speed will decrease linearly from V to zero. Thus, having the current distance to target, we can obtain the current speed:

$$speed = V \cdot \frac{distance\_to\_target}{nest\_range}$$

5.3.1   IMPLEMENTATION

Tuning global parameters on the go is not a good programming style, but in this case we can do it to quickly turn the "Dancing moth" simulation into "Homing pigeon". We will need a new global constant VMAX for the maximum allowed speed, while V will start receiving updates.

All we need to do is add a couple of declarations and a single line modifying V at the end of the loop:

```
V = 10
VMAX = V
NEST_RANGE = 70
...

def tick():
    if not sim_state.done:
        global v, V
        ...

        V = min(VMAX * length(bulb_direction) / NEST_RANGE, VMAX)
        turtle.update()
        turtle.ontimer(tick, SLEEP_MS)
...
```

If the bird is farther than NEST_RANGE from the nest (still called "bulb" here), the resulting value of V will be higher than VMAX, so we'll have to clamp it down.

Before wrapping up this example, I suggest one simple improvement. When the bird is about to arrive, its movement direction goes through a rapid series of little adjustments. They are almost invisible if we only look at trajectory, but the erratic turns of the turtle shape (bird's "beak") are annoying, so it makes sense to stop changing its visible orientation when the speed becomes small. This can be done by making the call to setheading() conditional:

```
# needs new global variable VMIN = 3 (for example)
# further suggestion: rename "moth" to "pigeon"
if V > VMIN:
    moth.setheading(moth.towards(x_new, y_new))
```

5.4   A FLOCK OF BOIDS

The most fascinating feature of the moth model is its ability to produce complex behavior patterns on the basis of very simple rules. All we have to do is implement several basic physical laws, and let the nature care about the rest.

This property is even more pronounced in simulations of interacting entities. Moths dancing around a lightbulb hardly interact with each other: each moth is more akin to a molecule of the ideal gas than to a member of a group. However, if we switch from moths to birds or fish, we'll see the examples of such "group behavior" immediately.

Numerous documentaries show how flocks of birds or schools of fish behave. Each bird or fish has a mind of its own, and yet they move in semi-chaotic semi-orderly patterns, ranging from blob-like crowds to perfect formations. In a sense, a flock also has a "mind of its own", which is hard to comprehend merely by studying the movements of its individual members.

This effect is known as *emergence*: a complex entity like a flock has properties that *emerge* only as a result of interaction of its constituents. Just like a dancing moth simulation, a complex system can be based on a handful of simple rules and exhibit emergent properties naturally, requiring no special programming efforts.

One of the most commonly cited examples of a simple emergent system is "Boids", developed by the already mentioned here Craig Reynolds [44]. According to Reynolds, *boids* are "bird-oid objects", representing generic simulated flocking creatures. Consequently, the goal of "Boids" is to simulate flocking behavior. Over years, this system was used in a variety of tasks, including the most obvious application: the simulation of birds or fish in animated movies and computer games.

Original "Boids" are based on merely three simple rules, applied to each boid independently. They are flexible in a sense that the original Reynolds's paper gives enough room to interpret them (and they work well under any reasonable interpretation). The rules are also stackable: it is easy to add new rules or modify any existing rule independently from the rest of the system.

I think this capability made the influence of "Boids" so enduring: once the original model becomes insufficient for whatever reason, it is not hard to improve it.

The three original rules can be summarized as follows:

- avoid being too close to another boid (*separation rule*);
- strive to keep the same speed and movement direction as nearby boids (*alignment rule*);
- strive to be in the center of the group formed by the nearby boids (*cohesion rule*).

The simulation we are about to develop shortly is based on the rules above, their interpretation by Conrad Parker[1], and implementation by Ben Eater[2]. This flavor of "Boids" relies on the following additional presumptions:

- a boid treats any flockmate within its VISUAL_RANGE as a "nearby" boid;
- a boid exhibits steering behavior;
- boid speed is limited to MAX_V;
- boids will steer away from the screen borders.

The implementation of steering behavior in this case is going to be simplified, but the general idea of controlling a boid via application of a force remains intact. The flocking model works equally well both in two-dimensional and three-dimensional case, so we will continue our work in a flat two-dimensional world.

5.4.1 IMPLEMENTATION

Since our new program will need a few functions from the "moth" simulation, let's take "moth" as a starting point, keeping only the necessary parts (see Listing 5.2).

Listing 5.2: A flock of boids (with Boid class missing).

```
import turtle
import math
from random import uniform
from dataclasses import dataclass
N = 100   # number of boids

WIDTH = 600
HEIGHT = 400
MARGIN = 50
R = 10
```

---

[1] Available at http://www.kfish.org/boids/pseudocode.html

[2] Available at https://eater.net/boids

```
SLEEP_MS = 20


@dataclass
class SimState:
    ...             # same as in moth

# also preserve the functions
# mult(), length(), scale(), vecsum(), vecdiff(), and setup_screen()

@dataclass
class Boid:
    ...             # to be created

sim_state = SimState.setup()
setup_screen("Boids")
boids = [Boid.create() for _ in range(N)]


def tick():
    if not sim_state.done:
        for b in boids:
            b.move()

        turtle.update()
        turtle.ontimer(tick, SLEEP_MS)


tick()
turtle.done()
```

Our next job would be to develop the class Boid, responsible for the actual behavior of flock members. As already noted, behavior rules in "Boids" are stackable, so we will deal with them one-by-one. Let's start with creating and moving a boid:

```
...
MIN_V = 5
MAX_V = 20


@dataclass
class Boid:
    m: turtle.Turtle
    v: tuple

    def move(self):
        self.rule_separation()
        self.rule_alignment()
        self.rule_cohesion()
        self.rule_limits()

        x_new, y_new = self.m.xcor() + self.v[0], self.m.ycor() + self.v[1]
        self.m.setheading(self.m.towards(x_new, y_new))
        self.m.goto(x_new, y_new)
```

```
@classmethod
def create(cls):
    x = uniform(-WIDTH / 2 + R, WIDTH / 2 - R)
    y = uniform(-HEIGHT / 2 + R, HEIGHT / 2 - R)
    m = turtle.Turtle()
    m.penup()
    m.goto(x, y)
    v = uniform(MIN_V, MAX_V)
    angle = uniform(0, 2 * math.pi)
    return cls(m, (v * math.cos(angle), v * math.sin(angle)))
```

This piece is very similar to the code we use for the moth simulation. A boid is created in a random screen location, and it has a random speed (within the given limits) and a random direction. To move a boid, we calculate its new coordinates using velocity constituents, point its head in the right direction, and update the current location. Velocity constituents are being updated on every simulation step according to the four rules. Three of them are the original rules proposed by Reynolds, while the fourth rule ("limits") keeps the flock within screen bounds, and limits movement speed to MAX_V.

Since three original rules rely on the concept of "nearby boids", we will need to be able to identify all the flockmates within a given distance:

```
@dataclass
class Boid:
    ...

    # returns all neighbors of the current boid within the given range
    def neighbors(self, dist):
        return [b for b in boids if b != self and self.m.distance(b.m) < dist]
```

Now we can finally proceed to the implementation of the flocking rules. Let's start with separation:

```
MIN_DISTANCE = 20
AVOID_F = 0.09
...

@dataclass
class Boid:
    ...
    def rule_separation(self):
        neighbors = self.neighbors(MIN_DISTANCE)

        if neighbors:
            vx = sum(self.m.xcor() - b.m.xcor() for b in neighbors)
            vy = sum(self.m.ycor() - b.m.ycor() for b in neighbors)
            target_v = (vx, vy)

            self.v = vecsum(self.v, mult(target_v, AVOID_F))
```

What is going on here? Let's consider a simple example of two neighbors within MIN_DISTANCE from "our" boid shown in Figure 5.3.

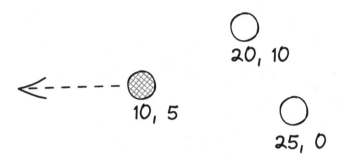

FIGURE 5.3: Calculating the target velocity.

First, we calculate the new target direction by summing up the vectors pointing away from each neighbor. In our case, vx = (10 - 20) + (10 - 25) = -25, vy = (5 - 10) + (5 - 0) = 0.

Since the boid cannot change its direction instantly, we will apply a force AVOID_F to modify its current course slightly on each simulation step. Note that the desired direction vector is multiplied by the force, so the resulting velocity would be higher for the boids located farther away from their neighbors. It is quite counter-intuitive: one would expect that nearby boids would be pushed away from each other harder. Parker argues that this approach produces smoother movements, because two boids rapidly approaching each other will not suddenly turn into the opposite directions. Instead, they will gradually slow down, turn around and gradually speed up.

Also note that the resulting velocity obtained with the separation rule is not restrained; we will need the final "limits" rule to make sure it does not exceed MAX_V.

The next rule is alignment:

```
VISUAL_RANGE = 200
VMATCH_F = 0.04
...

@dataclass
class Boid:
    ...
    def rule_alignment(self):
        neighbors = self.neighbors(VISUAL_RANGE)

        if neighbors:
            vx = sum(b.v[0] for b in neighbors) / len(neighbors)
            vy = sum(b.v[1] for b in neighbors) / len(neighbors)
            flock_v = (vx, vy)
            v_diff = vecdiff(flock_v, self.v)

            self.v = vecsum(self.v, mult(v_diff, VMATCH_F))
```

This one is simpler: we calculate the average velocity constituents (vx, vy) of the nearby boids and try to match them by applying the force VMATCH_F to the current boid.

The final original rule is cohesion:

```
CENTERING_F = 0.03
...

@dataclass
class Boid:
    ...
    def rule_cohesion(self):
        neighbors = self.neighbors(VISUAL_RANGE)

        if neighbors:
            cx = sum(b.m.xcor() for b in neighbors) / len(neighbors)
            cy = sum(b.m.ycor() for b in neighbors) / len(neighbors)
            center = (cx, cy)

            c_direction = vecdiff(center, (self.m.xcor(), self.m.ycor()))
            self.v = vecsum(self.v, mult(c_direction, CENTERING_F))
```

Here we calculate the center of the "local flock" (cx, cy) and steer the boid toward it by applying the force CENTERING_F.

Finally, we have to limit boid speed to MAX_V, and steer any boids away from the screen borders:

```
VRETURN_F = 3.0
RET_MARGIN = 70
...

@dataclass
class Boid:
    ...
    def rule_limits(self):
        ax, ay = 0, 0

        if abs(self.m.xcor()) > WIDTH / 2 - RET_MARGIN:
            ax = -math.copysign(VRETURN_F, self.m.xcor())
        if abs(self.m.ycor()) > HEIGHT / 2 - RET_MARGIN:
            ay = -math.copysign(VRETURN_F, self.m.ycor())

        self.v = vecsum(self.v, (ax, ay))
        if length(self.v) > MAX_V:
            self.v = scale(self.v, MAX_V)
```

A boid won't reflect from the screen border like a molecule of gas. Instead, we will apply the force VRETURN_F to steer the boid back. This force has to be negative for the boids flying toward the right and the top borders of the screen, and positive for the left and the bottom borders.

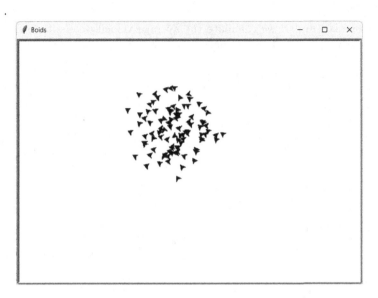

FIGURE 5.4: A flock of boids (screenshot).

If everything is assembled correctly, you will be able to enjoy a nicely moving flock of boids[3] (see Figure 5.4). The actual moving patterns in this simulation heavily depend on the chosen parameter values, so playing with them can be a nice pastime.

5.5 LINDENMAYER SYSTEMS

In the previous projects we observed how simple entities, controlled by simple rules, could produce intricate movements. Now we will take the opposite direction by looking into complexly organized immovable objects. The specific topic of our interest is going to be *Lindenmayer systems* (or *L-systems*), created for studying the developmental process of plants and similar organisms [42].

Among the most conspicuous properties of a plant shape are *symmetry* and *self-similarity*. Symmetry is a common feature of many living things: the left half of a beech leaf is the mirror image of its right half; two "pizza slices" of a daisy flower look alike. Self-similarity is a more elusive concept, used to describe a structure consisting of elements that look similar to the whole. For example, a tree is "self-similar" because it consists of branches, organized in the same way as the tree itself. Likewise, a compound leaf (such as a fern leaf) consists of leaflets that look similar to the whole leaf.

The complexity of plant structure appears to be an emergent property, arising naturally in the course of the normal plant growth. In other words, we again deal with a complex outcome, produced by a relatively simple process.

---

[3]Fun fact: remember that these boids are actually flying *turtles* in our case.

FIGURE 5.5: LRI plant.

FIGURE 5.6: ALRILRILRI plant (root element A is invisible).

While the original motivation for creating L-systems was to study and model the actual laws behind the process of plant growth, our goal is going to be more modest. In case of boids, we were interested in making the onscreen objects move somewhat like birds, and now we will try to generate patterns that look somewhat like plants.

In a nutshell, L-systems are based on three foundational ideas. The first idea is to represent plant structure with a string of characters. For example, suppose that a certain type of a plant is made of three kinds of elements: a trunk element I, a left leaf L, and a right leaf R. A little specimen of this plant, consisting of a single trunk element and two leaves, can be described with a string LRI (see Figure 5.5). Note that any particular image is just an illustration of one of many possible looks of the LRI plant. The textual description does not really dictate any particular appearance, it is only responsible for the internal structure of the entity we describe.

Having enough patience, one can create fairly complicated plants using this approach, but in practice the description strings quickly become long and difficult to work with. Thus, the second foundational idea is to specify the developmental rules of the plant in the form

predecessor → *successor*

We can make our LRI plant growable by introducing a new element A ("root") and specifying its developmental rule:

A → ALRI

Now let's "seed" the initial plant, consisting only of the root element A. After three applications of the developmental rule, we will obtain a "triple-LRI" plant (see Figure 5.6):

A → ALRI → ALRILRI → ALRILRILRI

Summing up, an L-system is a description of a plant structure, consisting of an initial string (called an *axiom*) and a set of *production rules* that determine how individual symbols "grow" into strings. On each "growth step" all the symbols of the current string are substituted according to the rules. It is also presumed that no rules are in conflict, so if we have a rule A → B, there should be no alternative rule A → C.[4]

As a more complex example, consider the evolution of the axiom g according to the production rule g → g[+g][-g]:

```
step 0: g
step 1: g[+g][-g]
step 2: g[+g][-g][+g[+g][-g]][-g[+g][-g]]
```

This way, every occurrence of g in the current string becomes g[+g][-g] at the next step. This process can go on forever, but in practice it is usually interesting to watch the evolution of a certain axiom over the predefined number of generations or simply visualize the final result.

The third and the final foundational idea of L-systems is to treat the textual description of a plant structure as a script, executable by a certain visualization module. While there is no single "right" approach to interpret plant description strings, a commonly suggested way to get started is to treat individual characters as turtle commands.

In our examples, we will use a "turtle dictionary" shown in Table 5.1. The values of constants DISTANCE and ANGLE are usually chosen separately for each plant. Advanced visualizers rely on more elaborate dictionaries that may include, for example, commands for movements in three dimensions and for drawing predefined images (such as leaves and flowers).

TABLE 5.1: Turtle commands for L-systems visualization.

Command	Description
any lowercase letter	Go DISTANCE points forward while drawing.
any uppercase letter	Ignore (do nothing).
+	Turn left by ANGLE degrees.
-	Turn right by ANGLE degrees.
[	Start a new branch (pass the control to a new turtle created here).
]	End a branch (pass the control to the previously active turtle).

---

[4]This is how *deterministic context free (DOL) systems* work. There are also other, more advanced flavors of L-systems.

Now let's look at the picture drawn by the visualization algorithm for the previously discussed L-system consisting of the axiom g and a single production rule g → g[+g][-g] (see Table 5.2). This picture is obtained with DISTANCE = 25, ANGLE = 20; the turtle is initially placed at the bottom of the screen, pointing upward.

TABLE 5.2: Visualized evolution of a simple L-system.

Last step	Plant string	Visualization
0	g	
1	g[+g][-g]	
2 ...	g[+g][-g][+g[+g] [-g]][-g[+g][-g]]	
6	...	

The initial plant string g is easy: by executing the command g, the turtle draws a single vertical line. The next string g[+g][-g] is more interesting. The first g corresponds to a vertical line, just like before. The next symbol [starts a branch: a new turtle appears in the current position, turns ANGLE degrees to the left (the + command) and draws a line (the g command). The branch ends here, and the control is passed to the previous turtle. Then the right branch is drawn in the same manner.

Clearly, these descriptions contain many unnecessary commands. For example, the next plant string starts with the already familiar fragment g[+g][-g]. After finishing it, the turtle proceeds to a more complex structure

[+g[+g][-g]][-g[+g][-g]], which is being drawn right over the previous fragment, so the same lines are being painted many times. To get rid of this
drawback, we can rewrite the L-system as follows:

Axiom: A.

Production rule: A → g[+A][-A].

The symbol A can be likened to a plant bud. From now on, plant development will take place only in buds:

```
step 0: A
step 1: g[+A][-A]
step 2: g[+g[+A][-A]][-g[+A][-A]]
step 3: g[+g[+g[+A][-A]][-g[+A][-A]]][-g[+g[+A][-A]][-g[+A][-A]]]
...
```

Being represented with uppercase letters, buds are ignored by the turtle
(and thus are invisible).

5.5.1 IMPLEMENTATION

Unlike our previous simulations, this program does not need animation, and
will finish its work as soon as the specified plant is drawn. Let's start with
the basic template, shown in Listing 5.3.

Listing 5.3: L-systems (incomplete).

```python
import turtle
from dataclasses import dataclass

WIDTH = 600
HEIGHT = 400

# example plant
AXIOM = "A"
RULES = {"A": "g[+A][-A]"}
ANGLE = 20
DISTANCE = 25
STEPS = 6


def setup_screen(title):
    turtle.setup(WIDTH, HEIGHT)
    turtle.tracer(0, 0)
    turtle.title(title)


@dataclass
class LSystem:
    script: str

    @classmethod
    def create(cls):
        ...
```

```
    def draw(self, drawer):
        ...

setup_screen("L-systems")

drawer = turtle.Turtle()   # place at the bottom, point upward
drawer.hideturtle()
drawer.penup()
drawer.goto(0, -HEIGHT / 2)
drawer.left(90)
drawer.pendown()

LSystem.create().draw(drawer)

turtle.done()
```

There are only two missing fragments in this code. The `create()` function will simulate STEPS iterations of plant development and save the resulting description string in the `script` variable. The `draw()` function will visualize the plant stored in `script`.

Let's create the plant growing functionality first:

```
...
@dataclass
class LSystem:
    script: str

    @classmethod
    def create(cls):
        r = cls(AXIOM)
        for _ in range(STEPS):
            r.transform()
        return r

    def apply_rule(self, c):
        return c if c not in RULES else RULES[c]

    def transform(self):
        self.script = "".join([self.apply_rule(c) for c in self.script])
    ...
```

The main work here is done inside `transform()`. It creates the next version of `self.script` by concatenating all the symbols obtained by applying a matching rule for each symbol c in the current `self.script`. The `apply_rule()` function returns the right-hand side of the matching rule for the given character, or the character itself if no matching rule is found.

The drawing functionality is longer but simple:

```
...
@dataclass
class LSystem:
    script: str
```

```
def draw(self, drawer):
    while self.script:
        c = self.script[0]
        self.script = self.script[1:]

        if c.islower():
            drawer.forward(DISTANCE)
            turtle.update()
        if c == "+":
            drawer.left(ANGLE)
        if c == "-":
            drawer.right(ANGLE)
        if c == "[":
            self.draw(drawer.clone())
        if c == "]":
            return
```

Here we set up a turtle first, and then proceed to executing the commands stored in `self.script`. Each step "eats up" the first character in `self.script`, so the drawing process ends when this string becomes empty. To make the visualization more fun to watch, `turtle.update()` is called every time something new appears on the screen.

The screenshot shown in Figure 5.7 shows the visualization of the following L-system:

```
# Prusinkiewicz & Lindenmayer, Fig. 1.24-f
AXIOM = "X"
RULES = {"X": "g-[[X]+X]+g[+gX]-X", "g": "gg"}
ANGLE = 22.5
DISTANCE = 5
STEPS = 5
```

You can also try out some other nice-looking L-systems:

```
# Prusinkiewicz & Lindenmayer, Fig. 1.24-d
AXIOM = "X"
RULES = {"X": "g[+X]g[-X]+X", "g": "gg"}
ANGLE = 20
DISTANCE = 2
STEPS = 7
```

```
# Prusinkiewicz & Lindenmayer, Fig. 1.24-c
AXIOM = "g"
RULES = {"g": "gg-[-g+g+g]+[+g-g-g]"}
ANGLE = 22.5
DISTANCE = 5
STEPS = 4
```

```
# Prusinkiewicz & Lindenmayer, Fig. 1.24-e
AXIOM = "X"
RULES = {"X": "g[+X][-X]gX", "g": "gg"}
ANGLE = 25.7
DISTANCE = 2
STEPS = 7
```

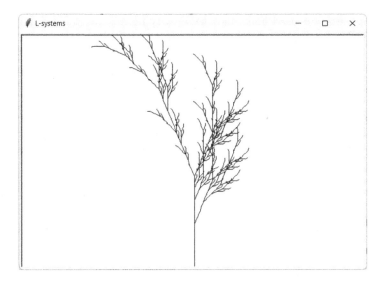

FIGURE 5.7: Visualizing an example L-system.

5.6 THE TRAGEDY OF THE COMMONS

Our next project shifts the focus from individual organisms and their groups to the level of large populations. It is inspired by the widely discussed essay "The Tragedy of the Commons", penned by ecologist G. Hardin in 1968 [18]. The main point of this text can be expressed as follows: people living in a condition of limited resources have to negotiate the principles of using these resources or face dire consequences.

In an "ultra-free" society with no restriction of individual behavior fishermen can catch all the fish, and factory owners can pollute air as much as they like. Here the "every man for himself" principle leads straight to a tragedy. In such cases, Hardin argues, it is important to recognize that some problems do not have a technical solution. For example, it is not possible to win the game of Tic-Tac-Toe against a reasonable opponent. In a sense, "victory" is achieved through abandonment of the whole game.

As a real-world example, Hardin examines the problem of overgrazing or overfishing (which is called "the tragedy of the commons" in the essay). Since the resource such as a pasture or a lake is nobody's property, everyone is free to catch as much fish or graze as many sheep as they please. While the community is small, and there is not much external trade, this policy may work fine. However, eventually people might start catching fish faster than it reproduces, and domestic animals might eat all the grass, meaning no more fish and no more pastures for the community. A "non-technical solution" here is, of course, to negotiate the rules of conscious resource use, such as introducing quotas for fishing.

Hardin's essay caused much debate, mainly because he was primarily concerned with the problem of overpopulation, and his idea was to agree on the rules of conscious *human* reproduction (the problem of overgrazing was discussed in literature long before). There is no surprise that such a proposal ignited quite a stir, with numerous researchers pointing out the differences between the actual cases where overgrazing occurs, and seemingly similar, but ultimately distinct scenarios. In any case, Hardin's main message to recognize the limits of common resources and to negotiate for the mutual good remains relevant, and in our next simulation we'll see how reasonable quotas help to prevent overfishing.

For starters, we need to be able to simulate the process of population growth. The simplest and perhaps most widely used approach is to employ *logistic function* [41]:

$$\Delta P = rP(1 - \frac{P}{K})$$

Here ΔP is the change of population per unit of time, r is the natural growth rate, P is the current population size, and K is the "carrying capacity", representing the maximum population size that can survive in the given environment.

For example, suppose that 100 tons of fish live in a basin that can support up to 3000 tons of fish, and the natural growth rate is 20% per year. After one year, the basin will receive additional

$$\Delta P = 0.2 \cdot 100 \cdot (1 - \frac{100}{3000}) \approx 19$$

tons of fish. After 40 years or so, the fish population will reach its natural limits (see Figure 5.8).

To examine the effects of fishing, let's remove a fixed amount of fish from the basin every year, and see what happens.

5.6.1 IMPLEMENTATION

Like the previous project, this one does not need animation. It is also quite simple, so we can proceed straight to the code (see Listing 5.4).

Listing 5.4: The tragedy of the commons.

```python
import turtle

WIDTH = 600
HEIGHT = 400

YEARS = 40
P = 100
r = 0.2
K = 3000
```

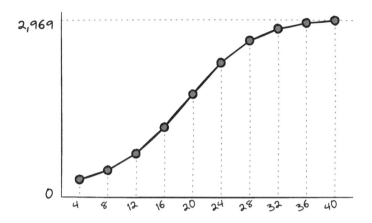

FIGURE 5.8: Growth of fish population over time.

```
HARVEST = 0

def setup_screen(title):
    turtle.setup(WIDTH, HEIGHT)
    turtle.tracer(0, 0)
    turtle.title(title)
    turtle.setworldcoordinates(0, 0, YEARS, K)


setup_screen("The tragedy of the commons")

drawer = turtle.Turtle()
drawer.hideturtle()

for year in range(0, YEARS):
    drawer.goto(year, P)
    P += r * P * (1 - P / K)
    P = max(0, P - HARVEST) # make sure the population is not negative

turtle.update()
turtle.done()
```

In the current form, the program draws the same chart as shown in Figure 5.8. The simulation becomes more interesting when the yearly catch of HARVEST tons of fish is introduced. Let's see what happens, for example, in a lake with an existing population of 1000 tons of fish and a yearly harvest of 120 tons (Figure 5.9).

This is "conscious consumption" scenario, good both for the people, and for the fish. However, the difference between this idyllic picture and predatory abuse is a mere 20 extra tons a year (see Figure 5.10).

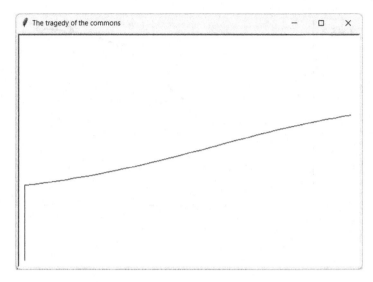

FIGURE 5.9: Dynamics of fish population (harvesting 120 tons of fish yearly).

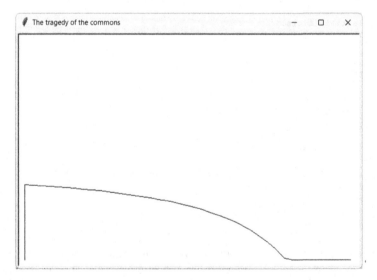

FIGURE 5.10: Dynamics of fish population (harvesting 140 tons of fish yearly).

I have a vague recollection of my university teacher mentioning a two-player game version of this simulation he was toying with back in the day. Both players knew the amount of fish in the lake on the current turn, and they had to secretly choose the amount they were going to catch. The player with the largest catch after N turns was declared a winner. Unfortunately, it turned out that a typical game session under such conditions ends quickly with no fish left in the lake. Someone "wins", of course, but the total catch isn't stellar. If I remember our conversation correctly, the teacher said he felt really ashamed after his first play session. He didn't expect everyone (including himself) to be so greedy and near-sighted. He learned his lesson, though, and so should we.

5.7 FURTHER IDEAS

1. Extend the "Dancing moth" program to simulate a group of independently moving insects.
2. Simulate the effect of wind in any of the "moth" simulations by applying a small force acting in the predefined direction to the moth. This force modifies the resulting moth velocity, allowing it to deviate from v. Therefore, flying with the wind is going to be faster than against it.
3. The "Boids" model can be extended in a variety of ways. Here are some ideas:
   - Introduce a predator, aiming to fly through the center of the flock like a moth in the "A moth and a lightbulb" simulation. The flock would respond by *evasion*: an additional evasive force would be applied to each boid, steering it away from the predator.
   - Designate a "leader" boid, aiming to reach the "nest". Other boids will experience an additional force, steering them toward the current location of the leader. Once the nest is reached, you can choose another random nest location.
   - Allow boids to rest by pausing a boid for up to R seconds with a certain (small) probability on each simulation step. After resting, the boid joins the flock.
4. Implement adjustable fishing quotas in "The tragedy of the commons" project. You can start with a simple idea: if this year's fish population is higher than last year's, increase the quotas by a certain percentage, and decrease them otherwise. It also makes sense to keep quotas low for a small fish population regardless of dynamics to facilitate its growth. Examine how different policies affect long-term fish population and harvest.

6 Grid worlds

The final program of the previous chapter, "The tragedy of the commons," aims to simulate the life of a population in a highly abstract manner. There is "fish," which is measured in "tons," and the only disruption it faces is a fixed yearly harvesting. The projects of the next batch will attempt to visualize the dynamics of populations by simulating the lives of their individual members. We will see how these hundreds and thousands of destinies form a picture of a much larger scale.

This formula echoes the portrayal of Monte Carlo methods as simulation of microscopic interactions between simple small moving parts of a complex system. This approach indeed turns out to be fruitful in the world of living beings, where emergent properties arising from encounters between the individuals are common, as we could see in the case of "boids".

A surprisingly large number of interesting scenarios can be simulated within simple grid-like environments, where individuals, occupying certain cells of the grid, interact with their immediate neighbors. Such "grid worlds" will be in the focus of our attention in the present chapter.

6.1 RABBITS AND WOLVES

Let's see how Monte Carlo simulation works in a grid world ecosystem, inhabited by three kinds of organisms. We will simulate a W × H patch of land with the following biota:[1]

- **Grass**. Each cell of the land initially contains a random amount of grass, ranging from 0 (no grass) to 1 (fully covered). On each simulation step grass grows by GRASS_GROWTH, but never exceeds 1.
- **Rabbits**. The patch is a home to RABBITS randomly scattered rabbits of random age (0 to max_age) and random fat resource (0 to 1). On each simulation step, a rabbit:
  - Gets one year older, exhausting fat_use units of fat, and dies if its age exceeds max_age or its fat reserve drops down to zero.
  - Eats grass on the current cell to fulfill its fat reserve (up to 1). When eating f units of grass, a rabbit accumulates f × fat_factor units of fat, and the amount of grass underneath is reduced by f.
  - Optionally moves to one of the neighboring cells, having no other rabbits, within a distance D.

---

[1] Adopted with modifications from
http://www.shodor.org/interactivate/activities/RabbitsAndWolves/

- Optionally delivers a baby rabbit in the previously occupied cell. In order to deliver, a rabbit must be at least `delivery_age` old and should have at least `MIN_DELIVERY_FAT` fat. The newborn rabbit has `NEWBORN_FAT` amount of fat and the age of zero.
- **Wolves.** The patch also contains `WOLVES` wolves generated and placed just like rabbits. Wolves behave according to the same pattern as rabbits with the following differences:
  - Wolves eat rabbits instead of grass and move to adjacent cells not occupied by other wolves.
  - A wolf will only eat a rabbit if it is "hungry enough", meaning this meal won't cause the wolf to exceed its fat capacity of 1.

Let's implement this project first, and then discuss the life of rabbits and wolves in more detail.

6.1.1 IMPLEMENTATION

The rules above are not a match for "boids" in terms of simplicity and elegance, so the final program is going to be relatively long and complicated. We'll start with the outline provided in Listing 6.1, which follows the scheme used in our previous animation-based projects.

Listing 6.1: Rabbits and wolves (incomplete).

```python
import turtle
from random import uniform, randint
from dataclasses import dataclass

H = 20   # grass patch size
W = 30
SLEEP_MS = 20

GRASS_GROWTH = 0.03   # units per step
RABBITS = 100
WOLVES = 10

MIN_DELIVERY_FAT = 0.7   # needed to deliver an offspring
NEWBORN_FAT = 0.5
D = 3

# fine-tunable parameters of rabbits and wolves
@dataclass
class RabbitCfg:
    fat_use: float = 0.20
    max_age: int = 10
    delivery_age: int = 3
    delivery_p = 0.6
    fat_factor = 1
    shape: str = "turtle"
    color: str = "rosy brown"
```

```python
@dataclass
class WolfConfig:
    fat_use: float = 0.04
    max_age: int = 17
    delivery_age: int = 4
    delivery_p = 0.4
    fat_factor = 0.6
    shape: str = "classic"
    color: str = "black"


# same as before
@dataclass
class SimState:
    done: bool

    def set_done(self):
        self.done = True

    @classmethod
    def setup(cls):
        r = cls(False)
        turtle.listen()
        turtle.onkeypress(r.set_done, "space")
        return r


@dataclass
class WorldState:
    ... # TODO

def setup_screen(title):
    turtle.setup(W * 20, H * 20)
    turtle.tracer(0, 0)
    turtle.title(title)
    turtle.setworldcoordinates(0, 0, W, H)


setup_screen("Rabbits and wolves")
sim_state = SimState.setup()
world_state = WorldState.setup()


def tick():
    if not sim_state.done:
        world_state.update()
        turtle.update()
        turtle.ontimer(tick, SLEEP_MS)


tick()
turtle.done()
```

The idea is to represent each onscreen entity (a grass plant, a rabbit, a wolf) as a turtle. Different entities will have different colors and shapes. Since the patch of grass to be modeled is a W × H board, it makes sense to set turtle world coordinates to the same dimensions.

Now let's take a look at WorldState class (see Listing 6.2).

Listing 6.2: Rabbits and wolves: WorldState class.

```python
@dataclass
class WorldState:
    grass: dict
    rabbits: dict
    wolves: dict
    cycle: int

    # get all non-None objects
    def animals(self, plane):
        return list((key, value) for key, value in plane.items() if value)

    def keep_alive(self, plane):
        animals = self.animals(plane)
        plane.update({k: None for k, v in animals if not v.is_alive()})

    def move_and_deliver(self, plane):
        for coords, v in self.animals(plane):
            x, y = coords
            newcoords = randint(x - D, x + D) % W, randint(y - D, y + D) % H
            if not plane[newcoords]:
                plane[newcoords] = v.moved_to(newcoords)
                plane[coords] = v.deliver_at(coords)

    def update(self):
        self.cycle += 1
        rabbits = self.animals(self.rabbits)
        wolves = self.animals(self.wolves)
        print(f"{self.cycle}\t{len(rabbits)}\t{len(wolves)}")   # for logging

        for v in self.grass.values():
            v.grow()

        for coords, v in rabbits:
            v.update_fat(self.grass[coords])

        for coords, v in wolves:
            v.update_fat(self.rabbits[coords])

        self.keep_alive(self.rabbits)
        self.keep_alive(self.wolves)

        self.move_and_deliver(self.rabbits)
        self.move_and_deliver(self.wolves)

    @classmethod
    def coords(cls, count):
        r = set()
        while len(r) < count:
            r.add((randint(0, W - 1), randint(0, H - 1)))
```

```
        return r

    @classmethod
    def setup(cls):
        coords = [(x, y) for x in range(W) for y in range(H)]

        grass = {c: Grass.create(c) for c in coords}
        rabbits = {c: None for c in coords}
        wolves = {c: None for c in coords}

        r = {c: Animal.create(RabbitCfg(), c) for c in cls.coords(RABBITS)}
        w = {c: Animal.create(WolfConfig(), c) for c in cls.coords(WOLVES)}
        rabbits.update(r)
        wolves.update(w)

        return cls(grass, rabbits, wolves, 0)
```

The simulation starts with the call to setup(). Biota lives in three separate "planes" grass, rabbits, and wolves, represented with dictionaries. A key in such dictionary is a pair of coordinates (x, y), and a value is a plant or an animal.

Since grass covers the whole plane, a Grass object is created for every possible pair of coordinates. To create rabbits and wolves, we start with preparing their planes filled with None values. Next, the necessary amount of random coordinate pairs is generated in coords(). Sets cannot contain duplicate values, so the function returns only after enough unique pairs are produced.

The call dic1.update(dic2) copies key/value pairs from dic2 into dic1, overriding existing keys. Thus, None values in rabbits and wolves will be replaced with Animal objects. Since the rules for both types of animals are nearly the same, we'll rely on the same class Animal with different settings.

World updates are handled in the update() function. It processes biota in a straightforward manner: first the grass grows, then rabbits and wolves update their fat reserves. A grass object does not need anything to grow, while the animals might eat their food located in the same cell. After this process, we update animal planes to keep only the animals that survived this round. Finally, each animal has a chance to move to a neighboring cell and deliver an offspring.

The coordinates for the target cell are determined randomly as follows:

```
newcoords = randint(x - D, x + D) % W, randint(y - D, y + D) % H
```

If an animal jumps off the board side, it appears at the opposite side, which means our patch of land actually has a shape of a torus (i.e., donut). If the target cell is empty, we move the animal there and possibly create a baby animal at the previous location.

Our next task is to design the Grass class (see Listing 6.3).

Listing 6.3: Rabbits and wolves: `Grass` class.

```
@dataclass
class Shape:
    drawer: turtle.Turtle

    def update(self, fat, is_alive):
        if not is_alive:
            self.drawer.hideturtle()
        else:
            self.drawer.shapesize(fat)

    def move(self, coords):
        self.drawer.goto(coords[0], coords[1])

    @classmethod
    def create(cls, shape, color, size, coords):
        r = turtle.Turtle()
        r.shape(shape)
        r.color(color)
        r.penup()
        r.shapesize(size)
        r.goto(coords[0], coords[1])
        r.right(90)
        return cls(r)


@dataclass
class Grass:
    shape: Shape
    amount: float

    def grow(self):
        self.amount = min(self.amount + GRASS_GROWTH, 1)
        self.shape.update(self.amount, True)

    def try_eat(self, to_eat):
        r = min(to_eat, self.amount)
        self.amount -= r
        return r

    @classmethod
    def create(cls, coords):
        amount = uniform(0, 1)
        color = "lawn green"
        return cls(Shape.create("circle", color, amount, coords), amount)
```

The utility `Shape` class is a simple wrapper for a turtle-based drawer. Its only capability is to create a turtle of the specified shape, size, and color in the given location, and update its location and size upon request.

`Grass` plants are represented with green circles. Note the `try_eat()` function: it will be called by an animal that wants to eat `to_eat` amount of grass. The

Grass objects will return the actual amount eaten (which cannot exceed the current amount available), and reduce its size accordingly.

Finally, let's consider the Animal class (see Listing 6.4).

Listing 6.4: Rabbits and wolves: Animal class.

```python
@dataclass
class Animal:
    shape: Shape
    fat: float
    age: int
    cfg: object

    def update_fat(self, food):
        self.fat = max(0, self.fat - self.cfg.fat_use)
        self.age += 1

        if self.is_alive() and food:
            food_needed = (1.0 - self.fat) / self.cfg.fat_factor
            if (r := food.try_eat(food_needed)) > 0:
                self.fat += r * self.cfg.fat_factor
        self.shape.update(self.fat, self.is_alive())

    def moved_to(self, coords):
        self.shape.move(coords)
        return self

    def try_eat(self, to_eat):
        r = 0 if to_eat < self.fat else self.fat
        self.fat -= r
        self.shape.update(self.fat, self.is_alive())
        return r

    def is_alive(self):
        return self.fat > 0 and self.age <= self.cfg.max_age

    def deliver_at(self, coords):
        fat_fail = self.fat < MIN_DELIVERY_FAT
        age_fail = self.age < self.cfg.delivery_age
        fail = fat_fail or age_fail or uniform(0, 1) > self.cfg.delivery_p
        return None if fail else Animal.create_newborn(self.cfg, coords)

    @classmethod
    def create_full(cls, cfg, age, fat, coords):
        shape = Shape.create(cfg.shape, cfg.color, fat, coords)
        return cls(shape, fat, age, cfg)

    @classmethod
    def create_newborn(cls, cfg, coords):
        return cls.create_full(cfg, 0, NEWBORN_FAT, coords)

    @classmethod
    def create(cls, cfg, coords):
        age = randint(0, cfg.max_age)
        return cls.create_full(cfg, age, uniform(0, 1), coords)
```

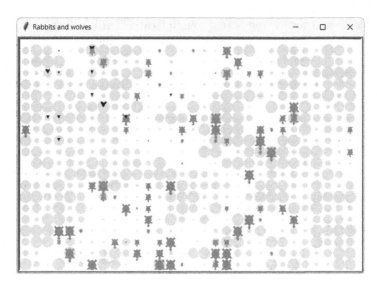

FIGURE 6.1: Rabbits and wolves (screenshot).

This class is not as complex as could be expected. During one step of simulation, an animal:

- Gets older and updates its fat reserves. It happens in update_fat() where the animal exhausts its fat_use fat and, if possible, tries to fulfill its vacant (1.0 - self.fat) fat reserve by consuming food_needed food. The actual amount of obtained food is returned by try_eat(), and converted to the accumulated fat by multiplying this value by fat_factor.
- Survives if it still has fat and its age does not exceed the limits, which is checked in is_alive().
- Moves via moved_to() and delivers via deliver_at(). If delivery is not successful due to insufficient fat, age, or bad luck, None is returned.

Perhaps, the most tricky function here is try_eat(), which is only called for rabbit objects. Here a rabbit escapes (zero is returned) if its fat reserve exceeds the hunting wolf's needs. Otherwise, all the fat is consumed, and the rabbit will be removed from the board on the next turn.

According to the RabbitCfg and WolfConfig classes, the rabbits are going to be represented with turtle shapes (because they vaguely resemble turtles), and the wolves will have "classic" shapes with pointy ears.

A running program should produce a picture similar to the one shown in Figure 6.1.

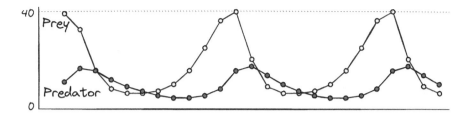

FIGURE 6.2: Predator-prey dynamics according to Lotka-Volterra model.

6.1.2 AFTERTHOUGHTS

It is fun to watch "Rabbits and wolves" running, and you can obtain very different outcomes by playing with the configuration. The big question is whether this little world has any relation to the real world, where actual rabbits and wolves live.

Clearly, a handful of arbitrary rules that reflect the most general ideas of a population lifecycle cannot reflect the complexities of reality. However, even thousands of rules cannot reflect these complexities either, meaning that the practical goal of a typical computer simulation should be to model *certain* aspects of reality with *certain* acceptable accuracy.

In "The tragedy of the commons", we could see how it works. The complex concept of a fish population was boiled down to a simple formula that makes no difference between individual fish, and it does not reflect any damages made by natural disasters or predators. Yet it is reasonably accurate in certain contexts, which makes it useful in practice. Broadly speaking, any scientific theory (and the fish population growth formula *is* a scientific theory) comes with clearly stated conditions where it is applicable.

Our "Rabbits and wolves" simulation belongs to a family of widely used *predator-prey* models. In the most commonly discussed scenario, there are only two populations: prey that always have enough food, and predators that depend on the prey. There is also a fairly standard approach to simulate their dynamics using Lotka-Volterra equations [19]. These equations produce a picture of growing prey population, which triggers the growth of predators, in turn, making the prey population shrink and, therefore, reduce the predator count. Both populations continue to oscillate in this manner indefinitely (see Figure 6.2)). By adjusting model parameters (such as predator or prey growth rate and their sensitivity to the size of the second population), it is possible to simulate different kinds of animals.

Just like the fish population model based on logistic function, the Lotka-Volterra model operates under strong constraints that are rarely seen in nature. Yet, similar cycles can be observed in reality. A very popular example is the life of the Canadian lynx and Snowshoe hare in Canada [9] (see

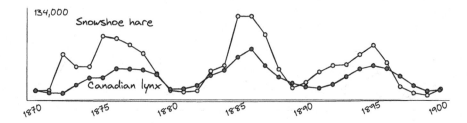

FIGURE 6.3: Predator-prey cycles (lynx and hare).

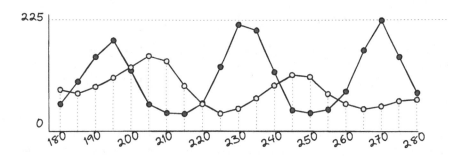

FIGURE 6.4: Population dynamics of rabbits and wolves (steps 180 to 280).

Figure 6.3). It is clear, however, that in the real world every cycle is different, and none of the peaks is destined to have a perfect twin in the future.

Now let's go back to "Rabbits and wolves". By experimenting with settings, it is easy to get a scenario where one of the population quickly dies due to lack of food. Rabbits can even go extinct without wolves if they propagate rapidly and eat too much. It seems, however, that any reasonable combination of parameters that allows both populations to survive a few hundreds of simulation steps, produces a chart, similar to the shown in Figure 6.3. For example, Figure 6.4 shows the life of rabbits and wolves obtained with the default configuration provided in Listing 6.1.

In the configuration used here, quite large fat reserves are allocated to wolves, so they react to the diminishing rabbit population with a delay. Smaller reserves would bring population peaks closer to each other, but they make wolves more vulnerable.

One interesting feature of our project, the model at *shodor.org*, and their earlier inspiration *Wa-Tor* [7] is the instability of the obtained ecosystem. A small change in a parameter or simply a streak of unlucky events may bring it to the verge of extinction. This effect can also be observed in classic predator-prey models, so our rabbits and wolves are in a good company. One interesting way to destabilize the ecosystem is to provide too much food to the prey, which triggers dangerous growth of predator population (this effect is known as the *paradox of enrichment* [46]).

Apparently, real-life populations are much more robust, being able to deal with shortages of food and natural disasters. There are also mechanisms protecting them against the "paradox of enrichment" scenario [47]. Now we will proceed to the next project, keeping in mind that "Rabbits and wolves" still has much room for further improvements.

6.2 EVOLUTION

Rabbits and wolves in our simulation never change. One population cycle follows another, but no rabbit and no wolf can learn anything from numerous generations of their ancestors. In contrast, creatures of our world *evolve*, and as a result, become better adapted to their environment.

Evolution we see in nature is a complicated process, but its effects can be observed even in very simple models. To create such a model, it's important to understand that the term "evolution" (or "adaptive evolution") might mean either the processes actually happening in the world of living beings, or the general idea of the mechanism that produces adaptive changes. It turns out that this mechanism kicks in when the following conditions are met [17]:

1. The members of population have individual differences.
2. These individual traits are inheritable, but random deviations occur during reproduction.
3. Population produces more descendants that can survive in the given environment.
4. The individuals better adapted for the environment are more likely to survive and reproduce.

There is no "single right way" to embody these principles. For example, humans achieve great individual diversity by combining traits received from both parents, but it is perfectly possible to evolve without this capability. Therefore, to observe evolutionary adaptations, it is enough to prepare a setup, where each element of the list above is somehow represented.

In our next project, we will see how organisms adapt to their environment in "Simulated Evolution" — an ingenious little world, created by M. Palmiter and popularized by A. K. Dewdney [8]. The rules of "Simulated Evolution" are very simple:

- The simulation takes place on a W × H bowl of "soup", initially seeded with PLANKTON_COUNT units of "plankton" and BUGS_COUNT "bugs". Each bug initially has INITIAL_ENERGY units of energy. Several bugs are allowed to occupy the same space.
- On each step of the simulation, new PLANKTON_GROWTH units of plankton appear in the random locations of the bowl.

- Next, each bug consumes one unit of energy and eats plankton beneath it (if available), obtaining FOOD_ENERGY units. Bug's energy cannot exceed MAX_ENERGY, and the bug dies if its energy drops down to zero. After eating, the bug makes a random turn and moves forward to one of the adjacent cells. There are eight possible directions of movement[2], so the bug might turn 0, 45, ..., 315 degrees to the left. The probability of each turn is determined by its *weight*; each bug receives a list of eight random weights upon creation.
- Bugs that survived MATURITY_AGE iterations and accumulated at least FISSION_ENERGY units of energy propagate by division ("fission"). The parent bug is replaced by two newborn bugs, each having one-half of their parent's energy. Direction weights are inherited with deviations: one descendant gets only a half of one randomly chosen weight, while another descendant gets a randomly chosen weight doubled.

The conditions for evolution are satisfied in the world of bugs as follows:

1. Bugs differ by their turning behavior. Some are more likely to turn left, for example, while others might prefer 180° U-turns.
2. Turning behavior is inheritable, but with random weight modifications.
3. Plankton can easily be made scarce by reducing PLANKTON_GROWTH, which makes life harder for the bugs.
4. Not every movement strategy is equally good to find food. Thus, the bugs with more successful behavior are more likely to propagate.

Before proceeding to implementation, let's discuss how to evaluate the final result. How would we understand that the bugs evolve over time? It turns out that devising a good criterion is not very easy. We can't expect the increase of the average bug lifespan, because at a certain age bugs fission. We can't expect the population to grow because scarce resources limit the size of sustainable colony. We can't even say that especially successful bugs produce more offspring because every passable individual is going to bear exactly two successors.

My proposal is to count the number of *unique* cells visited by a bug over its lifespan and report the average value for each generation. The rationale is simple: any successful foraging strategy should be based on harvesting existing plankton. Since new plankton units appear in random bowl areas, there is little sense in revisiting the same cells in the hope for luck.

There is no guarantee to find food by exploration, but we can check whether the bugs *at least tried*.

---

[2]In the original Palmiter's program, bugs move in six directions.

6.2.1 IMPLEMENTATION

Just like "Rabbits and wolves", "Evolution" is relatively long, so let's start with an outline (see Listing 6.5).

Listing 6.5: Evolution (incomplete).

```python
import turtle
from random import randint, choices
from dataclasses import dataclass

H = 40    # grass patch size
W = 70
SLEEP_MS = 20
VIS_SLEEP_MS = 500
CELLSIZE = 10    # pixels
SHAPE_SIZE = CELLSIZE / 20    # turtle size

INITIAL_ENERGY = 120
MAX_ENERGY = 400
FISSION_ENERGY = 250
MATURITY_AGE = 200
FOOD_ENERGY = 20
MAX_WEIGHT = 32
PLANKTON_GROWTH = 4
PLANKTON_COUNT = 300
BUGS_COUNT = 50


gen_count = []    # bugs in the given generation
gen_visited = []    # unique cells visited by bugs of a generation


@dataclass
class SimState:
    done: bool

    def set_done(self):
        self.done = True

    @classmethod
    def setup(cls):
        r = cls(False)
        turtle.listen()
        turtle.onkeypress(r.set_done, "space")
        return r


def clamp(v, min_v, max_v):
    return min(max_v, max(min_v, v))


@dataclass
class Plankton:
    ...
```

```
@dataclass
class Bug:
    ...

@dataclass
class WorldState:
    ...

def setup_screen(title):
    turtle.setup(W * CELLSIZE, H * CELLSIZE)
    turtle.tracer(0, 0)
    turtle.title(title)
    turtle.setworldcoordinates(0, 0, W, H)


setup_screen("Evolution")
sim_state = SimState.setup()
world_state = WorldState.setup()


def tick():
    if not sim_state.done:
        world_state.update()
        turtle.ontimer(tick, SLEEP_MS)


def tick_draw():
    if not sim_state.done:
        turtle.update()
        world_state.report_visits()
        turtle.ontimer(tick_draw, VIS_SLEEP_MS)


tick()
tick_draw()
turtle.done()
```

So far, it is just a generic prototype, very similar to the one used in "Rabbits and wolves". In this case, however, we have to strive for performance, since the goal is to examine dozens of generations of bugs. For this reasons screen update is moved into a separate function `tick_draw()`, which is called less frequently than the primary world update function `tick()`.

Let's implement the simplest missing class `Plankton` (see Listing 6.6).

Listing 6.6: Evolution: `Plankton` class.

```
@dataclass
class Plankton:
    shape: turtle.Turtle

    def energy(self):
        return FOOD_ENERGY if self.shape.isvisible() else 0
```

```
def show(self, s):
    if s:
        self.shape.showturtle()
    else:
        self.shape.hideturtle()

@classmethod
def create(cls, x, y):
    p = turtle.Turtle()
    p.penup()
    p.color("lawn green")
    p.shape("triangle")
    p.shapesize(SHAPE_SIZE)
    p.goto(x, y)
    p.hideturtle()
    return cls(p)
```

To avoid repeated creation of Plankton objects, we will "seed" the whole bowl from the very beginning, but we will make plankton on empty cells invisible. Plankton can be activated with the show(True) call. This will also make its food value non-zero.

Bugs are, naturally, more complicated (see Listing 6.7).

Listing 6.7: Evolution: Bug class.

```
@dataclass
class Bug:
    shape: turtle.Turtle
    dirweights: list
    energy: int
    generation: int
    visited: set
    age: int = 0

    def x(self):
        return clamp(round(self.shape.xcor()), 0, W - 1)

    def y(self):
        return clamp(round(self.shape.ycor()), 0, H - 1)

    def remove(self):
        gen_visited[self.generation] += len(self.visited)
        self.shape.hideturtle()

    def eat_and_move(self, food):
        self.visited.add((self.x(), self.y()))
        self.age += 1
        self.energy -= 1
        if self.energy == 0:
            self.remove()
        else:
            self.energy = min(MAX_ENERGY, self.energy + food)
            r = choices(list(range(8)), self.dirweights)[0]
            self.shape.left(45 * r)
```

```
        self.shape.forward(1)
        self.shape.goto(self.x(), self.y())

    def new_dirweights(self, dirs, d):
        idx = randint(0, 7)
        newdirs = list(dirs)
        newdirs[idx] = clamp(int(dirs[idx] * d), 1, MAX_WEIGHT)
        return newdirs

    def fission(self):
        if self.age > MATURITY_AGE and self.energy > FISSION_ENERGY:
            self.remove()
            e = int(self.energy / 2)
            dirs1 = self.new_dirweights(self.dirweights, 2)
            dirs2 = self.new_dirweights(self.dirweights, 0.5)

            return [
                Bug.create(self.x(), self.y(), dirs1, e, self.generation + 1),
                Bug.create(self.x(), self.y(), dirs2, e, self.generation + 1),
            ]
        return [self]

    @classmethod
    def create(cls, x, y, weights, energy, gen):
        if gen == len(gen_count):
            print(f"Generation: {gen}")
            gen_count.append(0)
            gen_visited.append(0)
        gen_count[gen] += 1

        p = turtle.Turtle()
        p.penup()
        p.shape("turtle")
        p.shapesize(SHAPE_SIZE)
        p.goto(x, y)
        return cls(p, weights, energy, gen, set())

    @classmethod
    def create_random(cls):
        x = randint(0, W - 1)
        y = randint(0, H - 1)
        weights = [randint(1, MAX_WEIGHT) for _ in range(8)]
        return cls.create(x, y, weights, INITIAL_ENERGY, 0)
```

A bug is created with one of the methods `create()` or `create_random()`. The first of them is more general, which is needed to implement fission. The second method is used to generate a random bug in the very beginning: it is created in a random cell of the bowl, and it has a random list of direction weights.

Two other principal methods, `eat_and_move()` and `fission()`, handle the respective activities of a bug. Both are quite straightforward.

When moving, a bug makes a random turn:

```
r = choices(list(range(8)), self.dirweights)[0]
self.shape.left(45 * r)
```

This fragment makes use of a Python built-in function `choices()` that generates a list of `k` random elements from the options taken from its first argument, using weights from its second argument. By default, `k=1`, so we obtain a single-element list, containing a certain value in the range 0-7. If you are interested in how weighted random choice works, check out, for example, detailed blog posts by Zhanliang Liu [25] and Keith Schwarz [48].

By moving forward via `self.shape.forward(1)`, a bug might end up being on the border between cells. Since cell coordinates of a bug are only needed to check for the plankton beneath, we can simply use a rounded bug's coordinates when necessary.

When a bug fissions, we create two versions of updated lists of direction weights:

```
dirs1 = self.new_dirweights(self.dirweights, 2)
dirs2 = self.new_dirweights(self.dirweights, 0.5)
```

The first version will have a random weight doubled, the second version will have a random weight halved. Bugs that don't fission are returned from the `fission()` method unchanged.

Bugs that fission or die are removed by the call to `remove()`. This function hides the bug and adds its unique visited cell count to the stats of its generation.

Finally, let's bind everything together using `WorldState` (see Listing 6.8).

Listing 6.8: Evolution: <code>WorldState</code> class.

```
@dataclass
class WorldState:
    plankton: list
    bugs: list
    cycle: int = 0
    mingen: int = 0

    def add_plankton(self, count=1):
        for _ in range(count):
            x, y = randint(0, W - 1), randint(0, H - 1)
            self.plankton[x][y].show(True)  # add to the bowl
        return self

    def update(self):
        self.cycle += 1
        self.add_plankton(PLANKTON_GROWTH)

        for b in self.bugs:
            food = self.plankton[b.x()][b.y()]
            b.eat_and_move(food.energy())
            food.show(False)

        self.bugs = [b for b in self.bugs if b.energy > 0]
        self.bugs = sum((b.fission() for b in self.bugs), [])
```

```
def report_visits(self):
    # report past generations only
    new_mingen = min(b.generation for b in self.bugs)
    if new_mingen != self.mingen:
        self.mingen = new_mingen
        visits = (gen_visited[i] / gen_count[i] for i in range(new_mingen))
        print([f"{v:.2f}" for v in visits])

@classmethod
def setup(cls):
    bugs = [Bug.create_random() for _ in range(BUGS_COUNT)]
    plk = [[Plankton.create(x, y) for y in range(H)] for x in range(W)]

    return cls(plk, bugs).add_plankton(PLANKTON_COUNT)
```

The logic of this class follows the original description of the project. On each simulation step, PLANKTON_GROWTH new instances of plankton are added to the "soup". If a cell chosen for the plankton turns out to be already occupied, nothing happens. Each bug eats and moves (hidden plankton objects give zero energy supply), then the bugs that did not survive are removed. To form the final list of bugs after fission, a little trick based on sum() is used. Suppose there are three bugs: a, b, and c. The bug b is about to fission into b1 and b2. In this case,

```
a.fission()   # returns [a]
b.fission()   # returns [b1, b2]
c.fission()   # returns [c]
```

The call to sum() sums up these lists, yielding [a, b1, b2, c]. The second argument of sum() is also added to the result. By default it equals zero, but adding numbers to lists is not allowed, so we have to pass an empty list instead.

The function report_visits() outputs the average number of unique cells visited by a bug of each generation. Only past generations (not currently present on the board) are reported, and nothing is reported if there were no changes since the last call to the function.

Now the program is complete and can be launched (see Figure 6.5).

The result of each test run is going to be different, and some runs might yield better results than others. We have to remember that evolution has no goals or purposes: the organisms that simply *happen* to survive and propagate pass their features to their descendants, ensuring the presence of these features in the future. As a result of evolution, organisms may become simpler or more complex, their size may increase or decrease, and their eating habits may change unpredictably.

In our case, "visiting as many cells as possible" is just a reasonable heuristics for successful foraging behavior. In reality, a skillful forager bug might get really unlucky if its surroundings are scarce, while a simple "jitterbug", moving back and forth inside a fertile area might live long and prosper. Still, most runs will likely produce many generations of impressive foragers.

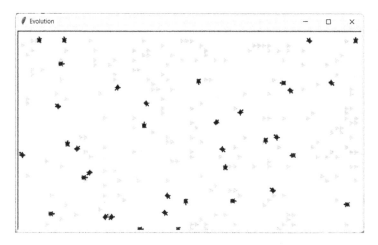

FIGURE 6.5: Evolution of bugs in a bowl of plankton soup.

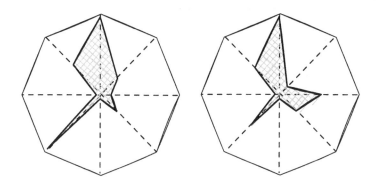

FIGURE 6.6: Forager bugs.

Consider, for example, two bugs having direction weights [32, 16, 2, 32, 2, 8, 4, 8] and [32, 16, 2, 16, 2, 8, 16, 4]. These lists can be visualized with radar charts (see Figure 6.6). Clearly, such bugs prefer moving forward, making occasional turns, which lets them cover large areas of unexplored space.

The average number of cells visited by the bugs of subsequent generations also go up (see Figure 6.7).

Aggressive foraging behavior, however, is only necessary in scarce environments. A bug created as a result of fission, gets at least 125 units of energy and has to survive 200 turns to reach maturity. The next goal is to accumulate 250 units of energy. Since the bug spends one energy unit on each turn, and plankton gives 20 units, it is enough to eat just 17 plankton during a lifetime in order to fission: 125-200+20×17=265.

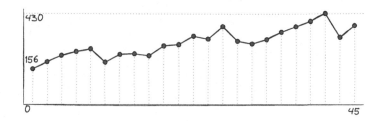

FIGURE 6.7: Cells visited by a typical bug in generations 0-45.

While demonstrating some basic principles of biological evolution, our little exercise also shows how the artificial evolutionary process can solve certain problems. Imagine we need to create AI-driven "bugs" able to survive food shortage. How to design such an AI system? It turns out that one of the possible ways is to employ evolution.

This idea is explored in the field of *evolutionary computation* and its specific methods, such as *genetic algorithms*. In our times, the term "AI" has almost became synonymous with neural networks, but they represent only one approach for creating intelligent systems. Genetic algorithms attempt to bootstrap the evolutionary process by simulating the natural mechanism of genes. The behavior of an individual is encoded as a sequence of traits ("genes"), and the diversity of future generations of individuals is ensured by mutating these sequences and mixing the sequences of several individuals (thus giving each individual two or even more "parents"). The use of genetic algorithms requires certain creativity: it is not always clear how to represent a certain task in terms of genes, mutations, and the ability of individuals to survive and propagate ("fitness"). To get an idea how it works in practice, check out a very beginner-friendly book [49].

6.3 RINGWORM INFECTION

After two relatively complex programs, let's do something simpler. Our next project will simulate the course of *ringworm infection*. A ringworm has nothing to do with worms: it is a fungus-caused skin disease.[3] The affected area looks like a circular itchy rash, expanding outward, while the skin inside the circle usually looks healthier. A typical disease will eventually go away, but of course it is recommended to treat it properly.

Ringworm infection spreads from the affected skin zone to the adjacent healthy tissue, so the infected "circle" gets bigger. However, the immune system quickly kicks in and makes the previously infected skin cells immune (for the time being), thus removing the rash inside the circle.

---

[3]From *Centers for Disease Control and Prevention (CDC)*:
https://www.cdc.gov/fungal/diseases/ringworm/

For our purposes, this process can be summarized as follows [56]:

1. Infection starts in the central cell of an W × H skin area.
2. On each simulation step, an infected cell infects each of its neighboring healthy cells with a probability of 0.5. Diagonally adjacent cells are considered neighboring.
3. After six steps, an infected cell becomes immune: it does not infect its neighbors and cannot be infected itself.
4. After four steps, an immune cell becomes healthy.

6.3.1 IMPLEMENTATION

This simulation relies on various ideas and techniques we used previously, so let's discuss its complete implementation right away (Listing 6.9).

Listing 6.9: Ringworm infection.

```python
import turtle
from enum import Enum
from random import randint
from dataclasses import dataclass

H = 41
W = 41
SLEEP_MS = 20
CELLSIZE = 15  # pixels
SHAPE_SIZE = CELLSIZE / 20  # turtle size


@dataclass
class SimState:
    done: bool

    def set_done(self):
        self.done = True

    @classmethod
    def setup(cls):
        r = cls(False)
        turtle.listen()
        turtle.onkeypress(r.set_done, "space")
        return r


class Status(Enum):
    HEALTHY = 1
    INFECTED = 2
    IMMUNE = 3


@dataclass
class Cell:
    shape: turtle.Turtle
```

```python
    status: Status
    count: int

    @classmethod
    def create(cls, x, y):
        p = turtle.Turtle()
        p.penup()
        p.shape("circle")
        p.shapesize(SHAPE_SIZE)
        p.goto(x, y)
        p.color("white")
        return cls(p, Status.HEALTHY, 0)

    def update_status(self, status, count):
        self.status = status
        self.count = count

        colors = {
            Status.HEALTHY: "white",
            Status.INFECTED: "red",
            Status.IMMUNE: "blue",
        }

        self.shape.color(colors[status])

    def update(self):
        self.count = max(0, self.count - 1)
        if self.count == 0:
            if self.status == Status.IMMUNE:
                self.update_status(Status.HEALTHY, 0)
            elif self.status == Status.INFECTED:
                self.update_status(Status.IMMUNE, 4)


@dataclass
class WorldState:
    cells: list

    def spread_from(self, x, y):
        r = []
        for xn in range(max(0, x - 1), min(x + 2, W)):
            for yn in range(max(0, y - 1), min(y + 2, H)):
                neighbor = self.cells[xn][yn]
                if neighbor.status == Status.HEALTHY and randint(0, 1) == 0:
                    r.append(neighbor)

        return r

    def update(self):
        for x in range(W):
            for y in range(H):
                self.cells[x][y].update()

        to_infect = []
        for x in range(W):
            for y in range(H):
```

```
                if self.cells[x][y].status == Status.INFECTED:
                    to_infect += self.spread_from(x, y)

        for c in to_infect:
            c.update_status(Status.INFECTED, 6)

    @classmethod
    def setup(cls):
        cells = [[Cell.create(x, y) for y in range(H)] for x in range(W)]
        cells[W // 2][H // 2].update_status(Status.INFECTED, 6)
        return cls(cells)


def setup_screen(title):
    turtle.setup(W * CELLSIZE, H * CELLSIZE)
    turtle.tracer(0, 0)
    turtle.title(title)
    turtle.setworldcoordinates(0, 0, W, H)


setup_screen("Ringworm infection")
sim_state = SimState.setup()
world_state = WorldState.setup()


def tick():
    if not sim_state.done:
        world_state.update()
        turtle.update()
        turtle.ontimer(tick, SLEEP_MS)


tick()
turtle.done()
```

We start by preparing a rectangular board filled with Cell objects:

```
cells = [[Cell.create(x, y) for y in range(H)] for x in range(W)]
```

The central cell becomes infected for six turns:[4]

```
cells[W // 2][H // 2].update_status(Status.INFECTED, 6)
```

On each simulation step, the board has to be updated in three stages. At the first stage, immune cells become healthy, and infected cells become immune when their "status counter" reaches zero. Healthy cells are displayed with (invisible) white turtles, infected cells are shown with red circles, and immune cells are represented with blue circles.

---

[4]Reminder: in Python, a // b is a shorter equivalent of math.floor(a / b) ("floor division").

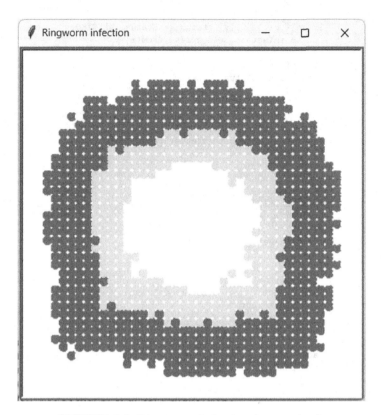

FIGURE 6.8: Ringworm infection (screenshot).

At the second stage, the list of cells to be infected is populated. We check the neighborhood of each infected cell and decide whether to add each healthy cell by "tossing a coin" with randint(0, 1).

Finally, each cell in to_infect becomes infected. As a result, the program draws a rough expanding circular pattern (see Figure 6.8).

6.4 FOREST FIRE

Many natural processes are strikingly similar in their inner workings. In our next project, we will see how "Ringworm infection" can serve as a basis for modeling events of a rather different scale, namely, forest fires. Let's presume that the fire starts from a single point and spreads in all directions. To make the simulation more interesting, let's also consider the effects of forest density and wind direction:[5]

---

[5]Inspired by "A Better Fire!!" simulation, available at
http://www.shodor.org/interactivate/activities/ABetterFire/

1. Fire starts in the central cell of an w × h forest area. The probability for a forest cell to contain a tree is PTREE.
2. On each simulation step, a burning cell may spread a fire to each of its neighboring cells with trees with a "base probability" of P (diagonally adjacent cells are considered neighboring). This probability is affected by two parameters WIND_DIRECTION and WIND_STRENGTH, so that stronger wind in the matching direction makes spreading fire more likely.
3. A burning cell burns for one turn then becomes empty.

The only new task that has to be solved here is the calculation of a wind effect. My proposal is to use the following logic:

- Suppose the current wind direction is A_w, and the fire is about to spread from the current cell in the direction A_f.
- The probability of spreading should be minimal if these directions are opposite ($A_w - A_f$ is coterminal to 180°), and maximal if they match ($A_w - A_f$ is coterminal to 0°).[6]
- The effect of wind direction should be amplified by the wind strength, ranging from 0 to 1.

A simple formula for the resulting probability of fire to be spread in the given direction would be

$$P_f = P + P \cdot WIND\_STRENGTH \cdot cos(A_w - A_f)$$

In case of opposite directions, $cos(A_w - A_f)$ becomes -1, so a strong wind of strength 1 would make the whole expression equal to zero ($P + P \cdot 1 \cdot (-1) = 0$), meaning that fire won't spread. Conversely, a matching wind direction would make $cos(A_w - A_f) = 1$ and thus double the original probability: $P + P \cdot 1 \cdot 1 = 2P$. Weak wind reduces this effect, and the wind of strength 0 makes no changes to the original probability.

This formula isn't perfect; for instance, it might yield probabilities of over 100%, but it is straightforward and sufficient for our modest purposes.

6.4.1 IMPLEMENTATION

"Forest fire" is even simpler than "Ringworm infection", because it does not need to keep track of counters that turn infected cells into immune cells, and then into healthy cells. Here every change takes just a single turn, which simplifies the whole logic (see Listing 6.10).

---

[6]Two angles are *coterminal* if they differ by some multiple of 360°.

Listing 6.10: Forest fire.

```python
import turtle
import math
from enum import Enum
from random import uniform
from dataclasses import dataclass


H = 41
W = 41
SLEEP_MS = 20
CELLSIZE = 15  # pixels
SHAPE_SIZE = CELLSIZE / 20  # turtle size
WIND_DIRECTION = math.pi / 4 # northeast
WIND_STRENGTH = 0.5
P = 0.6
PTREE = 0.6


@dataclass
class SimState:
    done: bool

    def set_done(self):
        self.done = True

    @classmethod
    def setup(cls):
        r = cls(False)
        turtle.listen()
        turtle.onkeypress(r.set_done, "space")
        return r


class Status(Enum):
    TREE = 1
    FIRE = 2
    EMPTY = 3


@dataclass
class Land:
    shape: turtle.Turtle
    status: Status = Status.EMPTY

    @classmethod
    def create(cls, x, y):
        p = turtle.Turtle()
        p.penup()
        p.shape("circle")
        p.shapesize(SHAPE_SIZE)
        p.goto(x, y)
        status = Status.TREE if uniform(0, 1) <= PTREE else Status.EMPTY
        return cls(p).update_status(status)
```

```
    def update_status(self, status):
        self.status = status
        c = {Status.TREE: "green", Status.FIRE: "red", Status.EMPTY: "white"}
        self.shape.color(c[status])
        return self


@dataclass
class WorldState:
    cells: list

    def spread_from(self, x, y):
        r = []
        for xn in range(max(0, x - 1), min(x + 2, W)):
            for yn in range(max(0, y - 1), min(y + 2, H)):
                a = math.atan2(yn - y, xn - x) - WIND_DIRECTION
                p = P + P * WIND_STRENGTH * math.cos(a)
                neighbor = self.cells[xn][yn]
                if neighbor.status == Status.TREE and uniform(0, 1) <= p:
                    r.append(neighbor)

        return r

    def update(self):
        to_burn = []
        for x in range(W):
            for y in range(H):
                if self.cells[x][y].status == Status.FIRE:
                    to_burn += self.spread_from(x, y)
                    self.cells[x][y].update_status(Status.EMPTY)

        for c in to_burn:
            c.update_status(Status.FIRE)

    @classmethod
    def setup(cls):
        cells = [[Land.create(x, y) for y in range(H)] for x in range(W)]
        cells[W // 2][H // 2].update_status(Status.FIRE)
        return cls(cells)


def setup_screen(title):
    turtle.setup(W * CELLSIZE, H * CELLSIZE)
    turtle.tracer(0, 0)
    turtle.title(title)
    turtle.setworldcoordinates(0, 0, W, H)


setup_screen("Forest fire")
sim_state = SimState.setup()
world_state = WorldState.setup()


def tick():
    if not sim_state.done:
```

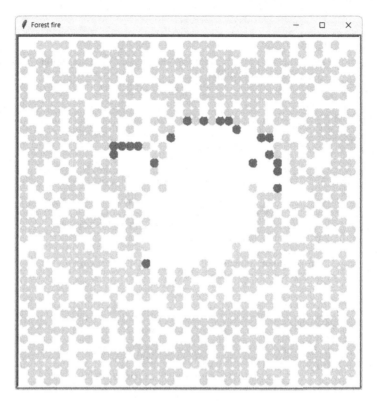

FIGURE 6.9: Forest fire (screenshot).

```
world_state.update()
turtle.update()
turtle.ontimer(tick, SLEEP_MS)

tick()
turtle.done()
```

The easiest (but not very efficient) way to calculate the current "fire direction" A_f is to use the already familiar `math.atan2()`. Each simulation step consists of two operations: we identify the neighbors to be ignited by each of the currently burning trees (and turn burning trees into empty spaces as we go), then mark all identified cells as burning. The result is shown in Figure 6.9.

6.4.2 AFTERTHOUGHTS

Just like in the case of rabbits and wolves, here we are dealing with an example, approximating a certain real-world process. How realistic is our model?

A number of advanced approaches have been designed to model forest fires and, in particular, natural regular *wildfires*, occurring mostly due to lighting strikes [31], [50]. These methods are fairly diverse, having roots in different branches of physics and mathematics.

Our approach has close relatives in the field of statistical physics—"forest-fire models", originally created to demonstrate and study a theoretical concept of "self-organized criticality", not directly related to the task of modeling natural processes. It turned out, however, that these generally simple algorithms are actually able to approximate the real forest fires fairly well [62].

The classic *Drossel-Schwabl forest-fire model*, for example, is no more complicated than our own simulation. It can be summarized as follows:

1. The $N \times N$ forest area is randomly covered with trees. The density of the forest can be adjusted.
2. A burning tree becomes an empty cell on the next step of simulation.
3. A non-burning tree becomes burning on the next step if *any* of its four (top/bottom/left/right) neighboring trees is burning.
4. A non-burning tree becomes burning with a probability f due to a lightning strike even if has no burning neighbors.
5. An empty cell becomes a home for a new tree with a probability p.

6.5 SPREAD OF DISEASE

Let's wrap up our family of disease-and-calamity simulations with another little program, modeling the spread of a contagious disease. It can be obtained by combining individual elements of "Ringworm infection" and "Rabbits and wolves" as follows.

We are going to have a "city" of W × H locations, inhabited by people constantly on the move in random directions. A person might be healthy but susceptible for a disease, infected, or immune. Infected people might infect their neighbors with a certain probability, who become infected themselves and then eventually turn immune. Let's take one further step and presume that immunity won't last forever, so eventually immune people become susceptible again.[7]

6.5.1 IMPLEMENTATION

Let's consider the complete listing of this simulation, obtained by modifying "Ringworm infection" a bit (see Listing 6.11). The required modifications are relatively minor. We'll need to take into account empty cells, because not all city locations are occupied with inhabitants. Then, we'll need to move each inhabitant to an adjacent random empty cell on every simulation step. Just

---

[7]Inspired by "Spread of Infection" simulation, available at
http://www.shodor.org/interactivate/activities/SpreadofDisease/

like in case of "Rabbits and wolves", we can presume toroidal shape of the city.

Listing 6.11: Spread of disease.

```python
import turtle
from enum import Enum
from random import randint, uniform
from dataclasses import dataclass

H = 41
W = 41
SLEEP_MS = 20
CELLSIZE = 10   # pixels
SHAPE_SIZE = CELLSIZE / 20   # turtle size

IMMUNE_DURATION = 15
INFECTED_DURATION = 7
PINHABIT = 0.4 # probability for a cell to be inhabited
PINFECT = 0.5 # probability for a cell to be infected by a neighbor


@dataclass
class SimState:
    done: bool

    def set_done(self):
        self.done = True

    @classmethod
    def setup(cls):
        r = cls(False)
        turtle.listen()
        turtle.onkeypress(r.set_done, "space")
        return r


class Status(Enum):
    HEALTHY = 1
    INFECTED = 2
    IMMUNE = 3


@dataclass
class Cell:
    shape: turtle.Turtle
    status: Status
    count: int

    def x(self):
        return int(self.shape.xcor())

    def y(self):
        return int(self.shape.ycor())

    @classmethod
```

```
    def populate(cls, x, y):
        if uniform(0, 1) > PINHABIT and not (x == W // 2 and y == H // 2):
            return None
        p = turtle.Turtle()
        p.penup()
        p.shape("circle")
        p.shapesize(SHAPE_SIZE)
        p.goto(x, y)
        p.color("green")
        return cls(p, Status.HEALTHY, 0)

    def update_status(self, status, count):
        self.status = status
        self.count = count

        colors = {
            Status.HEALTHY: "green",
            Status.INFECTED: "red",
            Status.IMMUNE: "blue",
        }
        self.shape.color(colors[status])

    def update(self):
        self.count = max(0, self.count - 1)
        if self.count == 0:
            if self.status == Status.IMMUNE:
                self.update_status(Status.HEALTHY, 0)
            elif self.status == Status.INFECTED:
                self.update_status(Status.IMMUNE, IMMUNE_DURATION)

    def moved_to(self, x, y):
        self.shape.goto(x, y)
        return self


@dataclass
class WorldState:
    cells: list

    def spread_from(self, x, y):
        r = []
        for xn in range(x - 1, x + 2):
            for yn in range(y - 1, y + 2):
                cell = self.cells[xn % W][yn % H]
                is_healthy = cell and cell.status == Status.HEALTHY
                if is_healthy and uniform(0, 1) <= PINFECT:
                    r.append(cell)

        return r

    def move(self, p):
        newx = randint(p.x() - 1, p.x() + 1) % W
        newy = randint(p.y() - 1, p.y() + 1) % H

        if not self.cells[newx][newy]:
            self.cells[p.x()][p.y()] = None
```

```
            self.cells[newx][newy] = p.moved_to(newx, newy)

    def print_stats(self, people):
        healthy = len([p for p in people if p.status == Status.HEALTHY])
        infected = len([p for p in people if p.status == Status.INFECTED])
        immune = len([p for p in people if p.status == Status.IMMUNE])
        print(f"{healthy}\t{infected}\t{immune}")

    def update(self):
        to_infect = []
        people = sum(([v for v in self.cells[x] if v] for x in range(W)), [])
        self.print_stats(people)

        for p in people:
            p.update()
            self.move(p)

            if p.status == Status.INFECTED:
                to_infect += self.spread_from(p.x(), p.y())

        for c in to_infect:
            c.update_status(Status.INFECTED, INFECTED_DURATION)

    @classmethod
    def setup(cls):
        cells = [[Cell.populate(x, y) for y in range(H)] for x in range(W)]
        cells[W // 2][H // 2].update_status(Status.INFECTED, INFECTED_DURATION)
        return cls(cells)


def setup_screen(title):
    turtle.setup(W * CELLSIZE, H * CELLSIZE)
    turtle.tracer(0, 0)
    turtle.title(title)
    turtle.setworldcoordinates(0, 0, W, H)


setup_screen("Spread of disease")
sim_state = SimState.setup()
world_state = WorldState.setup()


def tick():
    if not sim_state.done:
        world_state.update()
        turtle.update()
        turtle.ontimer(tick, SLEEP_MS)


tick()
turtle.done()
```

Let's review the most important changes that had to be introduced. The simulation starts with "populating" the city and infecting inhabitants of the central cell:

```
cells = [[Cell.populate(x, y) for y in range(H)] for x in range(W)]
cells[W // 2][H // 2].update_status(Status.INFECTED, INFECTED_DURATION)
```

Unlike `Cell.create()` method of "Ringworm infection", `Cell.populate()` creates an inhabitant only with a certain probability `PINHABIT`. It also makes sure to create an inhabitant in the central cell, because the infection starts there. Thus, the "unhappy path" of not creating an inhabitant looks like this:

```
def populate(cls, x, y):
    if uniform(0, 1) > PINHABIT and not (x == W // 2 and y == H // 2):
        return None
    ...
```

On each step of the simulation, we need to do something with each inhabitant. Thus, it is necessary to have a list of all non-empty cells in the system, which can be obtained as follows:

```
people = sum(([v for v in self.cells[x] if v] for x in range(W)), [])
```

Here we use the same `sum()` trick as in "Evolution": `cells` is a list of lists, so each element of `cells` is a list. It can be easily transformed into a list of non-empty cells:

```
[v for v in self.cells[x] if v]
```

Next, all these lists are concatenated into a resulting "flat" list using `sum()`.

Since the city we simulate has a toroidal shape, every time there is a chance to leave the city boundaries, a modulo operator is used to arrive from the opposite direction:

```
def move(self, p):
    newx = randint(p.x() - 1, p.x() + 1) % W
    newy = randint(p.y() - 1, p.y() + 1) % H
    ...

# similar logic is used in spread_from()
```

The screenshot of the running program is shown in Figure 6.10.

It is quite difficult to grasp the dynamics of this system by merely watching these dancing colored blobs, so let's look at some charts. Obviously, the course of the simulated epidemic heavily depends on the values of parameters. By giving the inhabitants prolonged immunity, we eradicate the disease after a single large outbreak (see Figure 6.11). Other reasonable combinations typically produce a familiar, to most of us, "seasonal" wave patterns (see Figure 6.12).

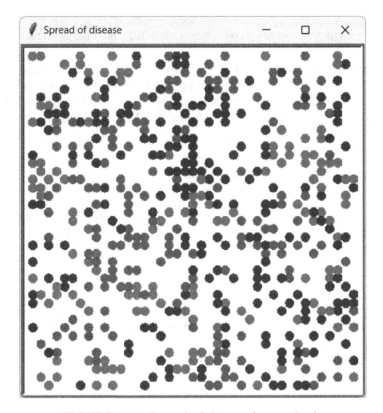

FIGURE 6.10: Spread of disease (screenshot).

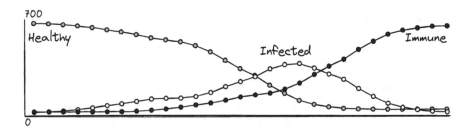

FIGURE 6.11: Population reaching immunity after a single disease outbreak.
IMMUNE_DURATION=22, INFECTED_DURATION=6, PINHABIT=0.4, PINFECT=0.5.

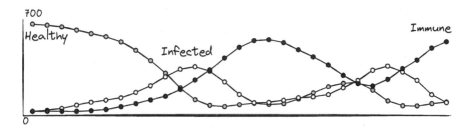

FIGURE 6.12: Wave patterns of disease spread. IMMUNE_DURATION=14, INFECTED_DURATION=7, PINHABIT=0.3, PINFECT=0.5.

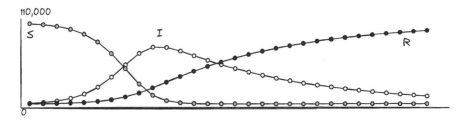

FIGURE 6.13: Example SIR chart.

6.5.2 AFTERTHOUGHTS

Once again, it would be good to discuss whether this simulation has any resemblance to the process of actual spread of disease. It turns out that yes, the basic spread scenario (without subsequent disease waves) produces the same pattern as can be obtained with conventional mathematical models, actually used for practical purposes.

The most basic such model is known as *SIR* (susceptible-infected-removed) [57]. It presumes that each individual belongs to one of three classes, just like in our case, but immune ("removed") people stay immune forever. SIR model consists of equations representing the change of each class size in a unit of time, and it has only two input parameters: the "disease transmission rate" and the "recovery rate". By varying these values, it is easy to obtain a picture similar to Figure 6.11 (see Figure 6.13).

Comparing our model with SIR makes sense because SIR is quite accurate under certain constraints if its parameters are set correctly (which can be a separate complicated task). There are more advanced variations of SIR that take into account other classes, such as "vaccinated" in the *SIRV* model, which helps modeling the effects of vaccination.

It is interesting to see how different approaches to the task of modeling a certain process produce so strikingly similar results. The SIR model, Lotka-Volterra equations, and the logistic function used in "The tragedy of the commons" consider populations from a "bird's eye" perspective. Our Python simulations usually start from an individual: a single rabbit, a wolf, or an infected person. We code just a few basic rules: rabbits move and eat grass; people walk through the city and possibly infect their neighbors. By simulating hundreds of individuals, we make visible emergent properties of the whole system.

Our models are more computationally expensive. Classic mathematical approaches can be seen as "computational shortcuts", replacing complex individual interactions with simple formulas. On the other hand, "individual-based" methods are more flexible: it is easy to add a new rule or to modify a certain behavior pattern and examine the outcome. As usual, there is no single right way to do it, but the growing availability of fast computing hardware makes simulation a viable option more often than before.

6.6 JOHN CONWAY'S "LIFE"

Our next "grid world" is a bit difficult to approach. Treat it lightly, and it gives an impression of a mere mathematical toy. Dig deeper, and it opens Pandora's box of related concepts and side discussions. To set a realistic goal, let's aim for a quick excursion to the world of biologically inspired computational models. They occupy an interesting middle ground between "biological models" that simulate living organisms and populations, and "computational models", attempting to formalize pure ideas of computing.

In our times, if mechanics of a certain process is well understood, designing its computer simulation is somewhat akin to writing a story: there is no need to invent words and rules of grammar; the only challenge is to arrange the right words in the right order. Likewise, turning theory into code requires talent and mastery, but at least we won't have to make our own tools before starting the actual work. Numerous powerful programming languages and extensive libraries are here already.

Early computing pioneers lacked such tools, and they had to struggle not only with the absence of computers in the modern sense, but also with inadequate means to express their ideas. One of such pioneers, John von Neumann, was interested in systems capable of achieving certain goals. In particular, he thought that the goal of *self-replication* is especially worthy of investigation [35]. But how to describe such as system—using logical formulas, equations, or electric circuits?

Among the ideas studied by von Neumann was *cellular automaton*—a biologically inspired abstract machine, "living" like a colony of cells. Such a device is "programmed" by specifying the initial configuration of cells, arranged as a two-dimensional grid, and supplying a set of rules governing the life of the colony. A cell can be in one of several possible states, and the rules specify how the cells switch from one state to another under influence of their neighborhood.

At this point, let's note that our "Ringworm infection" comes really close to be called a cellular automaton: it is enough to get rid of randomicity and presume that infected cells always infect their neighbors.[8] Initial configuration of this machine is a single cell in the "infected-1" state. At the next step, this cell switches to the state "infected-2", while its "healthy" neighbors become "infected-1". Cells reaching the "infected-6" state will switch into "immune-1", and so on. Thus, each cell can be in one of 11 states (one healthy, six infected, four immune), and switching between these states depends entirely on cell neighborhood (since a cell forms a part of its own neighborhood, unconditional switching, such as "infected-2" to "infected-3", still follows this principle).

Over the years, various kinds of cellular automata were proposed. One may tinker with the rules, the states, or even with the board, which does not have to be strictly two-dimensional. The variation known as "Life", proposed by John Conway in late 1960s, turned out to be especially popular [14]. The simplicity of its rules and the richness of cell colonies' developmental trajectories proved to be a great combination for its longevity and fame.

Cells in "Life" have two states: "populated" and "empty". They live in a two-dimensional grid, and the neighborhood of each cell consists of eight adjacent cells. "Life" has only three rules:

1. If a populated cell has less than two or more than three neighbors, it becomes empty ("dies").
2. If an empty cell has exactly three populated neighbors, it becomes populated.
3. Otherwise, the cell preserves its current state.

It is important to understand that births and deaths occur simultaneously. An empty cell with three neighbors *will become* populated on the next step. Likewise, a populated cell with one neighbor *will* die, but it is still alive and influences its neighborhood (see Figure 6.14).

Now let's implement "Life", and then discuss its fascinating world a bit longer.

6.6.1 IMPLEMENTATION

The complete program is shown in Listing 6.12. It follows the general structure of "Ringworm infection", but it adds some notable modifications.

Listing 6.12: The game of Life.

```
import turtle
from dataclasses import dataclass

H = 41
W = 41
```

---

[8]Randomicity is allowed in *stochastic* cellular automata.

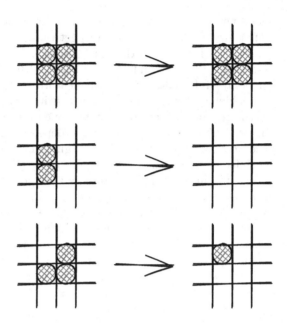

FIGURE 6.14: Typical developments in "Life".

```python
SLEEP_MS = 20
CELLSIZE = 10
SHAPE_SIZE = CELLSIZE / 20   # turtle size


@dataclass
class SimState:
    done: bool

    def set_done(self):
        self.done = True

    @classmethod
    def setup(cls):
        r = cls(False)
        turtle.listen()
        turtle.onkeypress(r.set_done, "space")
        return r


@dataclass
class CellShape:
    shape: turtle.Turtle

    @classmethod
    def create(cls, x, y):
        p = turtle.Turtle()
```

```
            p.penup()
            p.shape("circle")
            p.shapesize(SHAPE_SIZE)
            p.goto(x, y)
            p.color("black")
            p.hideturtle()
            return cls(p)

    def update(self, show):
        if show:
            self.shape.showturtle()
        else:
            self.shape.hideturtle()


@dataclass
class WorldState:
    shapes: list
    current: list
    next: list

    def neighbors_count(self, x, y):
        neighbors = -int(self.current[x][y])
        for nx in range(x - 1, x + 2):
            for ny in range(y - 1, y + 2):
                neighbors += int(self.current[nx % W][ny % H])
        return neighbors

    def next_status(self, x, y):
        neighbors = self.neighbors_count(x, y)

        if not self.current[x][y] and neighbors == 3:
            return True
        if self.current[x][y] and (neighbors < 2 or neighbors > 3):
            return False

        return self.current[x][y]

    def update(self):
        for x in range(W):
            for y in range(H):
                self.shapes[x][y].update(self.current[x][y])
                self.next[x][y] = self.next_status(x, y)

        self.current, self.next = self.next, self.current

    @classmethod
    def setup(cls, population):
        shapes = [[CellShape.create(x, y) for y in range(H)] for x in range(W)]
        current = [[False for _ in range(H)] for _ in range(W)]
        next = [[False for _ in range(H)] for _ in range(W)]

        for x, y in population:
            current[x][y] = True

        return cls(shapes, current, next)
```

```
def setup_screen(title):
    turtle.setup(W * CELLSIZE, H * CELLSIZE)
    turtle.tracer(0, 0)
    turtle.title(title)
    turtle.setworldcoordinates(0, 0, W, H)


setup_screen("Life")
sim_state = SimState.setup()
world_config = [(20, 20), (21, 20), (22, 20), (22, 21), (21, 22)]
world_state = WorldState.setup(world_config)


def tick():
    if not sim_state.done:
        world_state.update()
        turtle.update()
        turtle.ontimer(tick, SLEEP_MS)


tick()
turtle.done()
```

First let's note that the "cell" class `CellShape` merely works a container for a turtle that displays the current cell status (empty or populated). Since cells may have only two states, we can get away with a matrix of Boolean values instead of full-fledged cell objects.

Next, note that the `setup()` function of `WorldState` class creates two matrices: `current` and `next`. Since all the changes in "Life" have to occur simultaneously, we will store all the pending changes in the `next` matrix, and then swap it with `current`. This way, we always have the current game board and a buffer for the next configuration.

When counting neighbors, we have to exclude the current cell (otherwise, it will be counted as its own neighbor):

```
neighbors = -int(self.current[x][y])
```

Theoretically, the board of "Life" should be infinite. In practice, the opposite ends of the board are usually treated as adjacent, which gives the board a shape of a donut (just like in our "Rabbits and wolves" program). Thus, the neighbor counting code should wrap around the edges:

```
neighbors += int(self.current[nx % W][ny % H])
```

6.6.2 AFTERTHOUGHTS

The current implementation of "Life" comes with five alive cells:

```
world_config = [(20, 20), (21, 20), (22, 20), (22, 21), (21, 22)]
world_state = WorldState.setup(world_config)
```

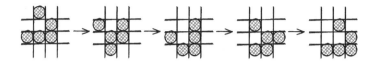

FIGURE 6.15: Glider movement.

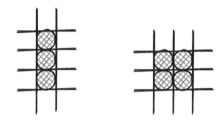

FIGURE 6.16: The blinker and the block.

This configuration is known as "glider", and its distinctive feature is the ability to move across the game board in a diagonal direction. Every fifth generation of the glider colony is a copy of its original ancestor, shifted to the bottom-right (see Figure 6.15).

A glider belongs to the category of patterns known as "spaceships". All of them are able to move, but they range in their size and speed. It takes four iterations for the glider to shift by one cell diagonally, and this is the highest diagonal speed achievable for a spaceship in "Life" [21].

Early experiments with "Life" revealed other interesting pattern types, such as "oscillators", reproducing themselves after a certain period, or "still life" configurations that never change. The simplest oscillator known as "the blinker" is a row of three alive cells. In one iteration, it produces a vertical line of cells (two new cells become populated, two old cells die), which, in turn, again produces a vertical line of cells, and the process repeats infinitely. An equally simple example of a still life pattern is "the block", consisting of four cells arranged as a square. No new cells can be populated here, and the existing cells survive forever (see Figure 6.16).

Currently, the connoisseurs of "Life" identify 11 "major" categories of patterns and more than 20 "minor" categories.[9] Patterns within the same category usually possess a certain kind of interesting property. For example, "glider guns" exhibit infinite population growth by periodically producing new gliders. "Gardens of Eden" are the patterns that must be created by the user, being unable to evolve from other configurations.

---

[9] From *LifeWiki*: https://conwaylife.com/wiki/Category:Patterns

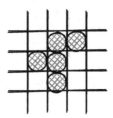

FIGURE 6.17: R-pentomino.

Just like in some of our previous simulations, "Life" exhibits emergent properties: simple configurations might yield unpredictably complex behaviors. One such example is a row of 10 populated cells that evolves into an oscillator having a period of 15 steps (known as "pentadecathlon"). Another good example is "R-pentomino" (see Figure 6.17), which goes through a lot of transformations before stabilizing after 1103 steps.

To wrap up the topic of "Life", let me come back to the beginning of this section. The original idea of John von Neumann was to employ a cellular automaton as a model of computation, as a "proto-computer". While not commonly employed, this idea is still alive, and cellular automata can be used to model certain processes in nature. Stephen Wolfram, who is probably the most active proponent of this direction today, dedicated a nearly 1200-page book to the study of cellular automata and their practical applications [60]. However, configurations in "Life" are often engineered and studied just for the fun of creation and challenge. The patterns shown here were already known in the 1970s, and numerous new discoveries have been made since then [22].

6.7 LANGTON'S ANT

Conway's "Life" is popular and famous, but just one specific example of a cellular automaton inspired by the image of a colony of cells. To make our discussion of this topic a bit deeper, let's consider another cellular automaton, which draws inspiration from the behavior of insects: Langton's ant.

Christopher Langton was interested in the study of *artificial life*, emerging from the interaction of inanimate "molecules" and other basic building blocks. The motivation for such studies is to model biochemical processes: living beings are made of inanimate substances, and the way life emerges from non-living elements is not really well understood. Some aspects of this mysterious transformation have to be connected with the chemical processes, specific for living creatures. However, it is clear that more universal principles are also at work here.

We have already seen that flocking behavior or adaptive evolution can be observed in simple virtual worlds inhabited by simple virtual creatures.

Langton proposed several cellular automata-based models, attempting to demonstrate other "life-like" features, such as self-reproduction and the "global" behavior of a society. The "society" described in his original work is actually a colony of ants, and the algorithm driving its individual members (virtual ants or "vants") is now known as "Langton's ant" [24].

A virtual ant lives on an infinite board, divided into square cells. Each cell can be either black or white. For starters, we can consider an empty (all-white) board with an ant residing in its arbitrary location. The ant operates according to the following rules:

1. If the cell under the ant is white, the ant turns 90° to the right, makes the cell black, and moves one cell forward.
2. If the cell under the ant is black, the ant turns 90° to the left, makes the cell white, and moves one cell forward.

At a glance, this description does not look quite right for a proper cellular automaton: the rules are supposed to specify how a cell switches from one state to another on the basis of cell neighborhood, rather than direct a moving creature over a board. However, the rules of Langton's ant can be rewritten to follow the usual conventions. Each cell of the board has 10 possible states: (white, no ant), (white, ant looks left), (white, ant looks up), and so on. In other words, a cell state is a combination of its color and ant status. Then the next state of a cell indeed entirely depends on its neighborhood. Say, a cell with the ant will have the opposite color and no ant on the next turn. Similarly, a cell having a left white neighbor with the up-looking ant will have the same color and the right-looking ant on the next turn.

Let's now implement this system and see what kind of behavior is exhibited by the virtual ant.

6.7.1 IMPLEMENTATION

A very straightforward implementation of the system is shown in Listing 6.13. The `CellShape` class, similar to the one used in "Life", is responsible for turning on and off black spots on the board. The ant does not even have its dedicated class: it behaves like a turtle (turn and go forward), so we can easily employ a `Turtle` object.

Listing 6.13: Langton's ant.

```
import turtle
from dataclasses import dataclass

H = 81
W = 81
SLEEP_MS = 20
CELLSIZE = 5
SHAPE_SIZE = CELLSIZE / 20  # turtle size
```

```python
@dataclass
class SimState:
    done: bool

    def set_done(self):
        self.done = True

    @classmethod
    def setup(cls):
        r = cls(False)
        turtle.listen()
        turtle.onkeypress(r.set_done, "space")
        return r


@dataclass
class CellShape:
    shape: turtle.Turtle

    @classmethod
    def create(cls, x, y):
        p = turtle.Turtle()
        p.penup()
        p.shape("circle")
        p.shapesize(SHAPE_SIZE)
        p.goto(x, y)
        p.color("black")
        p.hideturtle()
        return cls(p)

    def is_black(self):
        return self.shape.isvisible()

    def flip(self):
        if self.is_black():
            self.shape.hideturtle()
        else:
            self.shape.showturtle()


def make_ant(x, y):
    p = turtle.Turtle()
    p.penup()
    p.shape("turtle")
    p.shapesize(SHAPE_SIZE / 2)
    p.goto(x, y)
    p.color("red")
    return p


@dataclass
class WorldState:
    board: list
    ant: turtle.Turtle
    step: int = 0
```

```
    def update(self):
        self.step += 1
        if self.step % 1000 == 0:
            print(f"Performing step: {self.step}")

        x = round(self.ant.xcor())
        y = round(self.ant.ycor())
        turn = 90 if self.board[x][y].is_black() else -90

        self.board[x][y].flip()
        self.ant.left(turn)
        self.ant.forward(1)

    @classmethod
    def setup(cls):
        board = [[CellShape.create(x, y) for y in range(H)] for x in range(W)]
        ant = make_ant(W // 2, H // 2)
        return cls(board, ant)


def setup_screen(title):
    turtle.setup(W * CELLSIZE, H * CELLSIZE)
    turtle.tracer(0, 0)
    turtle.title(title)
    turtle.setworldcoordinates(0, 0, W, H)


setup_screen("Langton's ant")
sim_state = SimState.setup()
world_state = WorldState.setup()


def tick():
    if not sim_state.done:
        world_state.update()
        turtle.update()
        turtle.ontimer(tick, SLEEP_MS)


tick()
turtle.done()
```

The screenshot in Figure 6.18 shows the situation on the board after the first 1000 steps. This picture shows the lack of any conceivable patterns behind the ant's trajectory. This impression is even stronger if the ant is watched in real time: its nearly random movements do not seem to form regular shapes.

This effect shows the emergence of complex behavior from a set of simple rules, which is actually the whole point of the system. The situation becomes even more complex if we consider the interaction between several ants forming a colony. Interestingly, the trajectory of an ant on an empty board eventually stabilizes after around 10,000 iterations, when the ant begins building a

FIGURE 6.18: Screenshot of Langton's ant after 1000 iterations.

straight "path", consisting of smaller segments, each taking 104 steps to make (see Figure 6.19).

Later experiments showed that Langton's ant, like many other cellular automata (including "Life"), exhibits a property of *computational universality*. It means that an ant can theoretically perform *any* computational algorithm, encoded along with its input data in the initial configuration of the board [30].

6.8 CELLULAR SNOWFLAKES

"Ringworm infection" remains the only coincidental example of using a cellular automaton as a practical simulation and modeling instrument. Let's consider another task where a cellular automaton turns out to be the right tool for the job.

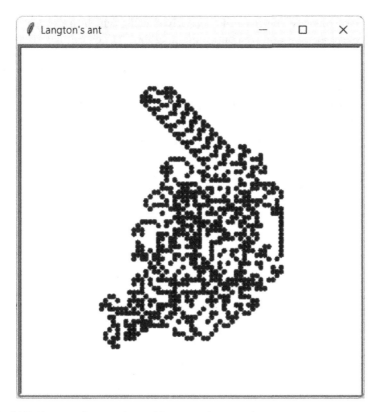

FIGURE 6.19: Screenshot of Langton's ant after $\approx 10,500$ iterations.

Our goal would be to model a process of *snow crystal growth*. Various kinds of snow crystals (known to most of us as mere snowflakes) are extensively studied, documented, and photographed.[10] While the physics behind crystal formation is far from being trivial, it turns out that a simple cellular automaton-based simulation can grasp its essential features, producing realistic snowflakes [43]. The proposed process works as follows.

1. We prepare an initial *hexagonal* grid of cells holding numeric values. Each cell is assigned the "background humidity" value β.
2. The central cell of the grid is "seeded" with a value of 1. Roughly speaking, values from zero to one represent various amounts of water in a certain location, while higher values correspond to the particles of ice.
3. On each simulation step, the following actions are performed:

---

[10]A good place to start exploring snowflakes is http://snowcrystals.com

- We identify the map of "receptive" cells, which are either ice or have at least one ice-containing neighbor. (Each cell has six neighbors.)
- We use the original (main) grid and the map of receptive cells to create a new "receptive" grid. Its cells are initially filled with zeroes, but for every location (x, y) found in the list of receptive cells the cell value is updated:

$$receptive\_grid[x, y] = main\_grid[x, y] + \gamma$$

The constant γ represents the amount of water coming from the outside world.

- Likewise, we create a new "non-receptive" grid, also initially filled with zeroes. Its locations, not found in the list of receptive cells, are updated with the values taken from the main grid:

$$non\_receptive\_grid[x, y] = main\_grid[x, y]$$

- Next, we create an averaged version of the non-receptive grid. Its locations are initialized according to the formula

$$averaged[x, y] = (1 - \frac{1}{2}\alpha) \cdot non\_receptive\_grid[x, y]$$

- Then we use the values of all six neighbors of $non\_receptive\_grid[x, y]$ to update its averaged version:

$$averaged[x, y] \mathrel{+}= \frac{1}{12}\alpha \cdot neighbor_k$$

Here α is the *diffusion constant*, controlling the fraction of water able to spill into the neighboring locations.

- Finally, new content of the main grid is obtained by summing up the corresponding elements of the receptive and the averaged grids.

It might sound a bit complicated, but at least all the steps are well defined and well separated, so we can proceed to implementation.[11]

6.8.1 IMPLEMENTATION

The first issue to sort out is hexagonal grid, which we never used before. The simplest approach for making it is to treat individual hexagonal cells as points on the regular square grid. When displayed, every second row is shifted to the right by one-half of a cell size (see Figure 6.20). This method allows to employ

---

[11] My code owes much to the version made by Stephen Fay, available at https://github.com/dcxSt/snowflake_automaton

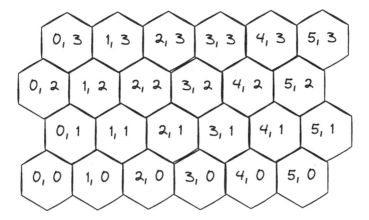

FIGURE 6.20: Building a hexagonal grid in Cartesian coordinates.

a regular Cartesian coordinate system with each cell addressed by its x and y coordinates.

Since growing snowflakes requires processing the immediate neighborhood of a cell, we need to be able to retrieve a list of neighbors for any specified location. As a concrete example, let's consider two such locations: (1, 1) and (4, 2). Four out of six neighbors can be obtained by looking to the left, to the right, up, and down (see Figure 6.21).

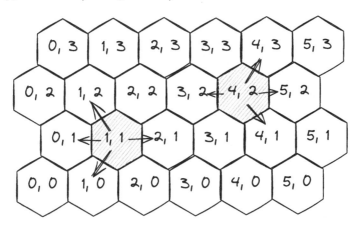

FIGURE 6.21: Retrieving four neighbors for each highlighted location.

Now it should be clear that the remaining two neighbors are harder to identify. For (4, 2), we need two cells lying diagonally to the left, while for (1, 1) the remaining cells lie diagonally to the right. The choice depends on the location's row: for even rows we have to look left, and for odd rows we have to look right (see Figure 6.22).

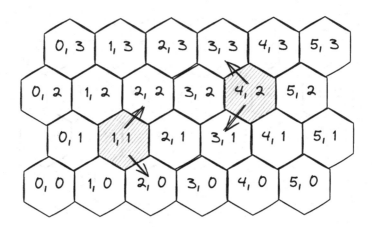

FIGURE 6.22: Retrieving the remaining neighbors for each highlighted location.

Now we can proceed to the preliminary version of the code, still having missing pieces (Listing 6.14).

Listing 6.14: Cellular snowflakes (sketch).

```python
import turtle
from dataclasses import dataclass

H = 201
W = 201
SLEEP_MS = 20
VIS_SLEEP_MS = 5000
CELLSIZE = 4
SHAPE_SIZE = CELLSIZE / 20   # turtle size

ALPHA = 2.03
BETA = 0.4
GAMMA = 0.0001


@dataclass
class SimState:
    done: bool

    def set_done(self):
        self.done = True

    @classmethod
    def setup(cls):
        r = cls(False)
        turtle.listen()
        turtle.onkeypress(r.set_done, "space")
        return r
```

```
@dataclass
class Drawer:
    shape: turtle.Turtle

    @classmethod
    def create(cls, x, y):
        p = turtle.Turtle()
        p.penup()
        p.shape("circle")
        p.shapesize(SHAPE_SIZE)
        p.goto(x + 0.5 * (y % 2), y)
        p.color("black")
        return cls(p)

    def update(self, v):
        self.shape.fillcolor(v, v, v)
        if SHAPE_SIZE * v == 0:
            self.shape.hideturtle()
        else:
            self.shape.showturtle()
            self.shape.shapesize(SHAPE_SIZE * v)


@dataclass
class WorldState:
    cells: list = None
    step: int = 0
    ...


def setup_screen(title):
    turtle.colormode(1.0)
    turtle.setup(W * CELLSIZE, H * CELLSIZE)
    turtle.tracer(0, 0)
    turtle.title(title)
    turtle.setworldcoordinates(0, 0, W, H)


def update_shapes(shapes, cells):
    for x in range(W):
        for y in range(H):
            shapes[x][y].update(min(1, cells[x][y]))


setup_screen("Cellular snowflakes")
sim_state = SimState.setup()
world_state = WorldState.setup()
shapes = [[Drawer.create(x, y) for y in range(H)] for x in range(W)]


def tick():
    if not sim_state.done:
        world_state.update()
        turtle.ontimer(tick, SLEEP_MS)
```

```
def tick_draw():
    if not sim_state.done:
        print(f"step {world_state.step}")
        update_shapes(shapes, world_state.cells)
        turtle.update()
        turtle.ontimer(tick_draw, VIS_SLEEP_MS)


tick()
tick_draw()
turtle.done()
```

This code follows the same scheme as used in "Life". There is a list of cell contents (world_state.cells) and a separate collection of turtle-based Drawer objects used to display the grid. This simulation is quite computationally demanding, so the graphics is updated in a separate function tick_draw(), just like in "Evolution". Note that the Drawer objects are created to form a hexagonal grid by shifting every second row to the right:

```
@classmethod
def create(cls, x, y):
    p = turtle.Turtle()
    ...
    p.goto(x + 0.5 * (y % 2), y) # shift by half a cell for odd rows
    ...
```

To visualize cell content, we will use both turtle shape size (larger circles correspond to higher values) and color. Each circle will have a black border and will be filled with a shade approaching white as the cell value increases:

```
self.shape.fillcolor(v, v, v) # 0 <= v <= 1
```

Values higher than 1 are clamped down to one in update_shapes(). To use values from 0 to 1 as RGB color components, the corresponding color mode has to be activated:

```
turtle.colormode(1.0)
```

Next, let's implement the missing class WorldState (see Listing 6.15).

Listing 6.15: Cellular snowflakes (class WorldState).

```
@dataclass
class WorldState:
    cells: list = None
    step: int = 0

    def make_cells(self, v):
        return [[v for _ in range(H)] for x in range(W)]
```

```python
def average(self, cells):
    avg = self.make_cells(0)

    for x in range(W):
        for y in range(H):
            e = cells[x][y]

            avg[x][y] += (1 - ALPHA * 0.5) * e
            for nx, ny in self.neighbors(x, y):
                avg[nx][ny] += e * ALPHA / 12
    return avg

def neighbors(self, x, y):
    even_neigh = [((x - 1) % W, (y - 1) % H), ((x - 1) % W, (y + 1) % H)]
    odd_neigh = [((x + 1) % W, (y - 1) % H), ((x + 1) % W, (y + 1) % H)]
    add_neighbors = even_neigh if y % 2 == 0 else odd_neigh

    return [
        (x, ((y + 1) % H)),
        (x, (y - 1) % H),
        ((x - 1) % W, y),
        ((x + 1) % W, y),
    ] + add_neighbors

def receptive_cells_map(self):
    is_receptive = self.make_cells(False)

    for x in range(W):
        for y in range(H):
            if self.cells[x][y] >= 1:
                for nx, ny in self.neighbors(x, y) + [(x, y)]:
                    is_receptive[nx][ny] = True

    return is_receptive

def rec_nonrec_grids(self, is_receptive):
    receptive = self.make_cells(0)
    non_receptive = self.make_cells(0)

    for x in range(W):
        for y in range(H):
            e = self.cells[x][y]
            if is_receptive[x][y]:
                receptive[x][y] = e + GAMMA
            else:
                non_receptive[x][y] = e
    return receptive, non_receptive

def update(self):
    self.step += 1

    is_receptive = self.receptive_cells_map()
    receptive, non_receptive = self.rec_nonrec_grids(is_receptive)
    non_receptive = self.average(non_receptive)
```

```
        for x in range(W):
            for y in range(H):
                self.cells[x][y] = receptive[x][y] + non_receptive[x][y]

    def fill_cells(self):
        self.cells = self.make_cells(BETA)
        self.cells[W // 2][H // 2] = 1.0
        return self

    @classmethod
    def setup(cls):
        return cls().fill_cells()
```

This code follows the description of the simulation quite closely. First, each cell of the grid `cells` is initialized with the value of `BETA` in `setup()`. The central cell gets the value of 1. The main simulation loop creates a map of receptive cells and two grids: `receptive` and `non_receptive`. The non-receptive grid is then averaged, and both grids are added together to form a new version of the main grid `cells`.

The complexities of dealing with a hexagonal grid are hidden in the function `neighbors()`. It returns the list of neighboring locations of the given cell taking into account the differences between odd and even rows. It also "wraps around" the board, so the edge locations are treated as adjacent to the locations on the opposite side (the same technique was used in "Life").

The result of a test run of the program after 900 steps is shown in Figure 6.23.

Naturally, the appearance of the resulting snowflake highly depends on the value of input parameters, so try playing with them. The original paper [43] shows a number of interesting examples.

This simulation is more complex than "Life", but it still satisfies the criteria of a regular cellular automaton. It operates on a two-dimensional grid, and its cells switch between their states according to the rules that take into account the immediate cell neighborhood. The cells here hold real numbers, so from a mathematical point of view the number of cell states is infinite. However, in Python, real numbers are stored in 64-bit variables, so there are at most 2^{64} states per cell. I believe the snowflake model does not need such high precision, so in practice the number of required states can be greatly reduced further.

6.9   FURTHER IDEAS

1. Examine the changes in grass volume over time in the "Rabbits and wolves" simulation. Consider also the case without wolves.
2. As already mentioned, the ecosystem of "Rabbits and wolves" (and Wa-Tor) is quite unstable and suffers from the paradox of enrichment. Check how various natural protective mechanisms work in the simulation. Here are some simple ideas to try [47]:

FIGURE 6.23: Sample snowflake.

- Inedible prey. Add another grass-eating population similar to rabbits but not eaten by wolves. This second population would compete with rabbits for grass, preventing rabbit overpopulation.
- Invulnerable prey. Create a square region inside the map where wolves cannot eat rabbits or even cannot visit. This "inconvenient hunting area" protects rabbits from extinction.
- Density-dependent predator mortality. Make the lifetime of a wolf dependent on wolf population size: members of a large population should live shorter (due to more frequent internal conflicts). It would help to keep wolf population under control even if food is abundant.

3. The original Palmiter's version of "Simulated Evolution" takes place on a hexagonal grid. Rewrite our "Evolution" for this setup. Each cell will have only six neighbors.

4. Print out the "family history" of the most successful bug of each generation. It should show how the radar chart of preferred movement directions was changing all the way back to the very first bug in the line.

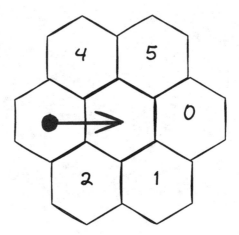

FIGURE 6.24: Starting movement of a worm and its next options.

5. Modify "Evolution" by including several zones of especially fertile areas. Find out what kind of bugs will eventually thrive there.

6. Implement the Drossel-Schwabl "Forest Fire" model.

7. Introduce vaccinated people into our "Spread of disease" simulation. Vaccination can be modeled by turning a constant percentage V of "healthy" people into "immune" on each iteration of the simulation.

8. Study the effect of lockdowns in the "Spread of disease" simulation. Simply stop moving infected people around the city and see how it changes the course of the epidemic.

9. Implement the "Paterson's worms" cellular automaton [15]. This system is somewhat similar to Langton's ant: it simulates the path of an artificial "worm" moving according to certain rules. Each worm, however, can be controlled by its own individual ruleset.

   A worm starts its journey in an arbitrary cell of an infinite hexagonal grid[12] and moves one cell forward, leaving a trail behind. To make the next move, the worm checks its surroundings and chooses a path to follow according to the rulebook. Each rule suggests the next movement direction for a certain six-cell neighborhood. Neighbor directions and movement directions are coded with integers, using the worm's point of view. Forward is 0, slight right turn is 1, sharp right turn is 2, slight left turn is 5, sharp left turn is 4 (see Figure 6.24). A rule, for example, might look like this: "if neighbors in directions 0, 1, 2, 4, 5 are empty, move in direction 5". A worm is not allowed to

---

[12]This setup is more commonly described as a triangular grid, where vertices of equilateral triangles represent cells.

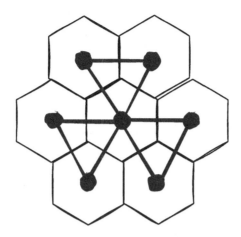

FIGURE 6.25: Trail of the "2 0 0" worm.

follow any of its previous trails, so the simulation is stopped as soon as it has no valid paths to continue.

An easy way to specify a rule is to provide the direction the worm must take next time it encounters a new situation with two or more possible paths available. An ordered list of these directions forms a ruleset. For example, a ruleset "2 0 0" means "in the next previously unseen situation take direction 2, next time choose direction 0, next time choose 0 again". The worm obeying this rule draws a simple path composed of three triangles (see Figure 6.25). Try also more interesting rulesets, like "1 5 2 5 4 1 2", "1 0 4 0 1 5", or "2 0 1 4 1 4 2" [40].

7 States and transitions

The final projects of the previous chapter can be called "systems for modeling systems". Artificial worlds of "Life" and Langton's ant are interesting on their own, possessing surprisingly complex and intricate properties. "Cellular snowflakes" demonstrated how a cellular automaton can model natural processes.

In this chapter we will add a couple of new shiny items to our toolbox of "systems for modeling systems". Our main focus is going to be on the tools, based on the same general idea: states and transitions. Cellular automata consist of "cells", switching to certain states depending on their neighborhood. Now we'll consider devices with only one "active unit" having a state. However, the state's "neighborhood" and rules controlling switching from one state to another are going to be far more flexible.

7.1 FINITE STATE MACHINE

Finite state machines (FSMs) serve as a great example of an important theoretical construction that also turns out to be a useful tool for everyday programming. In its basic form, an FSM performs only one kind of job: it processes an input string of symbols and decides whether it should be accepted or rejected. A sketch of this virtual device is shown in Figure 7.1.

An FSM always resides in a certain state (pointed by the needle in the sketch). One of them is chosen as the initial state. One or more states are also chosen as "favorable". The machine shown in the figure starts its work in state 3, and its only favorable state is 2.

The machine operates according to the transition rules, specifying the target state for each possible combination of the current state and the next input symbol. Thus, the machine reads the input string symbol-by-symbol and switches between the states. If, after reading the whole input, it happens to be in one of the favorable states, the string is accepted.

Instead of actually writing down a rule for every combination of state and symbol, it is usually presumed that unexpected situations cause the input string to be rejected. For example, in our case there is no rule for the combination (3, A). Thus, any input string starting with A is going to be rejected.

Let's see what happens during processing of the example string CAAB:

1. Machine reads C and switches to 1 using rule (3, C) → 1.
2. Machine reads A and switches to 5 using rule (1, A) → 5.
3. Machine reads A and switches to 2 using rule (5, A) → 2.
4. Machine reads B and switches to 1 using rule (2, B) → 1.

The final state is not favorable, and the input string is therefore rejected.

DOI: 10.1201/9781003455295-7

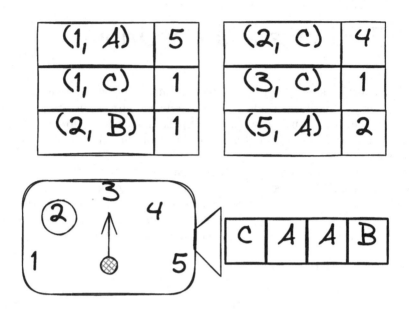

FIGURE 7.1: Finite state machine processing the input string CAAB.

Each FSM accepts certain strings and rejects other strings. Our device will accept a variety of strings, including, for instance, CCAA, CCCAA, and CCAABAA. Thus, an FSM divides all possible strings in the world into two classes: the strings it accepts and the strings it rejects.[1] Unsurprisingly, FSMs are often used in practice specifically for this purpose: to figure out whether an input string belongs to a class of our interest or not. For example, it is possible to construct a device that would only accept strings forming a time description in a 24-hour format (such as 12:35 or 00:15) or a valid Python variable name.

Some classes of strings, however, turn out to be an unreachable target for FSMs. Say, it is impossible to construct an FSM that would accept any string that reads the same both ways (a *palindrome*), such as "kayak" or "racecar". Intuitively, it is not hard to see why: an FSM has states, but no writable memory, so it cannot keep track of incoming symbols to check whether the same symbols reappear in the reverse order later.

This observation is an important result in theoretical computer science, where distinction is made between the sets of strings that can be recognized by an FSM, and the sets of strings requiring more powerful computational devices. Thus, FSMs mark a certain threshold of computational capacity. Note that "strings of symbols" do not necessarily mean "strings of characters":

---

[1]Some useful terminology: the given FSM *recognizes* the set S, consisting of all the strings, *accepted* by this FSM.

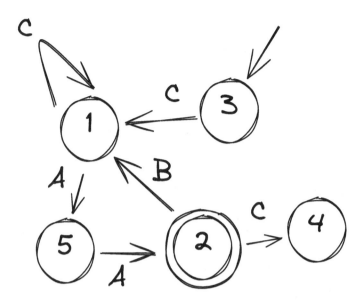

FIGURE 7.2: Finite state machine shown as a transition diagram.

FSMs process sequences of arbitrary elements, which makes them useful far beyond the tasks of text processing.

Before we move on, let me add that FSMs are typically visualized with diagrams, depicting their states and transitions between them. Such a diagram for the FSM shown in Figure 7.1 is provided in Figure 7.2.

7.1.1 IMPLEMENTATION

We'll discuss some practical applications of FSMs shortly, but now let's see how to use Python to simulate a basic FSM, defined with a provided set of rules. For the sake of simplicity, we'll presume that FSM states are coded with numbers, and the input string consists of ordinary ASCII characters (see Listing 7.1).

Listing 7.1: Finite state machine simulator.

```python
def accepts(rules, favstates, start, input):
    state = start
    try:
        for c in input:
            state = rules[(state, c)]
        return state in favstates
    except KeyError:
        return False
```

```
rules = {
    (3, "C"): 1,
    (1, "C"): 1,
    (1, "A"): 5,
    (5, "A"): 2,
    (2, "B"): 1,
    (2, "C"): 4,
}

favs = {2}
start = 3

print(accepts(rules, favs, start, "CAAB"))    # prints False
print(accepts(rules, favs, start, "CAABAA"))  # prints True
```

This approach for simulating an FSM might be perfectly fine for some tasks and inadequate for others. One notable property of these devices is their *linear processing time*: on each step, an FSM processes exactly one symbol of the input string. Thus, if the length of the string is N, we are guaranteed to obtain a solution after N steps. This makes FSMs useful for fast string processing. However, our implementation is not particularly fast: each step here requires to retrieve a value from a dictionary, which comes at a cost.

7.2   TIME MACHINE

The goal of our next little exercise is to create an FSM actually doing something useful. As mentioned in the previous section, it is possible to design an FSM that accepts strings forming time descriptions such as 12:35. Imagine an input box where the user has to supply a time value. The program must make sure the value is valid before using it.

Let's create such a device. To make things a bit more interesting, let's presume the time format is

```
HH:MM[:SS[.fff]]
```

There are two digits for hours, two digits for minutes, an optional two-digit part for seconds, and in case it is present, an additional optional part for milliseconds (ranging from 000 to 999). Thus, these are valid time strings: 00:30, 13:45:59, 23:03:15.003.

This particular data format is quite simple, so the corresponding FSM can be drawn without much preparation (see Figure 7.3).

A valid string starts with a digit 0, 1, or 2. Since the highest value for hours is 23, the digit after 2 must be no larger than 3. Then we expect a colon and a minutes chunk, which is a digit in a range 0-5 followed by a digit in a range 0-9. Since a valid string may end here, state 7 is favorable. Seconds work in the same way as minutes, and there is yet another favorable state after their chunk. The trailing part of the string, milliseconds, consists of a dot and three digits.

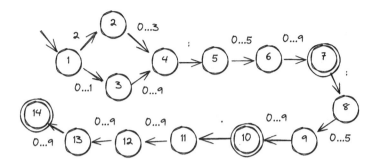

FIGURE 7.3: Finite state machine for time string recognition.

To save space, most transitions in Figure 7.3 are labeled with ranges like
0...3. Every such transition denotes a list of rules:

```
# the transition "(2, "0...3") → 4" represents four rules:

(2, "0") → 4
(2, "1") → 4
(2, "2") → 4
(2, "3") → 4
```

7.2.1 IMPLEMENTATION

Let's incorporate the rules shown in the diagram into our FSM simulator to
obtain the "time machine" (Listing 7.2).

Listing 7.2: "Time machine" FSM.

```
def accepts(rules, favstates, start, input):
    state = start
    try:
        for c in input:
            state = rules[(state, c)]
        return state in favstates
    except KeyError:
        return False


def rules_range(state_from, state_to, minchar, maxchar):
    r = range(ord(minchar), ord(maxchar) + 1)
    return {(state_from, chr(c)): state_to for c in r}


# hours
rules = {(1, "2"): 2}
rules.update(rules_range(1, 3, "0", "1"))
rules.update(rules_range(2, 4, "0", "3"))
rules.update(rules_range(3, 4, "0", "9"))
```

```
rules.update({(4, ":"): 5})

# minutes
rules.update(rules_range(5, 6, "0", "5"))
rules.update(rules_range(6, 7, "0", "9"))

rules.update({(7, ":"): 8})

# seconds
rules.update(rules_range(8, 9, "0", "5"))
rules.update(rules_range(9, 10, "0", "9"))

rules.update({(10, "."): 11})

# milliseconds
rules.update(rules_range(11, 12, "0", "9"))
rules.update(rules_range(12, 13, "0", "9"))
rules.update(rules_range(13, 14, "0", "9"))

start = 1
favs = {7, 10, 14}

print(accepts(rules, favs, start, "23:15"))        # True
print(accepts(rules, favs, start, "24:15"))        # False
print(accepts(rules, favs, start, "09:37"))        # True
print(accepts(rules, favs, start, "23:95"))        # False
print(accepts(rules, favs, start, "00:15:23"))     # True
print(accepts(rules, favs, start, "05:23:59.234")) # True
```

As you can see, apart from the utility function `rules_range()` that generates a separate FSM rule for each character in the given range, this code follows the same approach as used in the previous example.

7.2.2 AFTERTHOUGHTS

Being just a long and monotonous list of rules, this code possesses a particular kind of beauty: it accurately represents the original transition diagram from Figure 7.3. It is easy to imagine such a code being *automatically generated* from a diagram, and indeed, there are tools able to do it.[2]

What about the previous step? We had to create a state machine diagram from the format string `HH:MM[:SS[.fff]]`. Can this work be automated as well? It turns out that it can. There is a widely used approach to specify such "matching patterns", known as *regular expressions* [11].[3] Any given regular expression can be automatically transformed into a runnable FSM, and this is exactly the mechanism under the hood of Python module `re`.[4]

---

[2] Just to name one: https://github.com/pbosetti/gv_fsm

[3] This book is a good *comprehensive* guide. Numerous shorter tutorials are easy to find online.

[4] Note that Python regular expressions implement several extensions that require computational capabilities beyond the scope of basic FSMs.

7.3 NEEDLE IN A HAYSTACK

Regrettably, it is hard to showcase enough visually impressive simulations in this chapter, and the only way to restore the balance is to employ overly catchy project titles. However, I'd insist that the systems discussed here are *structurally* impressive, and hopefully they are as interesting to play with as our previous studies.

The task of the "Time machine" was to make sure that the input string conforms to a certain format. Our next goal will be to find the location of the given string (*pattern*) in another, larger string (*text*). If it sounds like a mundane task, it is because it is mundane. It is precisely the task performed by the Python `find()` function:

```python
print("mundane".find("dan")) # prints 3
```

Yet, there are countless variations of a *string matching* problem, and plenty of opportunities to improve existing methods for the benefit in certain specific cases. We will consider just one kind of optimization, driven by an FSM.

Consider the simplest possible *brute-force* implementation of `find()`:

```python
text = "mundane"
pattern = "dan"

for i in range(len(text) - len(pattern)):
    for j in range(len(pattern)):
        if pattern[j] != text[i + j]:
            break
    else:
        print(f"found at {i}")
        break
```

This code tries to find `pattern` in every location of `text`, proceeding to the next location in case of failure. (The little-known `else` clause of `for` kicks in if the loop ends normally, not due to `break`). Unfortunately, this approach suffers from a potential performance issue.

Consider the case of pattern `AAAAX` and text `AAAAAAAAX`. Our code will match four `A` characters in the beginning of the text, then fail to match `X` and restart from the second character of text. It will fail there again after matching four `A`s, and proceed to the third character of text. Thus, working in this fashion, this routine will perform `len(pattern)` operations every time inside the outer `for`-loop. If both strings are very long, the resulting performance might become unacceptable.

Let's note that such scenario is quite unlikely in practice, and for the absolute majority of real-world situations the brute-force approach is quite good. It is simple and requires no additional memory, which also might be an important factor. However, there are practical cases where the chances of facing poor performance are high. For example, DNA sequences consist of repetitive patterns of characters `A`, `T`, `G`, and `C`:

```
# "SV40 ORI" sequence

CTGTGGAATGTGTGTCAGTTAGGGTGTGGAAAGTCCCCAGGCTCCCCAGCAGGCAGAAGTATGCAAAGCATGCATCTCAA
TTAGTCAGCAACCAGGTGTGGAAAGTCCCCAGGCTCCCCAGCAGGCAGAAGTATGCAAAGCATGCATCTCAATTAGTCAG
CAACCATAGTCCCGCCCCTAACTCCGCCCATCCCGCCCCTAACTCCGCCCAGTTCCGCCCATTCTCCGCCCCATGGCTGA
CTAATTTTTTTTTATTTATGCAGAGGCCGAGGCCGCCTCTGCCTCTGAGCTATTCCAGAAGTAGTGAGGAGGCTTTTTTGG
AGGCCTAGGCTTTTGCAAAAAGCTC
```

These sequences can be long (billions of characters), and searching for matches inside large banks of sequences is a common task.

The actual Python function `find()` plays it safe by relying on the *two-way algorithm*[5], immune to random slowdowns [6]. It is a combined method, using the *Knuth-Morris-Pratt (KMP) algorithm* as one of its building blocks. My proposal is to implement a simplified version of KMP.

7.3.1 IMPLEMENTATION

Let's discuss how the brute-force approach can be improved. The key idea is simple: if we fail to match `pattern` at the current location of `text`, there is no need to restart from the very beginning of `pattern`. When our routine fails to match `AAAAX` at the beginning of `AAAAAAAAX`, it already knows that the first five characters of `text` are `AAAAA`, so it can simply check whether the sixth character is `x` to figure out whether `AAAAX` ends there (and therefore starts at the second character of `text`). On the other hand, when the routine fails to match the same pattern `AAAAX` at the beginning of `AAAXAAAAX`, it can conclude that there is no chance the pattern starts before `x`, so the search has to be restarted from the fifth character of `text` (right after `x`).

In general, a mismatch should be treated as "let's switch to our backup plan" rather than "let's start from scratch again". A mismatch at the earlier location can be a part of a later match. The tricky part is to understand that each combination of a successfully matched substring and the next character of `text` that caused a mismatch requires its own backup plan. Such plans can be shown on a diagram, where circles denote matched substrings, and arrows show how the next character of `text` changes the situation (see Figure 7.4). Naturally, this is a sketch of an FSM.

Any situation not covered by the rules switches the machine into its starting state. Once the favorable state is reached, the pattern is found, we can stop the routine.

All transitions rules of this FSM follow the same principle. For any pair of the source state S and the input character c, the destination state R should be labeled with the longest string, satisfying two conditions:

1. The pattern to be matched starts with R.
2. The string Sc ends with R.

---

[5]See https://github.com/python/cpython/pull/22904

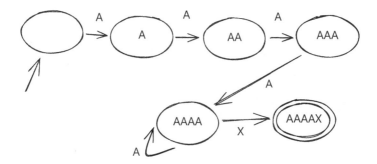

FIGURE 7.4: Finite state machine for matching the pattern AAAAX.

For example, consider the state AAAA. If the next input character is X, we need to switch to a state labeled with the longest string R, so that:

1. The original pattern AAAAX starts with R.
2. The string AAAA+X ends with R.

Clearly, the best candidate available in our FSM is the state AAAAX. Now, suppose the next input character is A. Then we are looking for the string R, so that:

1. The original pattern AAAAX starts with R.
2. The string AAAA+A ends with R.

In this case, our best option is AAAA.

Note this method also produces correct transitions to the starting state. For instance, if we apply it to a character not present in the pattern (such as z), the only option for R would be the empty string. However, it is easier to omit such rules altogether and simply presume that unhandled cases are equivalent to the transitions to the starting state. Also note that in the actual FSM we can use integers instead of strings as state labels: each state represents the number of pattern characters successfully matched so far.

The FSM for the pattern AAAAX is quite straightforward. More interesting rules arise for the patterns having repeated subsequences, such as banana (see Figure 7.5).

The code for both brute-force and FSM-based search routines is provided in Listing 7.3.

Listing 7.3: Brute-force and FSM-powered search routines.

```
def bf_search(pattern, text, start):
    for i in range(start, len(text) - len(pattern)):
        for j in range(len(pattern)):
            if pattern[j] != text[i + j]:
                break
```

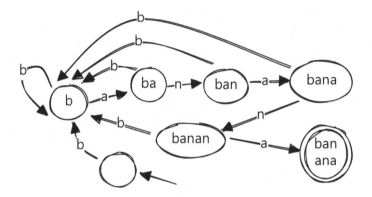

FIGURE 7.5: Finite state machine for matching the pattern `banana`.

```
        else:
            return i
    return -1


def fsm_search(rules, pattern, text, start):
    state = 0
    for i in range(start, len(text)):
        c = text[i]
        state = rules[(state, c)] if (state, c) in rules else 0
        if state == len(pattern):
            return i - (state - 1)
    return -1


def rules_for_pattern(pattern):
    rules = {}
    for c in set(pattern):
        rules.update(rules_for_char(pattern, c))
    return rules


def rules_for_char(pattern, c):
    rules = {}
    for sl in range(len(pattern) + 1):
        S = pattern[:sl]
        maxlen = 0
        for rl in range(1, len(pattern) + 1):
            R = pattern[:rl]
            if pattern.startswith(R) and (S + c).endswith(R) and rl > maxlen:
                maxlen = len(R)
                rules[(sl, c)] = rl
    return rules
```

The brute-force search is modified a bit here to return -1 if `pattern` is not found in `text` when searched from `start` onward. In case of success, the location of `pattern` is returned. This way it is easy to retrieve all matches of `pattern` by calling `bf_search()` in a loop until -1 is returned.

The `fsm_search()` function, in turn, is a slightly modified version of the FSM simulator. Instead of raising an exception, it treats any missing transition as a transition to the starting state 0. Once the pattern is found (this state is labeled with the number equals to `len(pattern)`), we return the index of the beginning of the match, which is `len(pattern)` - 1 characters away backward.

The code for generating FSM transition rules is more interesting. The main function `rules_for_pattern()` merely combines the rules obtained for each unique character in `pattern`. The real work takes place in `rules_for_char()`. This function goes through all possible pairs of FSM states (S, R) and checks whether a transition from S to R must be made according to the labeling rules. If all the necessary conditions are satisfied (R is the longest string so that `pattern` starts with R and $S+c$ ends with R), the transition is created.

It's easy to confirm this code works, but since the whole point of constructing the FSM was to achieve better performance, let's compare the speed of both routines. To do it, we'll generate random `pattern` and `text` sequences and measure the time taken by each method separately:

```python
from random import choice
from time import time


TEXTLEN = 1000000
PATTERNLEN = 6
CHARS = "abcde"
text = "".join((choice(CHARS) for _ in range(TEXTLEN)))
pattern = "".join((choice(CHARS) for _ in range(PATTERNLEN)))

rules = rules_for_pattern(pattern)

# find all the matches using bf_search()
start = time()
i = 0
cnt = 0
while (i := bf_search(pattern, text, i)) != -1:
    cnt += 1
    i += 1
bftime = time() - start

# do the same with fsm_search()
start = time()
i = 0
cnt = 0
while (i := fsm_search(rules, pattern, text, i)) != -1:
    cnt += 1
    i += 1
fsmtime = time() - start

print(f"matches found: {cnt}")
print(f"fsm speedup: {(bftime/fsmtime):.03}")
```

The typical output of this benchmarking looks like

```
matches found: 63
fsm speedup: 1.92
```

Therefore, the FSM-based routine works nearly twice faster.

7.3.2 AFTERTHOUGHTS

I have to say that the results of our performance measurements should be taken with a large grain of salt. It is very likely that significant slowdowns of the brute-force routine are caused by the mere *existence* of the nested loop. Initialization and teardown of loops are quite costly in Python, so by removing the loop, it is possible to achieve a significant benefit.

If `pattern` is short (say, five characters), the loop can be simply unrolled as follows:

```
def bf_search(pattern, text, start):
    for i in range(start, len(text) - 5):
        if (
            pattern[0] == text[i]
            and pattern[1] == text[i + 1]
            and pattern[2] == text[i + 2]
            and pattern[3] == text[i + 3]
            and pattern[4] == text[i + 4]
        ):
            return i
    return -1
```

You can benchmark this code and make sure it is even faster than our FSM implementation. However, the game doesn't stop here: it is possible to optimize `fsm_search()` as well by replacing dictionary lookup with faster 2D-array operations.

The real disadvantages of the FSM-based approach are different: constructing FSM takes time, and storing FSM takes space (which can be quite large for long patterns). The real KMP algorithm takes effort to minimize both, but still different approaches turn out to be more efficient in different scenarios of string matching. For example, searching the same pattern in multiple texts and searching multiple patterns in the same text are completely distinct scenarios.

7.4 ROBOT CONTROL

While the previous examples of practical FSM applications are hopefully convincing, they are not particularly relevant for everyday software development practice. It is true that FSMs are behind some basic string matching algorithms, but these algorithms are typically hidden somewhere in the standard libraries, and there is rarely a reason not to rely on them.

However, "FSM-style thinking" often comes handy as a general approach for structuring somewhat unpolished requirements to the system being developed. In this context, the term "finite state machine" is used not very rigorously. Rather than a memoryless machine switching between its states on the basis of built-in rules and incoming symbols, what is usually meant is a system organized as a collection of subsystems passing the control to each other upon certain events. This approach does not work equally well in different cases, but when it works, it produces a well-structured and easy to understand program architecture.

Let's take a small detour and consider a real-life analogy. Suppose the task is to make your own homemade scale. The general requirement is simple but somewhat vague: the scale should be able to weigh small things, and high precision is not required.

At this point, the possibilities are too wide even to come up with a list of items needed to create the scale. Is a spring or a lever necessary? Do we need planks or a set of weights? By choosing a specific design of the scale, we can focus on a clearly defined final result and identify a list of subtasks to accomplish. Suppose our design of choice is a simple spring scale. In a nutshell, it consists of a spring with one end attached to a gauge, and another (loose) end equipped with a hook and a pointer. The item to be weighed is hung on a hook of a vertically oriented scale, and the pointer on a stretched spring shows the weight on a gauge.

The choice of this design dictates the list of the next actions. It is necessary to obtain the right kind of a spring, to think how to connect the pieces together and how to calibrate the gauge. Doing these things right requires technical skill, but the real challenge is to choose the right design.

Finite state machine-based design is just one of many possible designs to choose from, and with some experience it is not too hard to spot situations where it will be able to do a good job.

Nystrom discusses a great example of such a case [37]:

"We're working on a little side-scrolling platformer. Our job is to implement the heroine that is the player's avatar in the game world. That means making her respond to user input. Push the B button and she should jump. Simple enough."[6]

```
def handleInput(Input input)
    if input == PRESS_B:
        yVelocity_ = JUMP_VELOCITY
        setGraphics(IMAGE_JUMP)
```

Spot the bug? There's nothing to prevent 'air jumping': keep hammering B while she's in the air and she will float forever. The simple fix is to add an

---

[6]The original code is in C++.

isJumping_ Boolean field to Heroine that tracks when she's jumping, and then do:

```
def handleInput(Input input)
    if input == PRESS_B:
        if not isJumping_:
            isJumping_ = True
            # Jump...
```

There should also be code that sets isJumping_ back to False when the heroine touches the ground. I've omitted that here for brevity's sake.

Next, we want the heroine to duck if the player presses down while she's on the ground, and stand back up when the button is released:

```
def handleInput(Input input)
    if input == PRESS_B:
        # Jump if not jumping...
    elif input == PRESS_DOWN:
        if not isJumping_:
            setGraphics(IMAGE_DUCK)
    elif input == RELEASE_DOWN:
        setGraphics(IMAGE_STAND)
```

Spot the bug this time? With this code, the player could:
1) Press down to duck.
2) Press B to jump from a ducking position.
3) Release down while still in the air.
The heroine will switch to her standing graphic in the middle of the jump. Time for another flag..."

Nystrom's sad story goes on and on in the same manner until it is crystal clear that every new capability or a bugfix makes the code even more brittle and harder to understand.

What makes this case especially confusing is that there is nothing inherently wrong in the chosen approach: all we see here is an honest attempt to "grow" the required functionality by gradual implementation of features and handling of edge cases. However, in the given circumstances it is like trying to build a tower of bricks simply by placing every next brick on top of the previous one: after a while, the whole structure collapses.

This problem can be also considered from another perspective. The code itself may be perfectly fine, but its logic based on numerous nested conditional statements and Boolean flags is too complicated for our limited cognitive abilities. Finite state machines provide the right kind of tool to cut this complexity into bite-size slices.

In the Nystrom's example, Heroine behaves differently in different modes, such as "standing", "jumping", "ducking", and "diving". The transitions between these modes are well defined: for example, ducking mode can only be activated from standing mode, and it is only possible to come back to stand-

FIGURE 7.6: Sketch of a box-sorting robot.

ing from ducking. This FSM-like diagram can be directly implemented in the code, and the end result will probably look repetitive but not convoluted.

To see the whole road from the idea to the implementation, let's consider a simpler scenario. Suppose our task is to design a control module for the industrial robot that sorts incoming boxes into two types: small and large (see Figure 7.6). The robot recognizes the type of the next box on the conveyor belt, and places it to the left or to the right with its robotic arm.[7]

The robot can lift its arm up and down, as well as open and close its grabber. The robot body can be in one of three positions: neutral, turned to the left, and turned to the right. Let's also presume that body rotation can only be performed with the arm lifted up (say, for safety reasons). When the robot is straight with its arm lifted up, its camera can be used to recognize

---

[7]There are robots doing exactly this kind of work, just search for "robotic pallet sorting".

the type of the next box on the conveyor. To formalize the task further, let's presume the robot is able to execute the following commands:

- **L**: turn 45° to the left (arm must be in upper position).
- **R**: turn 45° to the right (arm must be in upper position).
- **U**: move arm up.
- **D**: move arm down.
- **O**: open grabber.
- **C**: close grabber.
- **I**: identify next box (returns SMALL or LARGE).

The control module consists of two subsystems. The first subsystem executes individual commands by actually turning on and off electric motors. It is also its job to prevent illegal movements: what if the robot tried to open even wider its already open grabber? It might get damaged! The second subsystem issues chains of commands like "OLDCU", representing high-level functionality. Using this subsystem, a robot can be reprogrammed to sort incoming boxes differently, say, to place all the boxes into the same-side pile.

7.4.1   IMPLEMENTATION

Since we can't program real-life robots here, let's employ the turtle as a virtual robot to illustrate how the control module is doing its job. We will start by drawing all possible states of the robot and the transitions between them (see Figure 7.7). The robot starts operation in its "nuo" state: its body is in (n)eutral position, the arm is (u)p, the grabber is (o)pen. By turning right, the robot switches to the "ruo" position, and so on.

This diagram might look overly complicated for the task, but remember that *all* the complexity of robot operation is localized here, and in case of any changes in requirements we won't have to look anywhere else. Such changes are also easy to incorporate. Suppose that while designing a modified robot with a large grabber, we realize it is unsafe to turn the body with the grabber open. This new requirement can be easily introduced into the system by removing the corresponding transitions from the diagram.

Our code will execute the following loop:

```
while space key is not pressed
    recognize the next box
    in case of a large box, run the "DCULDOUR" sequence
    in case of a small box, run the "DCURDOUL" sequence
```

The type of the next box will be chosen randomly.

Let's start with an incomplete version shown in Listing 7.4.

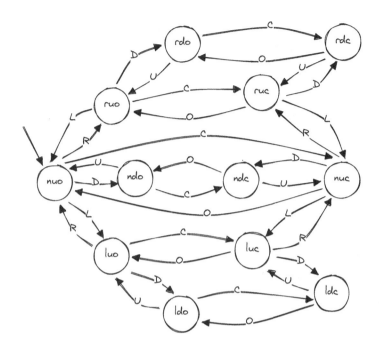

FIGURE 7.7: Scheme of sorting robot behavior.

Listing 7.4: Robot control (incomplete).

```python
import turtle
from dataclasses import dataclass
from random import randint

WIDTH = 600
HEIGHT = 400
MARGIN = 50
SLEEP_MS = 1000


@dataclass
class SimState:
    done: bool = False

    def set_done(self):
        self.done = True

    @classmethod
    def setup(cls):
        r = cls()
        turtle.listen()
        turtle.onkeypress(r.set_done, "space")
        return r
```

```
@dataclass
class WorldState:
    # display the current robot position
    def draw_state(self):
        ...

    # execute the next command (return False if no command available)
    def next(self):
        ...

    # recognize the next box and activate the corresponding command sequence
    def next_box(self):
        ...

    @classmethod
    def setup(cls):
        ...


def setup_screen(title):
    turtle.setup(WIDTH + MARGIN, HEIGHT + MARGIN)
    turtle.tracer(0, 0)
    turtle.title(title)


setup_screen("Robot control")
world_state = WorldState.setup()
sim_state = SimState.setup()


def tick():
    if not sim_state.done:
        try:
            if not https://linkprotect.cudasvc.com/url?a=https%3a%2f%2fworld_
            state.next&c=E,1,PYe0vh_SoaKa190exmjPcPEVUVtmc-q_anI1IgNb6Pdi1Jfq7j
            YFYQgThUvGN0fQ512q_--G1-5zV0jnfuhwArlpDYYZpM2c4ihJhwvxtPrcSgKPxTc,
            &typo=1():
                world_state.next_box()

            world_state.draw_state()
            turtle.update()
            turtle.ontimer(tick, SLEEP_MS)
        except KeyError:
            print("Illegal command")


tick()
turtle.done()
```

This code follows our usual approach to turtle-based simulation by performing certain activities on each `tick()` call. In this case, `tick()` either executes the next robot command or recognizes the next incoming box type and generates the next chain of commands.

Now let's consider the implementation of `WorldState` class (Listing 7.5).

Listing 7.5: Robot control (WorldState class).

```python
@dataclass
class WorldState:
    input: str = ""
    state = "nuo"
    index: int = 0
    body = turtle.Turtle()
    arm = turtle.Turtle()
    box = turtle.Turtle()
    rules = {}

    def draw_state(self):
        self.arm.reset()
        self.arm.left({"l": 45, "r": -45, "n": 0}[self.state[0]])
        self.arm.color("red" if self.state[1] == "u" else "black")
        self.arm.shape("classic" if self.state[2] == "o" else "arrow")
        self.arm.forward(30)
        self.arm.left(180)

    def next(self):
        if r := self.index < len(self.input):
            print(f"Running {self.input[self.index]} in {self.state}")
            self.state = self.rules[(self.state, self.input[self.index])]
            self.index += 1
        return r

    def add_rules(self, src, dest, c1, c2):
        self.rules[(src, c1)] = dest
        self.rules[(dest, c2)] = src

    def add_all_rules(self, lst):
        for src, dest, c1, c2 in lst:
            self.add_rules(src, dest, c1, c2)

    def next_box(self):
        self.index = 0
        if randint(0, 1) == 0:  # small box
            self.box.shapesize(0.8)
            self.input = "DCURDOUL"
        else:
            self.box.shapesize(1.5)
            self.input = "DCULDOUR"

    @classmethod
    def setup(cls):
        r = cls()
        r.body.shape("circle")
        r.body.shapesize(2)
        r.arm.shapesize(3)
        r.box.penup()
        r.box.shape("square")
        r.box.forward(55)

        r.add_all_rules(
            [
```

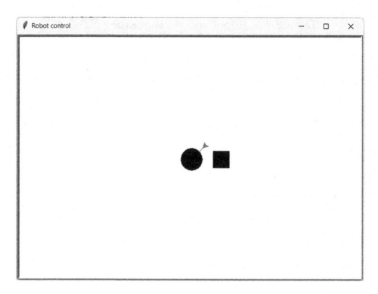

FIGURE 7.8: Box-sorting robot in its "luo" state.

```
        ("nuo", "ndo", "D", "U"),
        ("ndo", "ndc", "C", "O"),
        ("ndc", "nuc", "U", "D"),
        ("nuo", "nuc", "C", "O"),
        ("nuo", "ruo", "R", "L"),
        ("ruo", "rdo", "D", "U"),
        ("ruo", "ruc", "C", "O"),
        ("rdo", "rdc", "C", "O"),
        ("ruc", "rdc", "D", "U"),
        ("ruc", "nuc", "L", "R"),
        ("nuo", "luo", "L", "R"),
        ("luo", "ldo", "D", "U"),
        ("luo", "luc", "C", "O"),
        ("luc", "nuc", "R", "L"),
        ("luc", "ldc", "D", "U"),
        ("ldo", "ldc", "C", "O"),
    ]
)

    return r
```

The visual part of this simulation is supported by three turtles. The immovable circle `body` draws robot body, a square `box` draws a box of either size, and the `arm` shows both the robot arm and the grabber. It can be turned left or right, and its shape can resemble an arrow (open grabber) or a "classic" triangle (closed grabber). Red color is used to represent the arm in its lifted state (see Figure 7.8).

Helper functions `add_rules()` and `add_all_rules` simplify the task of listing all FSM transitions, but the FSM itself works exactly like our very first FSM project from the "Finite state machine" section.

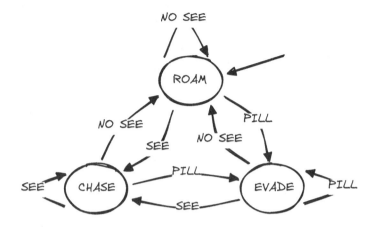

FIGURE 7.9: Pac-Man ghost finite state machine.

7.4.2 AFTERTHOUGHTS

I think while the "Robot control" project is a passable illustration of "FSM-based" design, it still feels overly complicated for the task. In our program, a relatively complex (12 states) FSM is used to control simple operations like turning motors on and off. In practical software engineering FSM-inspired design (or "state pattern") shines in the opposite situation, when a relatively simple state machine is used to switch between complex subsystems.

In Nystrom's example, each "state" of Heroine (such as standing, jumping, or ducking) is associated with its own (complex) unique capabilities and actions, but the state machine itself is simple, consisting just of a handful of states. This approach is very commonly employed in game programming, especially for creating autonomous non-playing characters.

For example, Pac-Man ghosts can be considered as FSMs, switching between "roaming", "chasing", and "evading" states (see Figure 7.9) [4]. On every timer tick the system checks state variables (whether Pac-Man is visible and whether "power pill" is active), and possibly switches the ghost to another state. Switching logic does not need to be as rigid as in the basic FSM: what to do if the current state is "evade", the power pill is active, and the ghost sees Pac-Man? We can prioritize conflicting rules by checking the pill status first, so the ghost would stay in "evade" until the pill is inactive, without even checking whether Pac-Man is visible.

The role of FSM as a design tool here is to separate and isolate these types of behavior, so they can be examined and implemented independently.

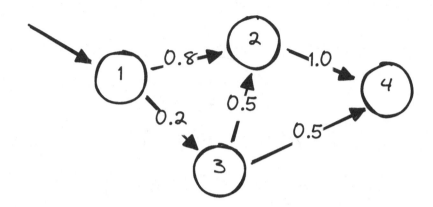

FIGURE 7.10: State diagram with probabilistic transitions.

7.5 MARKOVIAN WEATHER

The "Pac-Man state machine" is good enough for modeling the intelligence of a cartoony ghost, but more complex creatures (and even more advanced forms of ghosts) are hardly so deterministic. *Determinism* is an integral feature of FSMs: if there is a rule $(1, A) \rightarrow 2$, the command A will aways switch the machine from state 1 to state 2.

The real world tends to be less predictable, and an option to specify different outcomes of the same command would be handy. The most obvious use of such a capability is to model the processes taking place *in time*: what if our system receives no input commands, but its state might change as clock ticks? In a regular FSM, every tick is the same command ("tick"), so the system is destined to go over the same sequence of states every time we restart it.

A natural way to deal with uncertainty is to introduce probabilistic rules. In the simplest case, we can imagine an FSM-like device having no commands but clock ticks associated with probabilities (see Figure 7.10).

This device starts its operation in state 1. The next clock tick switches it either to state 2 (80% chance) or to state 3 (20% chance). There is just one option to go from state 2, but state 3 has two equally probable paths.

This kind of device is known as a *Markov process* or *Markov chain*. Its primary function is to represent certain processes rather than to control something: there is no command sequence in a Markov chain model, so we can only watch it switching from state to state.

A Markov chain can be derived from observations to model some real-life process or handcrafted to represent something artificial. In our next project we will make a simple weather simulator, say, for a role-playing computer game. Every time our team of heroes wakes up, it faces new weather conditions. Simply picking up random weather would be too unrealistic: a heavy rainfall

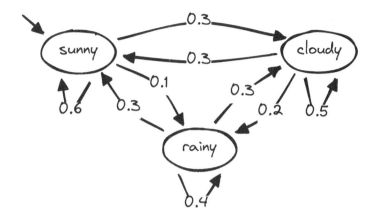

FIGURE 7.11: Markov chain-based weather model.

hardly comes after a sunny day with no cloud in sight. A Markov process suits this task much better (see Figure 7.11).

Let's implement this model and see what kind of climate it produces.

7.5.1 IMPLEMENTATION

This project can easily be done in the text mode, but to make the output easier to grasp, let's add some simple turtle-powered visuals (Listing 7.6).

Listing 7.6: Markovian weather.

```python
import turtle
from random import choices

CELLSIZE = 20
SHAPE_SIZE = CELLSIZE / 20
DAYS = 20


def setup_screen(title):
    turtle.setup(800, 600)
    turtle.tracer(0, 0)
    turtle.title(title)
    turtle.setworldcoordinates(-1, -10, DAYS, 10)


setup_screen("Markovian weather")


def next_day(state):
    rules = {
        "sunny": (("sunny", "rainy", "cloudy"), (0.6, 0.1, 0.3)),
        "cloudy": (("cloudy", "sunny", "rainy"), (0.5, 0.3, 0.2)),
```

FIGURE 7.12: Markovian weather (20 days).

```
    "rainy": (("rainy", "sunny", "cloudy"), (0.4, 0.3, 0.3)),
}
states, weights = rules[state]
return choices(states, weights)[0]


state = "sunny"
colors = {"sunny": "gold", "cloudy": "gray", "rainy": "black"}

for day in range(DAYS):
    drawer = turtle.Turtle()
    drawer.penup()
    drawer.shapesize(SHAPE_SIZE)
    drawer.shape("circle")
    drawer.forward(day)
    drawer.color("black", colors[state])
    state = next_day(state)

turtle.update()
turtle.done()
```

This code is similar to the implementation of the basic FSM. However, commands are not used anymore. The dictionary of rules for each source state now keeps a pair of tuples, containing (1) all possible destination states; (2) the weights (probabilities) of the respective transitions.[8] Thus, the job of the main `next_day()` function is to extract both elements by the given key and perform a weighted random choice using Python's `choices()` function. Different weather is shown with different colors (yellow, gray, black). A sample output is shown in Figure 7.12.

---

[8]Weights are relative: if an element has triple the weight of another element, it is three times more likely to be chosen. Probabilities are absolute and must add up to 1. In Markov chain-based projects we employ probabilities as weights, so these words are used interchangeably.

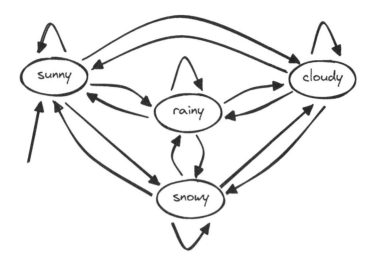

FIGURE 7.13: Markov chain-based weather model with four weather types.

7.6   THE FOUR SEASONS

It is easy to declare our weather model "good enough" and do something else, but you might have noticed one subtle yet major issue. It works fine with weather categories like "rainy" and "sunny" that belong to the same season, but once you try to add something like "snowy", the model will fall apart (see Figure 7.13). Like FSMs, Markov processes have no memory: when the system resides in a certain state, it does not know how exactly it arrived there. Thus, this device is suitable for modeling processes that satisfy *Markov property*: future evolution of a process should not depend on its history. In our case, the system has no tools to figure out that after a certain number of steps our game world should approach winter season with its snowy days.

Fortunately, Markov chains are powered with probabilities that *do not* have to remain constant. A Markov process can serve as the final decision-making module that determines the day weather, while the season-switching logic is implemented elsewhere. One may argue that "snowy" is just a winter version of "rainy", and our existing approach would still work. However, the problem of seasons is not limited to snow: the proportion of sunny days should be higher in summer than in autumn, which is also not reflected in the model.

Imagine a scenario where the probabilities of individual transitions change every day. As winter fades away, the proportion of sunny days goes up, while snowy days gradually disappear. The simplest way to achieve this effect is to create a list of complete Markov chain configurations for each day of the year, at the expense of substantial manual work. As it usually turns out in computing, the way to reduce manual work is to write additional code. In this case, we can manually specify certain "reference points" and *interpolate*

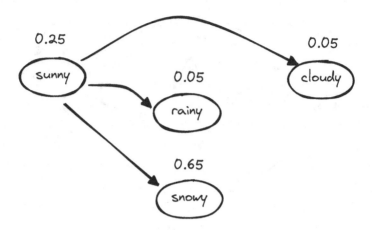

FIGURE 7.14: Outgoing transitions from "sunny".

values between then. For example, if the likelihood of moving from "sunny" to "snowy" is 0.4 somewhere in mid-winter, and only 0.1 somewhere in mid-spring, it should be around 0.25 in late winter or early spring.

Still, there are 16 transitions in our model, meaning we'll have to specify 16 numbers for each reference point. Thus, I propose pushing automation even further by specifying a probability for each state S (let's denote it $p(S)$), and use the following method to calculate the probabilities of all outgoing transitions of S:

1. Sum up the probabilities of all the states except S.
2. To obtain the probability of transition from S to any state R, multiply $p(R)$ by $1 - p(S)$ and divide the result by the sum obtained at the previous step.

The basic idea here is to use state probabilities for self-transitions and distribute the remaining values proportionally. Let's consider a specific example of a mid-winter day (see Figure 7.14).

Here $p(sunny) = 0.25$, $p(rainy) = 0.05$, $p(snowy) = 0.65$, and $p(cloudy) = 0.05$. Our task is to find the probabilities of outgoing transitions from "sunny". The sum of all the probabilities except $p(sunny)$ is $p(rainy) + p(snowy) + p(cloudy) = 0.05 + 0.65 + 0.05 = 0.75$. Note that our formula assigns $p(sunny)$ to the transition from "sunny" to "sunny": $p(sunny) \times (1 - p(sunny))/0.75 = 0.25$

Now we have to distribute the remaining probability $1 - p(sunny) = 0.75$ among three transitions. It would be reasonable to assign the highest value to the transition from "sunny" to "snowy", while the remaining transitions to "rainy" and "cloudy" receive the same smaller probabilities. Let's see how our formula tackles this task:

1. "Sunny" to "rainy": $p(rainy) \times (1 - p(sunny))/0.75 \approx 0.017$.
2. "Sunny" to "cloudy": same as above.
3. "Sunny" to "snowy": $p(snowy) \times (1 - p(sunny))/0.75 \approx 0.217$.

Equipped with this method and our previous experience, we can proceed to the code.

7.6.1 IMPLEMENTATION

The program in Listing 7.7 builds on our previous project. Instead of 20 days of the same season, we now have four 40-day "seasons" and four reference points, setting the values to be achieved at the middle of each season. The simulation starts on a sunny day in mid-winter and ends in mid-winter of the next year.

Remember that there are two places where our manually specified weights are used to generate the actual Markov chain. The function weight_to() can calculate the weight of any requested transition, but this only gives us the chain for the days where the reference weights are available, and they are available for mid-season days only.

For any other day, reference weights have to be interpolated first. Suppose a certain weight at the beginning of the current season is beg, and at the end of the season its value is end. Then for any day within the season, the corresponding weight value can be calculated with the function lerp():

```
# linear interpolation
def lerp(beg, end, day):
    return beg + (day / (DAYS_IN_SEASON - 1)) * (end - beg)
```

If unsure, note that for the first (zeroth) day of the season this function returns beg, for the last day (DAYS_IN_SEASON - 1) its value is end, and for anything in between its value is also between beg and end.

Listing 7.7: The four seasons.

```
import turtle
from random import choices

CELLSIZE = 20
SHAPE_SIZE = CELLSIZE / 20
DAYS_IN_ROW = 20
DAYS_IN_SEASON = 40
DAYS = 4 * DAYS_IN_SEASON

state = "sunny"
seasons = ("sunny", "rainy", "cloudy", "snowy")
colors = {"sunny": "gold", "cloudy": "gray", "rainy": "black", "snowy": "snow"}
winter = {"sunny": 0.25, "cloudy": 0.05, "rainy": 0.05, "snowy": 0.65}
spring = {"sunny": 0.4, "cloudy": 0.28, "rainy": 0.3, "snowy": 0.02}
summer = {"sunny": 0.64, "cloudy": 0.18, "rainy": 0.18, "snowy": 0}
autumn = {"sunny": 0.3, "cloudy": 0.28, "rainy": 0.4, "snowy": 0.02}
```

```python
def setup_screen(title):
    turtle.setup(800, 600)
    turtle.tracer(0, 0)
    turtle.title(title)
    turtle.setworldcoordinates(-1, -16, DAYS_IN_ROW, 4)


def weight_to(pweights, src, dest):
    r = 1.0 - pweights[src]
    wsum = sum(pweights[k] for k in pweights if k != src)
    return r * pweights[dest] / wsum


def next_day(src, pweights):
    wlist = [weight_to(pweights, src, dest) for dest in seasons]
    return choices(seasons, tuple(wlist))[0]


def lerp(beg, end, day):
    return beg + (day / (DAYS_IN_SEASON - 1)) * (end - beg)


def pweights_for(day):
    year = [winter, spring, summer, autumn, winter]
    cur_season = day // DAYS_IN_SEASON
    season_day = day % DAYS_IN_SEASON

    pweights = year[cur_season]
    nxt_pweights = year[cur_season + 1]

    return {k: lerp(pweights[k], nxt_pweights[k], season_day) for k in seasons}


setup_screen("The Four Seasons")

for day in range(DAYS):
    drawer = turtle.Turtle()
    drawer.penup()
    drawer.shapesize(SHAPE_SIZE)
    drawer.shape("circle")
    drawer.forward(day % DAYS_IN_ROW)
    drawer.right(90)
    drawer.forward(day // DAYS_IN_ROW)
    drawer.color("black", colors[state])
    state = next_day(state, pweights_for(day))

turtle.update()
turtle.done()
```

Interestingly, these formulas make keeping the complete Markov chain in the memory unnecessary: every time the function next_day() has to decide the next day's weather, it only needs to calculate the options for the current source state.

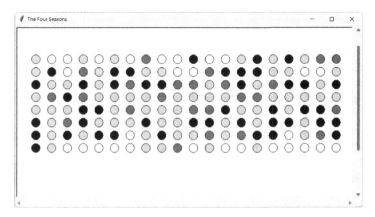

FIGURE 7.15: Visualization of a four-season year.

The turtle-based visualization is also nearly the same as before. After DAYS_IN_ROW days, the turtles are moved to the next row, so our calendar still has 20 horizontal cells (see Figure 7.15).

Perhaps, a meteorologist might find numerous flaws in this simulation, but I think for a game world it is reasonably convincing. Snowy mid-winter days nearly disappear by the beginning of spring, summer is sunshiny, and autumn is full of cloudy and rainy times. Thus, a task too challenging for simple formulas or Markov processes can be accomplished with the help of their combined power.

7.7 TEXT GENERATOR

Our previous projects show that Markov chains are quite good for the task of weather simulation. However, in both cases we had to design the states and transitions of the chain manually. More often than not, modeling real-world processes involves *deriving* the structure from actual data. A simple example of this process is *text generation*. It is probably used a bit too often in the literature; but being a perfect demonstration of the underlying idea, it is well worth our attention.

The task of the next program will be to produce a string that looks like a realistic fragment of English text. It might sound fun, but why would anyone need to do it? The most obvious application is the generation of realistic test data. For instance, as mentioned above, the benefit of choosing a FSM-based method over a naïve search procedure for searching substrings in a longer text depends on the nature of the text. For the strings composed entirely of random characters, the improvement is likely going to be much less noticeable than for the strings containing numerous repeating patterns. If a sample of real test data is available, it can be used to study its regularities and reproduce them in artificially generated texts.

The same logic can be applied to other kinds of test data. Say, it is possible to rely on user behavior data to generate a realistic sequence of clicks on various elements of a website to measure its performance or check whether it crashes in certain unlucky scenarios.

Derivation of a Markov chain from observations can be useful in cases like the ones discussed in our previous project, "The four seasons". It is possible to simulate the climate of a particular region by collecting transition probabilities from actual weather data.

In any case, the idea of deriving the configuration of the computing machine from data is not new for us: the FSM for searching substrings in "A needle in a haystack" was autogenerated as well. Now let's create a Markov chain for English texts.

7.7.1 IMPLEMENTATION

A season is a sequence of days. Similarly, an English text is a sequence of words. In late spring, a chance of a sunny day after a rainy day is much higher than a chance of a snowy day. In the same manner, it is far more likely to encounter a singular noun after "a" ("a box") than a plural noun ("a boxes") or a verb in the past tense ("a jumped"). Thus, we can start by reusing our "weather" machine: let states be labeled with English words, while the transitions reflect the probabilities of various continuations of the text. This way, we'll have a system knowing that "a" can be followed by "box" or "fox", but not "clocks".

However, human language is more complex than a simple weather model. By using only the probabilities between the successive word pairs, we'll lose broader context of the sentence. For example, the phrase "five wooden" will be continued with anything valid as a continuation of "wooden" (including "wooden box"), because "five" is already lost at this point. An easy way to fix this issue to some degree is to extend the context by relying on *two* successive words. A pair of words will form a state, and transitions from this state will identify the next possible word in the sequence.

Next, to derive a Markov chain from English texts, we need to have some. I suggest relying on Python documentation, just like we did in the "Zipf's law" project.

The complete implementation of the text generator is shown in Listing 7.8.

Listing 7.8: Markov text generator.

```
from random import randint, choices
from collections import defaultdict
from pydoc_data.topics import topics

TOKENS = 50

input_text = " ".join(topics.values())
words_raw = input_text.split()
```

```
words = [w for w in words_raw if w.replace(",", "").replace(".", "").isalpha()]
freq = {}

for i in range(len(words) - 2):
    key, next_word = (words[i], words[i + 1]), words[i + 2]

    if key not in freq:
        freq[key] = defaultdict(int)

    freq[key][next_word] += 1

idx = randint(0, len(words) - 3)
next_pair = (words[idx], words[idx + 1])

for _ in range(TOKENS):
    w1, w2 = next_pair
    print(w1, end=" ")

    keys = list(freq[next_pair].keys())
    values = list(freq[next_pair].values())
    w3 = choices(keys, values)[0]

    next_pair = (w2, w3)
```

The code is quite straightforward. We read the documentation and keep only the tokens consisting of alphabetic characters and punctuation symbols comma and full stop. Next, for each pair of successive words found in the text, a dictionary of possible continuations and their frequencies is created.

All we have to do after that is choose a random pair of successive words from the text as a "seed", and use the frequency dictionary to generate the next word. Since three words are available at this point, we can take the last two as the next key for dictionary lookup and repeat the process until the target token count is produced.

A possible output may look like this:

```
The uppercasing algorithm used is described in section Exceptions, and
information on using When inheriting from a single at code position or
as operand of the end of the program, or returns to its instances. If
weak reference support is needed, then add to the object is retrieved
from a parent class, the exception that unbound local variables held by
the future statement contains a description of the new exception. If
the operands are of different types. For instance, if is in the boolean
negation.
```

Python documentation (around 48,000 tokens) is not large enough to provide many options for possible continuations. Still, some word pairs are like large crossroads with numerous outgoing paths. Just insert the following print() call before the final line of the program to count the choices:

```
print(len(values), end=" ")
```

Now, consider this fragment of the test run:

```
Virtual 1 subclassing 1 is 53 not 3 allowed.
```

Each of the pairs `Virtual subclassing` and `subclassing is` has only one possible continuation. (Our `print()` call displays the counters between the words comprising a pair.) The next pair, `is not` is more fruitful, having 53 possible continuations. Naturally, common phrases, especially with prepositions, are likely to be "larger crossroads" than rare word combinations like "virtual subclassing".

7.8   TIC-TAC-TOE CHAMPION

The following project binds together all the important concepts discussed in this chapter. Let's recap the main capabilities of our tools:

- A finite state machine expresses how the state of the system changes as a result of consuming the next element of the input sequence. This process is deterministic: if the current state and the next input element are known, the result is completely predictable. A good example is robot operation: by consuming the next command "open the grabber", the robot moves from a state where the grabber is closed to a state where the grabber is open.
- A Markov chain expresses how the state of the system changes "on its own", commonly as a result of passing time. This process is probabilistic: the next state of the system is not entirely predictable, but the possible outcomes and their probabilities are known. Our example of such a situation was weather modeling: we don't know the weather of the next day, but the options are not equally likely.

An FSM can be used to describe the changes of a certain system over time if these changes are deterministic. For example, consider a simple Python program:

```
a = 1
b = 5
a = 3
```

The execution of this code can be treated as a series of state changes. Every change takes place as a result of executing the next line of code. The program starts in an "empty" state: it is about to execute its first line, and the list of variables in the memory is empty. By executing the line, it moves into the state where one variable `a` is available, its value is 1, and the second line is about to be executed. The process continues in the same manner until the favorable state is reached (see Figure 7.16).

Admittedly, this is not a very interesting state machine: knowing its previous state, we can always predict the next one. Even branches and loops in a Python program won't produce branches or loops in the corresponding FSM

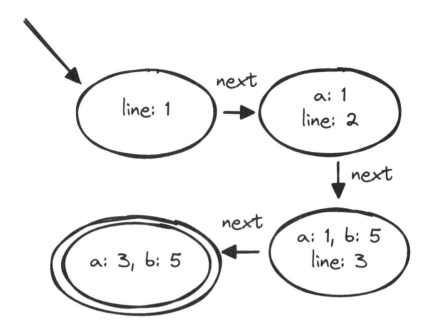

FIGURE 7.16: Python program as a state machine.

(a loop is possible if a program itself has an infinite loop, so it revisits the same states).

Summing up, we have seen FSMs with "real" commands and with mere "timer ticks", and we have seen Markov chains with timer ticks. It is time to combine Markov chains with instructions.

Imagine a situation where you execute a command, but the outcome is uncertain. Such situations are not uncommon: a soccer player making a shot on goal wants to score, but success is not guaranteed even to the most skillful professional.

Even in fully deterministic games like chess, the outcomes can be treated as probabilistic if we consider the game from "our side", treating opponent actions as weather changes: we can predict them to a certain extent, but not perfectly.

A Markov chain extended with probabilistically chosen actions having probabilistic outcomes is known as *Markov decision process (MDP)*. MDPs are used to model decision-making of an "active agent" operating in an uncertain world. At every point the agent may choose one of the possible actions to make. Some of these actions can be more or less preferable and lead to different outcomes. Figure 7.17 shows a simplified model of decision-making in a boxing-like sports game: the player may attack and hit the opponent, but in case of failure, may suffer from a counterattack. Alternatively, the player

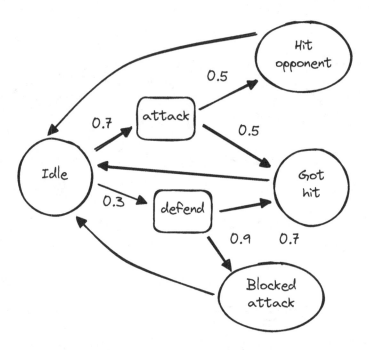

FIGURE 7.17: Boxing game MDP.

may choose a safer defensive move, which, however, makes no harm to the opponent.

The probabilities of attack and defense show the personality of the player: in this case, the boxer is quite aggressive, preferring to attack in 70% of cases. Other probabilities describe the reality of the game world: it is equally likely to hit and to get hit while attacking, while defense is mostly safe. The current skill of the player is included into this reality. It is possible that a more skillful player would be more successful while attacking.

Being a chart of actions and their outcomes, MDP is commonly used to optimize agent behavior to obtain certain desired properties. In case of boxing, it is desirable to arrive at the "hit opponent" state as often as possible, while minimizing the chances of getting into the "got hit" state. The only way for modifying agent behavior is to readjust action weights, just like we did in the "Four seasons" project.

To improve the choice of action weights, *reinforcement learning* algorithms are used. While this topic is far beyond the scope of the book, the general idea is to introduce numerical "rewards" for the different states in the MDP. In our case, the "hit opponent" state should be assigned a large positive, and "got hit" a large negative reward. The "blocked attack" can be slightly positive, and "idle" is neutral.

When an agent finds itself in a new situation, its reward is *backpropagated* to the actions that led the agent here. In effect, the probabilities of good actions are being increased, while bad actions are "punished". Relatively intricate schemes exist to calculate how exactly the rewards must be distributed. However, the general rule is to reward and punish the most recent actions most, reducing the amounts of distributed values as we go back to the past.

To demonstrate this idea, we'll write a self-learning program for playing the game of Tic-Tac-Toe (also known as "noughts and crosses"). I understand this might sound like the most boring choice ever, given that Tic-Tac-Toe is a solved game, where a good player never loses, and a match between two good players normally ends with a draw. However, it works fine as an example and demonstrates the concept of reinforcement learning very well.

Let's recap the rules. Two players, x and o, take turns placing their symbols on a 3 × 3 grid. Whoever managed to place three of their symbols to form a horizontal, vertical, or a diagonal line wins.

7.8.1   IMPLEMENTATION

Our program will work as follows. The MDP-powered player will engage in a series of matches against a "random player", placing their symbol into random empty cells. If a match ends with a victory of either player, the MDP player will be positively or negatively rewarded. The last move will receive the maximal reward, the previous move will receive a certain percentage of the full reward, and so on all the way back to the first move. Current move rewards will serve as weight for the weighted random choice procedure, so eventually good actions will have much higher chances to be selected.

For the sake of simplicity, we'll take the "brawn over brains" approach by ignoring the fact that many game positions in the game are identical, being mirror reflections or rotations of each other. Our learning algorithm is also quite basic, only slightly more advanced than the one used in the tic-tac-toe playing device MENACE, made entirely from matchboxes [28]. The original MENACE needs around 300 boxes; so if you are interested in trying out this technology, consider a simpler game of Hexapawn by Martin Gardner, which can be played with a 24-box device [12].[9] However, these early experiments are direct predecessors of more advanced algorithms like Q-Learning that power (with further improvements and variations) intelligent systems of the present day [20].

It is quite hard to break down the program into meaningful independent units, so let's consider the whole code at once (Listing 7.9).

---

[9]You can also play with the online version of MENACE, available at
https://linkprotect.cudasvc.com/url?a=https%3a%2f%2fwww.mscroggs.co.
uk%2fmenace%2f%7d%7d&c=E,1,1NxCeQBEkrGcncVh8XOmTHdIy9WrKQZQHJdgu83_
8RdoDogqn7-hext7w4viq2qjHxuBAjRKbeQvurDGT0c-eTqlwj23wqNGErgtHWNxjas,&typo=1

Listing 7.9: Tic-tac-toe champion.

```python
from random import choices
from dataclasses import dataclass

INIT_WEIGHT = 50
POS_REWARD = 5
NEG_REWARD = -5
NTR_REWARD = 0
LEARN_RATE = 0.8
PLAYER_SYMBOL = "X"
OPP_SYMBOL = "O" if PLAYER_SYMBOL == "X" else "X"


@dataclass
class Action:
    value: int
    weight: float


@dataclass
class State:
    value: list
    actions: list

    @classmethod
    def create(cls, val):
        acts = [Action(i, INIT_WEIGHT) for i, v in enumerate(val) if v == " "]
        return cls(val, acts)

    def random_action(self):
        w = [a.weight for a in self.actions]
        return choices(self.actions, w)[0]

    def key(self):
        return tuple(self.value)

    def next(self, action, symbol):
        next_value = list(self.value)
        next_value[action.value] = symbol
        return State.create(next_value)

    def full(self):
        return " " not in self.value

    def rc(self, row, col):
        return self.value[row * 3 + col]

    def victory(self, sym):
        for k in range(3):
            h = sym == self.rc(k, 0) == self.rc(k, 1) == self.rc(k, 2)
            v = sym == self.rc(0, k) == self.rc(1, k) == self.rc(2, k)
            d1 = sym == self.rc(0, 0) == self.rc(1, 1) == self.rc(2, 2)
            d2 = sym == self.rc(2, 0) == self.rc(1, 1) == self.rc(0, 2)
```

```python
            if h or v or d1 or d2:
                return True
        return False

    def game_over(self):
        return self.full() or self.victory("X") or self.victory("0")


def reward(history, score):
    r = score
    for action in reversed(history):
        action.weight = max(0.001, action.weight + r)
        r *= LEARN_RATE


knowledge = {}


def play_results():
    history = []
    sym = "X"
    state = State.create([" " for _ in range(9)])

    while not state.game_over():
        if sym == OPP_SYMBOL:
            action = State.create(state.value).random_action()
        else:
            if state.key() not in knowledge:
                knowledge[state.key()] = state

            action = knowledge[state.key()].random_action()
            history.append(action)

        state = https://linkprotect.cudasvc.com/url?a=https%3a%2f%2fstate.
        next&c=E1,y2pysBPWpmAWVMvol97Kq5Xn_PvxKX1VlJQc5wGMRXRTUBInZj8h_
        6KjWxJWVek4ygOluNoEfsSoBE00gqnLVPF2WoD_T2xLvPXkE4pciN7C&typo=1(action,
        sym)sym = "X" if sym == "0" else "0"

    pl_wins = state.victory(PLAYER_SYMBOL)
    opp_wins = state.victory(OPP_SYMBOL)
    is_draw = not (pl_wins or opp_wins)

    r = POS_REWARD if pl_wins else (NEG_REWARD if opp_wins else NTR_REWARD)
    reward(history, r)

    return [pl_wins, opp_wins, is_draw]


for _ in range(10):
    stats = [play_results() for _ in range(10000)]
    for k in range(3):
        print(sum(s[k] for s in stats), end=" ")
    print()
```

To understand this program, let's start with the basic elements of MDP: states and actions. A Markov decision process is a network of states. Each

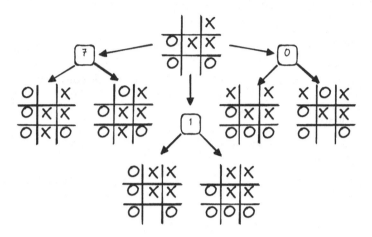

FIGURE 7.18: Possible actions of the player x.

state is associated with a list of possible actions, and each action leads to one or more states representing its outcomes.

In our case, an action is simply an index of a cell where the player places their symbol:

```
@dataclass
class Action:
    value: int
    weight: float
```

Cells are numbered from 0 to 8 (left to right, top to bottom). Initially, the weight of each action is INIT_WEIGHT, but weights will change over time.

State objects keep the actual gameboard configurations (list of cells and their values), so each state in our system represents a certain configuration:

```
@dataclass
class State:
    value: list
    actions: list
    ...
```

A cell value is one of three possible characters: x, o, or space.

This mechanism represents the game from a particular player's perspective, so all the configurations stored in MDP states show this player's turn, and all the actions are this player's actions (see Figure 7.18).

The State class implements the following methods:

- create(): creates the board from the given list of cells and generates an Action object for each empty cell.

- `random_action()`: returns a random action (action weights are taken into account).
- `key()`: returns cell values as a tuple so it can be used as a dictionary key.
- `next()`: returns a game configuration formed as a result of the given action.
- `full()`: returns True if the game board is full.
- `rc()`: returns a cell value in the given column/row.
- `victory()`: returns True if the given state satisfies victory conditions for the given player.
- `game_over()`: returns True if either player has won or the game board is full.

The `value` stored inside a state is the actual game board configuration.

The program plays 10 sessions of 10,000 games each between the MDP player and the random player, printing out stats after every session (victories of both players and draws). An individual game is played in `play_results()`. This function prepares an empty game field and alternates turns between the players. The random player simply creates a new `State` object and calls `random_action()` to perform the turn. The MDP player preserves the states between the calls, so the weights of the actions stored in states are never reinitialized. Every applied action is stored in the `history` list, so at the end of the game the reward can be propagated all the way backward. The reward is multiplied by `LEARN_RATE` on each step, so the first action in the list (the oldest one) gets the smallest reward by its absolute value.

Even though a game between two good players normally end with a draw, in a game between two players making random moves the first player has an advantage. The "baseline performance" can be obtained with a test run between two random players:

```
Wins Loss Draw
5837 2925 1238
5905 2814 1281
5817 2912 1271
...
```

Thus, roughly 58% of "random" games end with the first player victory, the second player wins in 29% of cases, and the remaining games end in a draw.

Now let's examine how well the MDP player behaves in both roles:

```
MDP is Player 1 (X):
Wins Loss Draw
6535 2290 1175
7260 1759 981
7610 1399 991
7935 1156 909
```

```
8242 946  812
8390 861  749
8531 774  695
8714 642  644
8785 587  628
8844 562  594

MDP is Player 2 (O):
Wins Loss Draw
3773 4910 1317
5950 2585 1465
6917 1811 1272
7457 1383 1160
7716 1205 1079
8036 911  1053
8327 742  931
8330 699  971
8491 581  928
8536 557  907
```

Even playing as O, the MDP player is able to raise its victory percentage to around 85%; so let's consider our goals accomplished.

7.9 FURTHER IDEAS

1. Use "Time machine" as a starting point to create a program able to recognize floating point numbers. As a simplification, you can consider only the following format:

   `[+|-]([digits].digits | digits[.])`

   Square brackets denote optional elements, a vertical bar stands for "or", and "digits" is one or more digit symbols. Thus, strings like "+.35", "75." and "-0.94" should be matched.

2. Transform the robot from the "Robot control" project into a cargo elevator installed in a two-storey building. By pressing the only button on the panel, the operator can send the elevator to another floor. The starting position is "ground floor, doors open". Button press closes the doors, moves the elevator up or down, and opens the doors. Make sure the elevator never moves with open doors.

3. Modify our "Text generator" project to solve the problem of *language identification*. Suppose you have a document in a language you don't know. How do you find out what language it is? One option is to use the following method. Download sample files for different languages (texts from Project Gutenberg[10] can be good candidates), and build a "probabilistic profile" for each language. In this case, it makes sense to model the level of individual letters, meaning that the profile would show the likelihood of appearance of a certain letter after a pair of two

---

[10]See https://www.gutenberg.org

other letters. Having these profiles, build a profile for your document and find the closest match. Profiles, converted to lists of probabilities, can be compared with each other using *dot product*:

$$similarity(prof_1, prof_2) = prof_1[0] \cdot prof_2[0] + ... + prof_1[N] \cdot prof_2[N]$$

4. Use real weather data from your favorite city to simulate its all-year climate with "The four seasons" project code.

5. It might be surprising why the learning rate of our artificial Tic-Tac-Toe player is so slow. The reason is simple: one can't master a game by playing against weak opponents. When playing against a "random player", our MDP optimization strategy rewards good actions; but it often rewards bad ones as well and leaves many bad moves without punishment. Try learning by playing against another self-learning MDP player and watch how they evolve in parallel. In this case, it makes sense to provide a small positive reward for the draw, since victory is going to be rare.

6. Create a self-learning player for an interesting Tic-Tac-Toe variation named Row call [38]. Here the players still attempt to complete a line of three symbols, but the game takes place on a 4 × 4 grid, and a player only picks the column or the row of the next symbol, while the opponent finalizes the move by pointing the target cell. In other words, every move except the very first one consists of two actions: (1) choose the final location for the opponent's symbol within the given row or column; (2) chose the row or column for the next symbol of your own. This game is far more complex than Tic-Tac-Toe, so make sure to reuse rotations and reflections of already known game situations.

References

1. Sidra Arshad, Shougeng Hu, and Badar Nadeem Ashraf. Zipf's law and city size distribution: A survey of the literature and future research agenda. *Physica A: Statistical Mechanics and its Applications*, 492:75–92, February 2018.

2. Marco Baroni. 39 Distributions in text. In Anke Lüdeling and Merja Kytö, editors, *Corpus Linguistics*, pages 803–822. Mouton de Gruyter, March 2009.

3. Alex F. Bielajew. History of Monte Carlo. In *Monte Carlo Techniques in Radiation Therapy*, pages 3–15. CRC Press, 2021.

4. David M. Bourg and Glenn Seemann. *AI for Game Developers*. O'Reilly, Sebastopol, CA, 1st edition, 2004.

5. George E. P. Box. Robustness in the strategy of scientific model building. In *Robustness in Statistics*, pages 201–236. Elsevier, 1979.

6. Maxime Crochemore and Dominique Perrin. Two-way string-matching. *Journal of the ACM*, 38(3):650–674, July 1991.

7. Alexander Keewatin Dewdney. Sharks and fish wage an ecological war on the toroidal planet Wa-Tor. *Scientific American*, 251(6):14–22, 1984.

8. Alexander Keewatin Dewdney. *The Magic Machine: A Handbook of Computer Sorcery*. W.H. Freeman, New York, 1990.

9. J. Patrick Finerty. Cycles in Canadian Lynx. *The American Naturalist*, 114(3):453–455, September 1979.

10. Michael Fowler. Kinetic Theory of Gases: A Brief Review. https://galileo.phys.virginia.edu/classes/252/kinetic_theory.html, 2008.

11. Jeffrey Friedl. *Mastering Regular Expressions*. O'Reilly Media, Sebastapol, CA, 3rd edition, September 2006.

12. Martin Gardner. Mathematical games: How to build a game-learning machine and then teach it to play and to win. *Scientific American*, 232 (126):592, 1958.

13. Martin Gardner. Mathematical games: Problems involving questions of probability and ambiguity. *Scientific American*, 201(4):147–182, 1959.

14. Martin Gardner. Mathematical games: The fantastic combinations of John Conway's new solitaire game "life". *Scientific American*, 223(4): 120–123, October 1970.

15. Martin Gardner. Mathematical games: Fantastic patterns traced by programmed "worms". *Scientific American*, 229(5):116–123, November 1973.

16. Thomas B. Greenslade. *Adventures with Lissajous Figures:*. Morgan & Claypool Publishers, June 2018.

17. T. Ryan Gregory. Understanding Natural Selection: Essential Concepts and Common Misconceptions. *Evolution: Education and Outreach*, 2(2): 156–175, June 2009.

18. Garrett Hardin. The Tragedy of the Commons: The population problem has no technical solution; it requires a fundamental extension in morality. *Science*, 162(3859):1243–1248, December 1968.

19. F. Hoppensteadt. Predator-prey model. *Scholarpedia*, 1(10):1563, 2006.

20. Beakcheol Jang, Myeonghwi Kim, Gaspard Harerimana, and Jong Wook Kim. Q-Learning Algorithms: A Comprehensive Classification and Applications. *IEEE Access*, 7:133653–133667, 2019.

21. Nathaniel Johnston. Spaceship Speed Limits in "B3" Life-Like Cellular Automata. http://www.njohnston.ca/2009/10/spaceship-speed-limits-in-life-like-cellular-automata/, October 2009.

22. Nathaniel Johnston and Dave Greene. *Conway's Game of Life: Mathematics and Construction*. Self-published, 2022.

23. Henry C. King and John R. Millburn. *Geared to the Stars: The Evolution of Planetariums, Orreries, and Astronomical Clocks*. University of Toronto Press, Toronto, 1978.

24. Christopher G. Langton. Studying artificial life with cellular automata. *Physica D: Nonlinear Phenomena*, 22(1-3):120–149, 1986.

25. Zhanliang Liu. Weighted Random: Algorithms for sampling from discrete probability distributions. https://zliu.org/post/weighted-random/, 2018.

26. Yuri Mansury and László Gulyás. The emergence of Zipf's Law in a system of cities: An agent-based simulation approach. *Journal of Economic Dynamics and Control*, 31(7):2438–2460, July 2007.

27. Koji Maruyama, Franco Nori, and Vlatko Vedral. The physics of Maxwell's demon and information. *Reviews of Modern Physics*, 81(1): 1–23, January 2009.

28. Donald Michie. Experiments on the mechanization of game-learning. Part I. Characterization of the model and its parameters. *The Computer Journal*, 6(3):232–236, 1963.

29. Bastian Molkenthin. Vector reflection at a surface. http://sunshine2k.de/articles.html, 2021.

30. Andrés Moreira, Anahí Gajardo, and Eric Goles. Dynamical behavior and complexity of Langton's ant. *Complexity*, 6(4):46–52, 2001.

31. Dominique Morvan. Wildfires Modelling: Short Overview, Challenges and Perspectives. *Journal of the Combustion Society of Japan*, 61(196):120–125, 2019.

32. Lloyd Motz and Jefferson Hane Weaver. The perfect gas law. In *The Concepts of Science: From Newton to Einstein*, pages 284–308. Springer US, Boston, MA, 1988.

33. Todd W. Neller and Clifton G.M. Presser. Optimal play of the dice game Pig. *The UMAP Journal*, 25(1), 2004.

34. Todd W. Neller and Clifton G.M. Presser. Practical play of the dice game Pig. *The UMAP Journal*, 31(1), 2010.

35. John von Neumann. *Theory of Self Reproducing Automata*. University of Illinois Press, first edition, January 1966.

36. Mej Newman. Power laws, Pareto distributions and Zipf's law. *Contemporary Physics*, 46(5):323–351, September 2005.
37. Robert Nystrom. *Game Programming Patterns*. Genever Benning, 2014.
38. Ben Orlin. *Math Games with Bad Drawings: 74 1/2 Simple, Challenging, Go-Anywhere Games-and Why They Matter*. Black Dog & Leventhal, New York, NY, first edition, 2022.
39. Seymour Papert. *Mindstorms: Children, Computers, and Powerful Ideas*. Basic Books, New York, 2nd edition, 1993.
40. Ed Pegg. Paterson's Worms Revisited. https://www.mathpuzzle.com/MAA/Worms.html, 2003.
41. Eric R. Pianka. *Evolutionary Ecology*. Benjamin/Cummings Life Science Series. Benjamin/Cummings, San Francisco, sixth edition, 2000.
42. Przemysław Prusinkiewicz and Aristid Lindenmayer. *The Algorithmic Beauty of Plants*. The Virtual Laboratory. Springer-Verlag, 1996.
43. Clifford A. Reiter. A local cellular model for snow crystal growth. *Chaos, Solitons & Fractals*, 23(4):1111–1119, February 2005.
44. Craig W. Reynolds. Flocks, herds and schools: A distributed behavioral model. In *Proceedings of the 14th Annual Conference on Computer Graphics and Interactive Techniques*, pages 25–34, 1987.
45. Craig W. Reynolds. Steering behaviors for autonomous characters. In *Game Developers Conference*, pages 763–782, 1999.
46. Michael L. Rosenzweig. Paradox of Enrichment: Destabilization of Exploitation Ecosystems in Ecological Time. *Science*, 171(3969):385–387, January 1971.
47. Shovonlal Roy and J. Chattopadhyay. The stability of ecosystems: A brief overview of the paradox of enrichment. *Journal of Biosciences*, 32 (2):421–428, March 2007.
48. Keith Schwarz. Darts, Dice, and Coins: Sampling from a Discrete Distribution. https://www.keithschwarz.com/darts-dice-coins/, 2011.
49. Clinton Sheppard. *Genetic Algorithms with Python*. Self-published, 2018.
50. João Silva, João Marques, Inês Gonçalves, Rui Brito, Senhorinha Teixeira, José Teixeira, and Filipe Alvelos. A Systematic Review and Bibliometric Analysis of Wildland Fire Behavior Modeling. *Fluids*, 7(12):374, December 2022.
51. Stephen M. Stigler. Regression towards the mean, historically considered. *Statistical Methods in Medical Research*, 6(2):103–114, April 1997.
52. Yuki Sugiyama, Minoru Fukui, Macoto Kikuchi, Katsuya Hasebe, Akihiro Nakayama, Katsuhiro Nishinari, Shin-ichi Tadaki, and Satoshi Yukawa. Traffic jams without bottlenecks—experimental evidence for the physical mechanism of the formation of a jam. *New Journal of Physics*, 10(3): 033001, March 2008.
53. Dek Terrell. A test of the gambler's fallacy: Evidence from pari-mutuel games. *Journal of Risk and Uncertainty*, 8(3):309–317, May 1994.

54. Steven Tijms. Monty Hall and "the Leibniz Illusion". *CHANCE*, 35(4): 4–14, October 2022.

55. Richard Vaillencourt. *Simple Solutions to Energy Calculations*. River Publishers, sixth edition, 2021.

56. Dennie Van Tassel. *Program Style, Design, Efficiency, Debugging, and Testing*. Prentice-Hall, Englewood Cliffs, NJ, second edition, 1978.

57. Howard Howie Weiss. The SIR model and the foundations of public health. *Materials Matematics*, pages 1–17, 2013.

58. Charles Wetherell. *Etudes for Programmers*. Prentice-Hall, Englewood Cliffs, NJ, 1978.

59. Robert J. Whitaker. A note on the Blackburn pendulum. *American Journal of Physics*, 59(4):330–333, April 1991.

60. Stephen Wolfram. *A New Kind of Science*. Wolfram Media, Champaign, IL, 2002.

61. Ronald Wyllys. Empirical and theoretical bases of Zipf's law. *Library trends*, 30(1):53–64, 1981.

62. R. D. Zinck and V. Grimm. More realistic than anticipated: A classical forest-fire model from statistical physics captures real fire shapes. *The Open Ecology Journal*, 1(1), 2008.

Index

Printed in the United States
by Baker & Taylor Publisher Services